THE SOCIAL CONTEXT AND VALUES
Perspectives of the Americas

The Council for Research in Values and Philosophy

Cultural Heritage and Contemporary Life
Series V. Latin America, Volume 1
Series VI. Foundations of Moral Education, Volume 4

Edited by
George F. McLean
Olinto Pegoraro

UNIVERSITY
PRESS OF
AMERICA

Lanham • New York • London

THE COUNCIL FOR
RESEARCH IN VALUES
AND PHILOSOPHY

Library of Congress Cataloging-in-Publication Data

The Social context and values : perspectives of the Americas / edited
by George F. McLean, Olinto Pegoraro.
p.   cm.
(Cultural heritage and contemporary life. Series V, Latin America ; v. 1.
Series VI, Foundation of moral education ; v. 4)
Includes index.
1. Values. 2. Moral education. I. McLean, George F. II. Pegoraro,
Olinto Antonio. III. Series: Cultural heritage and contemporary life.
Series V, Latin America ; v. 1. IV. Series: Cultural heritage and
contemporary life. Series VI, Foundation of moral education ; v. 4.
BD232. S46   1989   88–37080 CIP
121'.8– –dc19
ISBN 0–8191–7354–1 (alk. paper).
ISBN 0–8191–7355–X (pbk. : alk. paper)

ACKNOWLEDGEMENT

Grateful acknowledgement is made to the scholars from many countries whose serious scholarship, personal sacrifice of time and resources, and high dedication have made the realization of this study an object lesson in interdisciplinary and international cooperation. They have demonstrated that scholars can do more than suggest tasks in need of realization, leaving to others the determination of whether and how their capabilities will serve. Working in bonds of shared concern, they themselves have determined what must be done and have shared their separate capabilities to develop insight possible only as the fruit of extended and intensive collaboration. If the truly new insight required for the future is to be generated, this team has shown how it can be done.

The scholars from the project on The Foundations of Moral Education gave generously of their time to provide seminars for the visiting scholars so that they might grasp better the pattern of research which had been done by those teams of philosophers, psychologists and specialists in education. In response with the present volume the scholars from Central and South America and from the Philippines have added a dimension of social experience and concern which probably could not have been realized by scholars in the less troubled atmosphere of North American. The result is a new level of North-South collaboration.

Acknowledgement is made also to Mrs. B. Kennedy for her tireless assistance in preparing materials for the discussions and for this volume, to Joseph Blaney for his careful reading and helpful suggestions, and to the James A. McLeans for their help in the realization of this study.

INTRODUCTION

Concern for values in education has developed rapidly in the last decade. Following a period in which people looked upon science as value-free and had confidence that it could solve all human problems, new sensibilities have developed. More attention is given now to the person as free and responsible and to the life of communities as reflecting their cultures, their rich experience and their deep commitments. This, along with serious problems of social life in society and hence in education, has generated new concern for the moral dimension of education and character development.

All of this generated an urgent need for an integrating understanding of the person and his or her growth and development. In response, The Council for Research in Values and Philosophy (RVP) designed and implemented a three level approach. First, over a two year period, a team of nine philosophers elaborated a volume on the multiple dimensions of the person as moral agent. This drew upon phenomenological insights to trace one's being from its very origins in order to overcome the characteristically modern dilemmas of relating mind to will, and body to spirit. The study worked to integrate also the classical concern for moral norms with more recent contemporary sensibility to human growth. Conversely, it attempted to situate the work done by Piaget and Kohlberg on developmental stages within a deeper metaphysical context which provided new grounding and enriched significance for the development of the human person. The resulting integrated understanding of the person in relation to moral growth is entitled: *Act and Agent: Philosophical Foundations for Moral Education and Character Development*.

A year later a companion team of eleven psychologists undertook to investigate the psychological dynamics of these themes. They not only brought together the relevant resources in their field, but added work on the psychology of such dimensions of moral life as emotions and responsibility which had emerged with new importance in the philosophy volume. This was integrated within an evolved psychological model which expanded and enriched that of Erickson. The implications were traced for moral education at each stage of life, from early childhood to old age. That volume is entitled: *Psychological Foundations of Moral Education and Character Development: An Integrated Theory of Moral Development*.

During the third year a team of thirteen professors of education initiated a two year effort to work out the educational implications of these investigations. In their studies central attention was given, of course, to curriculum implications for personal growth at the various grade, high school and college levels. As the contexts of meaningful personal interaction and of concrete moral challenge, the classroom, school and social environments were also studied.

In discussions of the above work with scholars from other continents it was pointed out, particularly by those in education in Latin America, that these studies focused upon personal growth. Its possibilities, difficulties and modalities, however, are affected fundamentally by the historical dynamics of the community which shape one's life. Hence, the above philosophical, psychological and educational studies needed to be continued in an explicit study of the ways in which society, in its strengths and weaknesses, is fundamental to the educational project.

Consequently, a team consisting largely of Latin American scholars carried out the present cooperative study. This approaches personal life as lived in community, through time, and thereby creating social life, history and culture. Education works with concrete persons and peoples as born into a history and culture which gives them their special capability for moral interaction. Thus, a hermeneutics or interpretation is basic for an education which would draw upon the values of a heritage and enable these to be shaped wisely in circumstances of great social change and hence psychological tension. This work is presented here under the title: *The Social Context of Values: Perspectives of the Americas.*

Part I on "Hermeneutics and the Socio-Historical Context of Values" first studies time, and hence the essentially historical character of the human person. This locates one in society, not as an external environment, but as one's source and destiny.

In this light, what the community has chosen in the past, how it has formed a pattern of values which constitutes its culture, and how it has ordered--and disordered--the structures of relations between persons and groups becomes a basic point of departure for learning appropriate moral relations and developing the capacity to take on the responsibilities of a moral life. To be able to look attentively at the pattern of values which makes human life possible for those growing up in a community and which shapes their destiny, Chapter II looks to hermeneutics.

This is seen both as interpretation of culture and as its critique, for through times of change tradition must be a liberating resource, rather than a set of chains holding a people to outmoded or possibly even exploitive structures. Hence, chapter II opens the way for attention to social analysis (ch III) and depth psychology (ch IV). Both are required in order to understand the external structures and the implied internal dynamics within which we shape our moral choices and build our relations to others.

On these foundations Part II, "Value Horizons and Liberation in Society," is able to look at some of the factors in the
dynamics of contemporary social change under the modernizing
influence of a technological rationalization of life (ch V). To
respond creatively it is necessary to bring to new awareness an
aesthetic striving for purpose, harmony and beauty in our life
(ch VI). In turn, the grounds for this must be found in our
histories as peoples and persons, that is, in our families and
communities. These must be understood then, not as means for
production or consumption, but as expression of human transcendence and hence of the Transcendent Itself (ch VII). This provides both the basis and the fulfillment of the search for liberation at the heart of social life (ch VIII).

The issues treated in this volume are vast. They have
important concrete modalities which require continued and more
detailed study. Such work is already in progress and single volumes in this and related series by The Council for Research in
Values and Philosophy will treat implied thematic issues: *The
Relation Between Cultures; Urbanization and Values; The Humanities, Moral Education and Character Development;* and *The
Personalization of Society: Community and Contemporary Life*;
and related resources in specific cultural traditions: *Moral Education in the Chinese Tradition; Man and Nature in Chinese
Thought; Culture, Human Rights and Peace in Central America;
Love, Community and Social Life in Venezuelan Culture; The
Person in the Cultures of Ghana;* and *Ethics and African Cul-
tures.*

The search to transform, humanize and thereby to deepen
and enrich social life is today the common heart of the search
of peoples, both young and old. This volume is part of that
search.

TABLE OF CONTENTS

PART I

HERMENEUTICS AND

THE SOCIO-HISTORICAL CONTEXT

OF VALUES

CHAPTER I

ETHICS AND HISTORICITY

OLINTO PEGORARO

Ethics as philosophical discourse studies the articulation and evolution of human behavior, especially the habits commonly accepted by the community at a certain cultural moment. This idea of ethics stresses two important dimensions of human behavior: the cultural and the temporal. Like the tongue we speak, our behavior is a living and developing reality; and as living it grows, matures and can die.

Being rooted structurally in both the cultural and the temporal, behavior is not based merely on human interiority or subjectivity, as has been taught in the history of ethics. Contemporary ethics considers community to be the most important and radical foundation of our behavior; it is the soil from which behavior grows.

In effect, the behavior of the community is prior to persons. Each person is born and grows in a preexistent setting and structure of behavior which, in turn, becomes the source of their own behavior. Consequently, the first source of ethics is not human nature characterized by intelligence and free will, but the cultural milieu formed by the living behavior that is approved in some way by the historical community.

Generally communities reflect two main trends in human behavior. The first is a conservative bent: persons react cautiously in matters of behavior. This conservatism is inspired by metaphysics which supports the concept of an immutable essence or nature of human beings, from which one deduces that human behavior will be immutable in its basic expressions.

The second tendency is innovative. This is the effect of new conditions of life in community, especially the recent concentration of millions of persons and the development of efficient media of communication. Due both to the numbers of persons and the mass media as impersonal masters of society, it has become difficult to transmit behavior by teaching principles, as was done in past generations. Especially in the last thirty years, our habits, knowledge and beliefs have been transformed. Despite new opportunities and better living conditions, we have created economic, cultural and military systems of domination. These new life conditions have created serious difficulties for a system of ethics which tends to preserve human behavior in the name of an immutable nature.

An ethics based upon a changing community must take account of the global sense of history, especially the new possibilities to be developed in the future. The second trend reflects this historicity of existence by considering ethics as a system which is historical and based upon the process of transforming the community. Indeed, such an ethics as historical will always be part of the process of the innovation and revelation of new behavior.

As these two tendencies have very different methods, goals and ideas, we shall present a summary of their roots and goals.

THE ROOTS OF ETHICS IN HISTORY

Characteristics of Metaphysical Ethics

In elaborating the first treatise on ethics Greek philosophers deeply influenced occidental culture. Their point of departure was metaphysics which defines the essence of human nature in relation to other beings. From this emerges the first principle of ethics, which can be announced as follows: ethical action is that which is controlled by a rational structure (intelligence and will). As the supreme goal of rational behavior is the contemplation of the supreme being, behavior directed by instinct and sensibility is excluded from the field of ethics.

Christian philosophy and theology operated with these same principles. Rather than creating a new philosophical model, Christian thinkers oriented Greek metaphysics to God as creator of every being and every nature. This relationship between Creator and creature is the basic idea of Christian philosophy. In ethics one finds the same reorientation. God is the basis of the morality of human action. The first pages of the Bible report the fall of man and the New Testament reports divine grace recreating human beings through the death and resurrection of Christ. Thus, this great interpretation of human behavior was supported by both metaphysical and theological structures.

Little by little this interpretation lost its capacity to explain the new ways of life created by scientific and philosophical cultural movements. Dominated by science, the modern age created its own way and proclaimed its independence vis a vis philosophy and theology. While theology became increasingly dogmatic, philosophy experienced a new beginning as philosophers tried to find new answers to the new problems proposed by science.

In this turbulent period, ethics, as the philosophical study of human behavior, became "temporary" and provisional. Descartes in his *Discourse on Method* was the first great thinker to question classical metaphysics and, consequently, the bases of ethics. Kantian criticism laid a new beginning of ethics by introducing the "categorical imperative," which in fact favored individual and formal ethics.

Consequently, ethics, founded in both metaphysics and individuality, became increasingly unable to interpret the movement of science and the cultural process. The scientific interpretation of the cosmos, the evolutionary theory of life and, recently, psychoanalytic therapy revealing the great role of instinct in human behavior shook the bases of rational ethics.

In contrast, contemporary socio-political theories about human existence suggest a new vision of human ethics. Many philosophers consider the new point of departure for ethics to be the personal existent living in community. In sum, cosmological, biological, psychological and sociological challenges all call for a new manner of philosophical and ethical thinking.

Trends in Contemporary Philosophy

Science and technology direct the organization of the contemporary world. Certain nations dominate the mass media and the sophisticated instruments of communication elaborated by electronic technology. Correlatively, nations and communities without technical development become increasingly dependent upon developed countries. Underdeveloped countries are dependent in such crucial areas as education, politics, economy and information. As a result, the power of decision becomes the privilege of a few nations.

Furthermore, the instruments of communication create artificial needs, after the manner of consumerism. This focuses human attention on secondary problems and leads to the neglect of such decisive questions as happiness, a sense of community, participation, justice, education, health for all, etc. The gigantic industrial structures benefit few people, while they exploit and destroy nature and its ecological equilibrium. The dissemination of technology and communication has transformed human behavior.

Contemporary society needs, therefore, to develop new premises, new principles, especially in the field of ethics. In this sense, phenomenology, existentialism, and social philosophy have articulated some very important questions about the sense of the person, community, history, temporality, and the human condition. Psychology and sociology have contributed extensively to the elaboration of these concepts. As a result, the person today is understood as a human existent in relation with other persons who, in turn, are related to nature and culture. This means that the person taken in his/her own interiority and subjectivity is insufficient and incomplete. The notion of person must be completed by relationships to other persons and to the community. Thus, persons find their fulfillment in community, which is integrated by political structures: political structures are the place of full realization of human beings living in a temporal process.

By moving from the concept of the individual to the analysis of the person living in a community and its political context, contemporary philosophy has developed the ontological structure of the historicity of human existence. Historicity and temporality have become the most important concepts in contemporary philosophy. Elaborated during a very long period beginning with Heraclitus, and extending through Augustine to Hegel, these concepts of temporality and historicity have thrust philosophical discourse into the flux of human existence. Philosophical reflection is no longer a strange discourse, coming after the events; it is contemporary to the events and, with its global vision, even anticipates in certain ways the general trends of the influence of culture upon civilization.

Temporality and historicity change the way of considering human beings. In this light the person is not merely an incarnate nature, nor a mere individual in and of him/herself (*in se et per se*), nor a mere thinker of subjectivity. The person is especially a being-in-the-world, an historic being so constituted by the movement of the culture.

The concepts of time and historicity enable one to form a better idea of history, not as a fated and cyclical process, but as the process of human creativity and liberty essential to the constitution of the person and the community. Through science and technique man sets free the forces of nature and integrates them into the global process of liberation.

This process of liberation is made difficult by many obstacles and contradictions, for the articulation of human history includes nonsense and negation. In other words, besides the impulse to create positive structures, we find the organization of destructive impulses appearing in dictatorship, economic oppression, and cultural hegemony. While the destructive impulses operate with a quantitative concept of time (here and now), the process of liberation works with a concept of temporality which involves the experience of tradition (the past), the contemporary situation (the present), and the dimension to come (the future). The creativity of freedom is not merely an idea, but especially an activity transforming and liberating human history. History is made by human work taken in a very large sense: work builds history.

Therefore, human beings, nature, culture and all kinds of technical organization make temporal existence a process of liberty. Temporal existence is a vivid totality formed by human experience of the past and human expectation and possibilities of the future, working in present conditions. The process of liberation reinterprets past human experience and projects temporal existence in the direction of new future possibilities.

TRENDS IN HISTORICAL ETHICS

The analysis of human behavior must be founded in an hermeneutic of human experience. Ethics can no longer depend upon the metaphysical concept of the nature and structure of the individual; today it must follow the process of creative and responsible freedom. Ethics is, so to speak, the eye of liberty and of the historical process; it foresees the direction of the movement of human existence.

As the light of history, ethics is not an ensemble of ethical rules, but a movement of human experience capable of bringing some light to bear upon the route of human pilgrimage. Our life is not determined, our world does not exist; we need to discover it and build it all the time. This discovery is possible through the historical experience of person and community. In fact, there is a deep analogy of human experience through the generations. This historical analogy relates human archeology, as articulation of the past, with teleology as articulation of the future or of new possibilities. Ethics is exactly a double view, both retrospective and prospective. From analyzing the experience of life retrospectively it enlightens decisions about the future possibilities of persons and community. These possibilities constitute the positive goals of history: happiness, liberty, peace, love and justice are the possibilities and goals of human beings in all cultures and ages.

When will humanity attain these goals? Is an historical moment of real peace and justice possible in the world? Intellectualist theories hold that only thinkers, especially philosophers, can attain a happiness which is had through contemplation. Religions reserve the eternal life for persons who live according to revealed principles. Contemporary philosophy developed the idea of achieving happiness and justice in the process of history. Happiness is a human possibility and human beings need to construct values in history during the process of the development of humanity. Liberty and happiness have sense only in the history of the human community.

In order to attain this goal, human beings need to develop work and all the systems and subsystems produced by science, culture, politics, and religion: all are necessary in order progressively to develop human historical existence. Cultural, technological and economic systems and subsystems should be coordinated politically, for politics is the center of decision-making by the community. Historical analogy and the contributions of science, philosophy, psychology, religion, and politics are needed to enlighten the teleological horizon of this human existence.

Man as Historical Being

Above we saw the study of ethics moving from metaphysics to historical analysis. This shifts the roots of ethics to human beings as, above all, temporal beings. Today the diverse sciences and methods, and the mutual collaboration between different systems of knowledge, help philosophy to analyze human existence as a temporal structure, ontologically finite and historically limited.

Historical ethics finds its roots in this human finitude; it depends upon the historicity of human beings. Teilhard de Chardin noted that thinking began when primordial energy attained its the "highest complexification" in human beings; with this began also history or the organization of meaning. Before human beings there existed only the blind movement of nature; the advent of thinking inaugurated a realm of liberty and indeterminism. From this moment on, things and events could be oriented in different ways according to the directions of thought. Science, culture, philosophy and religion summon nature to take part in the realm of liberty: the human mission is to construct a free world.

The evolutive process is founded in human thinking which transforms nature into the cultural world in which man lives. Human thinking also involves work in the cyclical relation or dialectic between thinking and work called *praxis*, which has built the sense of history. The historical process is not a triumphal procession; on the contrary, the process of liberty has many obstacles, questions, great darkness and conflicts. It can be concluded therefore that history does not have a definite route preestablished by divine powers, but is a field of liberty, constructing itself constantly through human experience.

Now and again in history there are new moments of insight. Thus, in philosophy, Kant raised new problems when he put the questions: What can we know; what should we do; what can we hope; what is a human being? Today we know that there are no answers to these questions, but that further insight is attained at certain periods. In science there is a new beginning with the theories of relativity. In religion there is a continual rethinking of the foundations in order to interpret new human situations. Philosophy, science, and religion all articulate historical experience with the aim of creating more liberty, autonomy and happiness in human community.

Knowledge is neither determined by a fatal power, nor spontaneous. Between these two extremes of determinism and relativism lies historical knowledge of the process of human existence. This is more practice than theory: it is the practice of elaborating concepts, dates and socio-political experience.

Today, a variety of sciences elaborate different interpretations of being human, some of which are described below.

Metaphysical Man (Homo Metaphysics). The metaphysics of human existence elaborated by Plato and Aristotle lasted more than 2000 years. It considered man, like other beings, to be composed of matter as the chaotic or indetermined element and form as the specific element. These two elements govern and command such potentialities of the human being as instinct, sensibility and imagination, especially linked with matter. Form especially commands intelligence and will, that is, rationality, which gives human beings their capacity for thinking and deciding. This is the divine (*intellectus agens*) and immortal power in human beings

Ancient philosophy never managed to link rationality with sensibility. It saw human behavior as governed by rationality, while all actions which cannot be controlled by reason were excluded from the field of ethics. This division between reason and the senses continued until the advent of psychoanalysis.

Psychological Man (Homo Psychicus). Along with metaphysics there developed the idea of the spirituality of the soul and of an interior life. In the Christian era, Augustine especially cultivated this tendency, seeing the soul and human interiority as the place of encounter with God who lives in human interiority: God is closer to me than I am to myself (*Deus est intimior meipso*). For Augustine temporality is a dimension of our interiority. Whereas in common life and language we speak about time as past, present and future, for Augustine the soul lives in three dimensions: memory, which keeps alive the experiences of the past; expectancy, which anticipates our future projects; and situation, which is the whole of present events. Therefore, time is precisely memory, expectancy and situation as living human experience vividly present in our interiority.

The study of human interiority gained new life with experimental psychology, which elaborated a more scientific and less metaphysical approach. Psychoanalysis carried the study of human interiority still further by giving a large place to instinct as governing much of the human behavior formerly considered a field of reason. Ethics would no longer be controlled simply by reason and metaphysics; the analysis of the unconscious would take a decisive place in judging human behavior.

Economic Man (Homo Oeconomicus). In the technological era human beings, especially on the material or sense level, are considered to have a great capacity for consumption. Industrial technology and mass media, linked with political power and concentrations of wealth, constitute a powerful system which acts upon the human being. This is the era of production, building and making (*homo-faber*) in which the human being is urged to consume what is produced. This distracts man from his subjectivity and interiority and makes him live on the surface, as it were, in terms of the common and external occurrences of everyday life. As a result, the quality of life has diminished and people are increasingly absorbed by the structures of production, industrialization and communication. Because our civilization lives in economic and military dependence, two thirds of humanity live in the misery of hunger, disease, ignorance, and bad housing. This situation has generated such suspicion and antipathy between persons, communities and nations that our civilization has lost its confidence.

In spite of this situation, economic man (*homo-oeconomicus*) has attained fantastic results in the scientific field, dominating the macro-cosmos by space travel, the micro-cosmos by dividing atoms, the biocosmos by genetic exploration. Today it seems possible to "construct" "artificial man"--a surrogate to serve as the slave of economic man.

Human behavior, formerly studied primarily by metaphysics and later in terms of psychoanalytical theories, today may become a scientific field in the department of genetics as the biological code reveals more of one's future behavior.

Therefore scientific and technological progress, on the one hand, and extreme human misery, on the other, have made ethical problems a universal challenge. They are questions of living and not merely theoretical problems; they regard personal and especially community life. Particular problems must be located in the broader context of community, and solved on the basis of broader principles which involve the social context. Science, technology and industrialization all need to be defined in terms of the community. The most important point of departure for contemporary ethics is the person-living-in-community and attempting to develop, above all, structures of justice, solidarity and participation as the major bases for a new society involving all nations and cultures.

Homo-historicus

Metaphysical ethics created a solitary man searching for happiness through the contemplation of the idea of perfection. Psychological ethics explored human interiority as distinct and separated from the external world. The ethics of economic man (*homo oeconomicus*) produced a crisis by the extreme exteriorization of man as a consumer of products and a slave in structures of domination. In this way mankind has been falling into the slavery to its own systems.

Today philosophers, psychologists and theologians are developing an ethical structure based upon the concept of the person involving, not only the rational, but the instinctive and sensitive dimensions as well. Unconscious sexual and biological tendencies are seriously considered: one's personality is accepted as a whole. Further, because one's personality is intrinsically incomplete and finite, we must be open to others, constituting thereby the interpersonal horizon in which persons understand one another.

The most recent development in ethics involves not only interpersonal relations, but especially the world of cultural-structures. Here, phenomenology helped unveil the structures of comprehension (*verstehen*): situatedness (*befindlichkeit*), openness (*erschlossenheit*), and truth (*warheit*) as human-beings-existing-with-others (*mitsein*). Through these structures we find temporality (*zeitlichkeit*) at the root of human existence. From them the human being emerges as a relational-being constituted of social relations in an historical process.

Life then is a process or movement which over the millennia has achieved the power of thought in human beings who are the result of both a natural process and historical development. Culture, science, politics, religion and philosophy were built through a dialectical relation of human thought and work. Natural determinism fell under the influence of historical indeterminism, manifested in freedom, creativity, science and technology. The human being became the conductor of history, as nature became culture; this, in turn, revealed new and hidden dimensions of nature.

Human beings can construct a just or unjust world, peace or war, liberty or slavery: nature and history can be humanized or de-humanized. In a positive sense, in building the world, human beings create liberty and transform the process into an immense movement of liberation realized by human work and thought. This process is based on a relation with nature and community, for without community there is no man, no nature, no process, no history. Community, therefore, is not the realm of impersonality, but the horizon of personalization. All this forms the idea of temporal or historical man (*homo-historicus*). Temporality is the radical force moving the human being and, through him/her, nature.

Historical time is evidently different from cosmological time. Cosmological or chronological time is quantitative and artificial; through it science and technology calculate the age of nature and the years of a human being. It can be an object that we buy and sell: 'time is money.' In contrast, languages and discourse are founded on chronological time: we can form a sentence using three times, but it is impossible to build a sentence without time.

Historical time is a living movement of liberation and is simultaneous. For example, our studies of the past are a present exercise of our culture: personal history and the history of community permit the living exercise here and now of our past experience. We can live here and now with sentiments provoked by future events. Consequently, historical time exists simultaneously as a living experience and as the wisdom of community.

Learning from historical wisdom enables a community to prepare future events. Though difficult, especially when we want to project the future, this is possible when science, technology, philosophy and economics are shaped by a broad political vision which is inspired by the experience of the community. The wisdom of the community needs help from thinkers and scientists in finding the path of liberation.

All this forms the ethical dimension of life which, in turn, sheds light upon the community. The ethical illumines both the general behavior of society and persons and the human-life-in-community as the first value and the basis of all others. Cultural movements, technical organizations and social structures will be ethically positive to the degree that they promote the life of community. Consequently, social behavior is more important than individual behavior. We need an historical awareness which enables us to see that personal realization is radically connected to the realization of the community inspired by a concept of justice.

FOUNDATIONS OF ETHICS

We saw that the human community as involved in the historical process of liberation is the foundation of contemporary ethics. Today we cannot speak of absolute and evident foundations. Science undergoes evolution even in its foundation and principles; logic, mathematics and philosophy also evolve. Therefore, the different fields of human knowledge prefer the model of an open space or field rather than of a foundation, for all modes of knowledge are open and progress indefinitely. Hence, the image of a substantial foundation is substituted by the image of future being (*advenant*) as a milieu or open space in which science, mathematics, philosophy and religion organize their scientific structures, which remain always temporary.

The image of a foundation is replaced also by the image of an abyss (*abgrund*). Knowledge is indefinite in its directions because reality is always moving and future (*advenant*). Events come and disappear in the process of time: reality as elaborated by human knowledge is precisely this movement of coming and disappearing. The same is true of the movement of culture: beyond the determinism of natural law we find that the world of freedom is organized by culture. This lifts nature from its foundations and situates it in the movement toward the future.

In this sense, the phenomenological movement tries to draw ethics beyond a static foundation. Ethics is based upon the community as it comes-to-be: community, historical conscience, and temporal process inspire the conception of an historical ethics which articulates human history as a process directed toward the general goal of creating liberty and happiness, but without definite structures. Its general orientation is found in the experience of community, in the sayings of philosophers and religious persons. It does not have a definite organization, but must be invented and re-invented by community in every historical situation.

Historical ethics, however, is not a spontaneous movement; on the contrary, it depends upon a serious analysis and reflection on human experience, the human condition and human aspirations. In this reflection, persons and the community find motivations for which it is worth living or dying. These, in turn, enable people to triumph over such historical deviations as dictatorship, commercialism, sensualism and other limited vision. In this, historical ethics must be aided by sociological, political, scientific and religious studies which can enlighten the human community in its movement toward a *telos* that is always present but never definitely attained. That *telos* is happiness in the most radical sense.

Universidad Federal do Rio de Janeiro
Rio de Janeiro, Brazil

CHAPTER II

HERMENEUTICS, HISTORICITY AND VALUES

GEORGE F. McLEAN

This chapter concerns the appropriation and realization of values by persons living with others in time. Optimistically, time might be seen as the opportunity for one to become aware of the good received in creation, to be attracted in turn to creative action, and therein to exercise one's freedom. More pessimistically, the history of human freedom has never been a tale simply of the good, for the human possibility to do good is correlatively the ability to fail and to do evil. Consequently, the task here is not simply to draw from history a vision of the good and of values, but to determine how to decipher these from a history of human ambiguities and to work with persons of other outlooks in applying these in new and creative ways. In a word the task is one of interpretation, that is to say, of hermeneutics.

DIMENSIONS OF THE PROBLEM

The term 'hermeneutics' is derived from the son of Zeus, Hermes, the messenger of the Olympian gods. This etymological root with its three elements--(1) a messenger, (2) from the gods and (3) to mankind--suggests three corresponding dimensions of our problem, namely, hermeneutics, values and historicity.

Hermeneutics. The circumstances of the Greek messenger make manifest the basic dilemma of hermeneutics and interpretation, which has come to be called the hermeneutic circle. This consists in the fact that any understanding of the parts requires an understanding of the whole, while the grasp of the whole depends upon some awareness of its parts. This appears in four ways. First, the herald had not merely to pass on a written text, but to speak or proclaim it. This could be done only by reading through all the parts of the message in sequence. But grasping these as parts requires some understanding of the whole message from the very beginning. How can a whole of meaning depend upon parts, which for their very meaning depend upon the whole? Secondly, the message had to be conveyed in a particular historical time and place, and with specific intonation and inflection. But this would convey only one particular sense from the many potentialities of the words. Thirdly, the messenger had not only to express, but also to explain the message and its ramifications or meaning. This required a certain awareness of the broader context of the issue and of the language as the repository of the culture within which the message was composed. In sum, in order to interpret, convey, or receive a message, some sense of the whole is required for assembling and interpreting its parts; but how can one know the whole before knowing its parts?

This appears also from the task of the messenger in translating or bearing the meaning of the text from the source in its own context, to others in their distinctive set of circumstances and with their projects and preoccupations. The etymology of the term underlines this task. 'Interpret' combines *praesto*: to show, manifest or exhibit, with the prefix *inter* to indicate the distinction of the one from whom and the one to whom the message is passed.[1] This difference could be between past and present, as when an ancient text is being reread today; between one culture and another, as when a text in another language than one's own is being interpreted; or indeed, between persons, even in the same culture and time, provided full attention be paid to the uniqueness of each person. But given this difference, how is communication and its implied 'community' between the two contexts possible? And were it not to be possible we would be left with never-ending violent clashes between persons, classes and values.

Values. The term 'value' was derived from the economic sphere where it meant the amount of a commodity required in order to bring a certain price. This is reflected also in the term 'axiology,' the root of which means "weighing as much" or "worth as much." This has objective content, for the good must really "weigh in"; it must make a real difference.[2]

But the term 'value' expresses this good especially as related to persons who actually acknowledge it as a good and respond to it as desirable. Thus, different individuals or groups, or possibly the same but at different periods, may have distinct sets of values as they become sensitive to, and prize, distinct sets of goods. More generally, over time a subtle shift takes place in the distinctive ranking of the degree to which they prize various goods. By so doing they delineate among objective moral goods a certain pattern of values which in a more stable fashion mirrors their corporate free choices. This constitutes the basic topology of a culture; as repeatedly reaffirmed through time, it builds a tradition or heritage.

By giving shape to the culture, values constitute the prime pattern and gradation of goods experienced from their earliest years by persons born into that heritage. In these terms they interpret and shape the development of their relations with other persons and groups. Young persons, as it were, peer out at the world through cultural lenses which were formed by their family and ancestors and which reflect the pattern of choices made by their community through its long history--often in its most trying circumstances. Like a pair of glasses, values do not create the object, but they do reveal and focus attention upon certain goods and patterns of goods rather than upon others.

Thus values become the basic orienting factor for one's affective and emotional life. Over time, they encourage certain patterns of action--and even of physical growth--which, in turn, reinforce the pattern of values. Through this process we constitute our universe of moral concern in terms of which we struggle to achieve, mourn our failures, and celebrate our successes.[3] This is our world of hopes and fears, in terms of which, as Plato wrote in the *Laches*, our lives have moral meaning and one can properly begin to speak of virtues.

The reference to the god, Hermes, in the term 'hermeneutics' suggests something of the depth of the meaning which is sought and its implication for the world of values. For the message borne by Hermes is not merely an abstract mathematical formula or a methodological prescription devoid of human meaning and value. Rather, it is the limitless wisdom regarding the source--and hence reality--and regarding the priorities--and hence the value--of all. Hesiod had appealed for this in the introduction to his *Theogony*: "Hail, children of Zeus! Grant lovely song and celebrate the holy race of the deathless gods who are forever. . . . Tell how at the first gods and earth came to be."[4]

Aristotle indicated this concern for values in describing his science of wisdom as "knowing to what end each thing must be done . . . ; and this end is the good of that thing, and in general the supreme good in the whole of nature." Such a science will be most divine, for: "(1) God is thought to be among the causes of all things and to be a first principle, and (2) such a science either God alone can have, or God above all others. All the sciences, indeed, are more necessary than this, but none is better."[5] Hence, rather than considering things in a perspective that is only temporal and totally changing--with an implied total relativization of all--hermeneutics or interpretation is essentially open to a vision of what is most real in itself and most lasting through time, that is, to the perennial in the realm of being and values.

Historicity. In undertaking his search for unchanging and permanent guides for human action Socrates had directed the attention of the Western mind away from the temporal and changing. In redirected attention back to this changing universe, the modern mind still echoed Socrates by searching for the permanent structures of complex entities and the stable laws of change. Nevertheless, its attention to the essentially temporal character of mankind and hence to the uniqueness of each decision, individual and corporate, opened important new horizons.

In the term hermeneutics, the element of translation or interpretation by stresses the presentation to the one who receives the message. This makes their historical situation, and hence the historical character of human life, essential. It brings into consideration not merely the persuit of general truth, but those to whom truth is expressed, namely, persons in the concrete circumstances of their cultures as these have developed through the history of human interaction with nature, with other human beings and with God.

This human history sets the circumstances in which one perceives the values presented in the tradition and then mobilizes his or her own project toward the future. Given the admixture of good and evil in human action the process of realizing the good in human history always has been compromised with evil. Consequently the past as well as the present must always be deciphered or interpreted in order to identify its value content--as well as the contradictions of that content. Projections towards the realization of values in the future must provide also for encountering and overcoming evil.

THE CHALLENGE TO HERMENEUTICS

In working upon these three themes: hermeneutics, values and historicity, there are two major problems. One concerns truth; it is the rationalist/enlightenment ideal of clarity for all knowledge worthy of the name. The other concerns the good as the object of our will; it is our penchant for considering either only what is good or of value, or only what is evil.

Truth

The enlightenment ideal focuses upon ideas which are clear and distinct both in themselves and in their interconnection. As such they are divorced--often intentionally--from existential or temporal significance. Such an ideal of human knowledge, it is proposed, would be achieved either through an intellect working by itself from an Archemedian principle or through the senses drawing their ideas from experience and combining them in myriad tautological transformations.[6] In either case the result is an a-temporal and consequently non-historical ideal of knowledge. This revolutionary view was adhered to even by the romantics who appeared to oppose it, for in turning to the past and to myths they too sought clear and distinct knowledge of human reality. Thinking that this could be attained if all was understood in its historical context and sequence, they placed historicity ultimately at the service of the rationalist ideal.

In the rationalist view any meaning not clearly and distinctly perceived was an idol to be smashed, an idea to be bracketed by doubt, or something to be wiped clean from the slate of the mind as irrational and coercive. Any type of judgment--even if provisional--made before all had been examined and its clarity and distinctness established would be essentially a prejudgment or prejudice, and therefore a dangerous imposition by the will.

This raises a number of problems. First, absolute knowledge of oneself or of others, simply and without condition, is not possible, for the knower is always conditioned according to his or her position in time and space and in relation to others. But neither is such knowledge of ultimate interest for the reality of human knowledge, as of being, develops in time and with others. This does not exclude the more limited projects of scientific knowledge, but it does identify these precisely as limited and specialized views: they make specific and important--but not all-controlling--contributions.

Secondly, as reason is had by all and completely according to Descartes,[7] authority could be only an entitlement of some to decide issues by an application of their will rather than according to an authentic understanding of the truth or justice of an issue. Further, the limited number of people in authority means that the vision of which they disposed would be limited by restricted individual interests. Finally, as one decision constitutes a precedent for those to follow, authority must become fundamentally bankrupt and hence corruptive.[8]

Hermeneutics will need to relocate knowledge in the ongoing process of human discovery as taking place within a still broader project of human interaction.

Good

A second problem area for hermeneutics concerns the good, for it is important to avoid the danger of attempting to take either the good or the bad--values or their negations--in isolation one from another. In considering only the good, or values, there is danger of abstracting from human life; one loses the sense of the struggle to realize values and tends to supplant this with an idealistic simplicity and inhumane rigor. Ultimately this can only discourage and then destroy authentically human efforts toward the realization of values. Further, recognizing that the values we experience have been embodied in our traditions, by considering only values we are in danger either of considering as an absolute norm a tradition which in human history can only be ambiguous--thereby continuing its disvalues as well--or upon recognizing evil therein of rejecting the tradition as a whole.

Finally, it is sometimes observed that the tendency to turn to tradition gives a priority to conservatism in personal ethos or public politics. Those who by privileged education have been able to become familiar with that tradition are constituted thereby as an elite in relation to which others, rather than being encouraged in their freedom, are pressed into a state of dependency.

Other problems derive from treating the negation of value without the broader context of the good--that is, of making evil the context for the consideration of the good. The meaning of evil is dependent upon the good and cannot be understood without some notion thereof. On the one hand, one might surreptitiously suppose a pattern of values which, being unarticulated and uncriticized, is in danger of being partial or false--and later disasterously misleading in our effort to realize a society worthy of mankind. On the other hand, and still worse, one might have no notion of the human good and thus reduce the description of evil to the simply factual. In that case, it would be no more than a structure described by a value-free theory, without relation to the area of human freedom or responsibility. The antithesis, evil, without its thesis, good, is either blind to, or devoid of, value concern.

Finally, where all, including evil, is a mere state of affairs, one cannot hope to generate a sense of the good or of value. When the horizon becomes one of mere psychological manipulation of the ego, the response can be only by further manipulation. This allows the ego to dominate the self and thereby excludes human freedom. Politically, for lack of an horizon adequate for the appreciation of freedom no progressive liberation can occur. Instead socio-political changes become mere substitutions of one manipulator for another until there arrives one whose permanence is due to his or her success in repressing others.

The problem then is how to understand or interpret human values in a tradition, which, in its human ambiguity, contains not only its classical ideals, but its historical contradictions. This enables one, in the words of John Dewey, to discover

> in thoughtful observation and experiment the method of administering the unfinished processes of existence so that frail goods shall be substantiated, secure goods be extended and the precarious promises of good that haunt experienced things be more liberally fulfilled.[9]

The response here will follow a dialectical pattern. The thesis will concern the hermeneutics of value discovery in history and tradition. The critique or antithesis will look at the way contradictions of value also are integral to the dynamics of human social structures and the problems this generates for deciphering the values in one's tradition, for sharing in the vision of other people and for working together toward a future which more fully realizes human values. The final step will look for the ways in which tradition and critique are mutually interdependent, working as thesis and antithesis toward the elaboration of a synthesis in which each person can make his/her full and proper contribution to life in our times.

TRADITION

This section will attend: first to tradition as the normative locus and summation of the ambiguous human experience of values; second, to the notion of application as the progressive revelation of meaning and of value in the concrete circumstances of history; and third to hermeneutics as a method for making positive use of the distinctiveness of one's own point in history in order more broadly to appreciate this content of human experience.

To situate and emphasize the relation of meaning to tradition John Caputo, in *Act and Agent: Foundations for Moral Education and Character Development*, notes that from its very beginnings before birth one's experience is lived in and with the biological rhythms of one's mother. Upon birth there follows a progressively broader sharing in the life of parents and siblings; this is the context in which one is fully at peace, and hence most open to personal growth and social development. In a word, from its beginning one's life has been historical: it has been lived in time and with other persons. In the family human life and learning is realized in relation to prior life and learning upon which it depends for development and orientation. This is the universal condition of each person, and consequently of the development of human awareness and knowledge.

In terms of this phenomenological understanding interpersonal dependence is not unnatural--quite the contrary. We depend for our being upon our creator, we are conceived in dependence upon our parents, and we are nurtured by them with care and concern. Through the years we depend continually upon our family and peers, school and community. Beyond our personal and social group we turn eagerly to other persons whom we recognize as superior, not basically in terms of their will, but in terms of their insight and judgment precisely in those matters where truth, reason and balanced judgment are required. The preeminence or authority of wise persons in the community is not something they usurp or with which they are arbitrarily endowed, but is based upon their capabilities and acknowledged in our free and reasoned response. Thus, the burden of Plato's *Republic* is precisely the education of the future leader to be able to exercise authority, for while the leader who is wise but indecisive may be ineffective, the one who is decisive but foolish is bound upon destruction.

From this notion of authority it is possible to construct that of tradition by adding to present interchange additional generations with their accumulation of human insight predicated upon the wealth of their human experience through time. As a process of trial and error, of continual correction and addition, history constitutes a type of learning and testing laboratory in which the strengths of various insights can be identified and reinforced, while their deficiencies are corrected and complemented. The cumulative results of the extended process of learning and testing constitute tradition. The historical and prophetical books of the Bible constitute just such an extended concrete account of one's people's process of discovery carried out in interaction with the divine.

The content of a tradition serves as a model and exemplar, not because of personal inertia, but because of the corporate character of the learning by which it was built out of experience and the free and wise acts of succeeding generations in reevaluating, reaffirming, preserving and passing on what has been learned. The content of a long tradition has passed the test of countless generations. Standing, as it were, on the shoulders of our forebears, we are able to discover and evaluate situations with the help of their vision because of the sensitivity they developed and communicated to us. Without this we could not even choose topics to be investigated or awaken within ourselves the desire to investigate those problems.[10]

Tradition, then, is not simply everything that ever happened, but only what appears significant in the light of those who have appreciated and described it. Indeed, this presentation by different voices draws out its many aspects. Thus tradition is not an object in itself, but a rich source from which multiple themes can be drawn according to the motivation and interest of the inquirer. It needs to be accepted and embraced, affirmed and cultivated. Here the emphasis is neither upon the past or the present, but upon mankind living through time.[11]

But neither is tradition a passive storehouse of materials to be drawn upon and shaped at the arbitrary will of the present inquirer; rather, it presents insight and wisdom that is normative for life in the present and future. Just as prudence (*phronesis*) without law (*nomos*) would be as relativistic and ineffectual as muscular action without a skeletal substructure, so law built simply upon transcendental or abstract vision, without taking account of historicity, would be irrelevant idealism. Hence, there is need to look into historicity to see if human action in time can engender a vision which sufficiently transcends its own time to be normative for the present and directive for the future.

This would consist of a set of values and goals which each person should seek to realize. Its harmony of measure and fullness would suggest a way for the mature and perfect formation of man.[12] Such a vision would be both historical and normative: historical because arising in time and presenting an appropriate way to preserve and promote human life through time; normative because presenting a basis upon which to judge past ages, present actions and options for the future. The fact of human striving manifests that every humanism, far from being indifferent to all, is committed to the realization of some such classical and perduring model of perfection.

It would be erroneous, however, to consider this to be merely a matter of knowledge, for then it would engage, not entire peoples, but only a few whom it would divide into opposing schools. The project of a tradition is much broader and can be described only in terms of the more inclusive existential and phenomenological horizon of Samay and Caputo in *Act and Agent*[13], namely, as including both body and spirit, knowledge and love. It is, in fact, the whole human dynamism of reaching out to others in striving toward ever more complete personal and social fulfillment through the realization of understanding and love, and thereby of justice and peace.

Finally, the classical model is not drawn forward artificially by overcoming chronological distance; rather, it acts as inspiration of, and judgment upon, man's best efforts. Through time it is the timeless mode of history. We do not construct it, but belong to it, just as it belongs to us--for it is the ultimate community of human striving. Hence, historical and cultural self-criticism is not simply an individual act of subjectivity, but our situatedness in a tradition as this fuses in us past, present and future.[14]

As mentioned in the introduction, the sense of the good or of value which constitutes tradition is required also in order to appreciate the real impact of the achievements and deformations of the present. Without tradition, present events become simply facts of the moment, succeeded by counter-facts in ever succeeding waves of contradiction. This would constitute a history written in terms of violence in which human despair would turn to a Utopian abstraction of merely human origin--a kind of *1984* designed according to the reductive limitations of a modern rationalism.

This stands in brutal contrast to the cumulative richness of vision acquired by peoples through the ages and embodied in the figure of a Bolivar or Lincoln, a Gandhi or Mother Theresa, or a Martin Luther King. They certainly were not mere matters of fact, but eminently free and unique. As concrete universals they exemplified the above-mentioned harmony of measure and fullness which is at once classical and historical, ideal and personal, normative and free. Living in their own times, they emerge out of history to judge and inspire peoples of all times and places.

APPLICATION

In entering upon application we turn, as it were, from the whole to its parts, from tradition to its particular meaning for each new time as we turn to ordering the present and sconstructing the future. This is a matter, first of all, of taking time seriously, that is, of recognizing that reality includes authentic novelty. This contrasts to the perspective of Plato for whom the real is the ideal, the forms or ideas transcending matter and time, of which physical things and temporal events are but shadows. It also goes beyond rationalism's search for clear and distinct knowledge of eternal and simple natures and their relations. A fortiori, it goes beyond method alone without content.

In contrast to all these, Gadamer's notion of application[15] means that tradition, with its inherent authority or normative force, achieves its perfection in the temporal unfolding of reality. Secondly, it shows human persons, not as detached intellects, but as inextricably enabled by, and formative of, their changing physical and social universe. Thirdly, in the area of moral values and human action it expresses directly the striving of persons to realize their lives, the orientation of this striving and its development into a fixed attitude (*hexis*). Hence, as distinct from the physical order *ethos* is a situation neither of law or of lawlessness, but of human and therefore developing institutions and attitudes which regulate, but do not determine.[16]

There are certain broad guidelines for the area of ethical knowledge which can serve in the application of tradition as a guide for historical practice. The concrete and unique reality of human freedom when lived with others through time constitutes a distinctive and ever-changing process. This is historicity and means that our responses to the good are made always in concrete and ever changing circumstances. Hence, the general principles of ethics as a philosophic science of action must not be purely theoretical knowledge or a simple accounting from the past. Instead, they must help people exercise their conscious freedom in concrete historical circumstances which as ever-changing are ever new

Here an important distinction must be made between techné and ethics. In techné action is governed by an idea as an exemplary cause which is fully determined and known by objective theoretical knowledge (epistéme). Skill consists in knowing how to act according to that idea or plan; and when it cannot be carried out perfectly some parts of it are simply omitted in the execution.

In ethics the situation, though similar in the possession of a practical guide and its application to a particular task, differs in important ways. First, in action as moral the subject constitutes oneself, as much as one makes the object: agents are differentiated by their action. Hence, moral knowledge as an understanding of the appropriateness of human action cannot be fully determined independently of the subjects in their situation.

Secondly, adaptation by moral agents in their application of the law, does not diminish, but rather corrects and perfects it. In relation to a world which is less ordered, the law is imperfect for it cannot contain in any explicit manner the response to the concrete possibilities which arise in history. It is precisely here that the freedom and creativity of the person is located. This does not consist in an arbitrary response, for Kant is right in saying that without law freedom has no meaning. Nor does it consist simply in an automatic response determined by the historical situation, for then determinism and relativism would compete for the crown in undermining human freedom. Human freedom consists rather in shaping the present according to a sense of what is just and good, and in a way which manifests and indeed creates for the first time more of what justice and goodness mean.

Hence, the law is perfected by its application in the circumstances. Epoché and equity do not diminish, but perfect the law. Without them the law would be simply a mechanical replication doing the work not of justice, but of injustice. Ethics is not only knowledge of what is right in general, but the search for what is right in the situation and the choice of the right means for this situation. Knowledge about the means then is not a matter of mere expediency; it is the essence of the search for a more perfect application of the law in the given situation. This is the fulfilment of moral knowledge.[17]

It will be important to note here that the rule of the concrete (of what the situation is asking of us) is known not by sense knowledge which simply registers a set of concrete facts. In order to know what is morally required, the situation must be understood in the light of what is right, that is, in the light of what has been discovered about appropriate human action through the tradition with its normative character. Only in this light can moral consciousness as the work of intellect (*nous*) rather than of sensation go about its job of choosing the right means.

Hence, to proceed simply in reaction to concrete injustices as present negations of the good, rather than in the light of one's tradition, is ultimately destructive. It inverts the order just mentioned and result in manipulation of our hopes for the good. Destructive or repressive structures would lead us to the use of correspondingly evil means, truly suited only to producing evil results. The true response to evil can be worked out only in terms of the good as discovered by our people, passed on in tradition and applied by us in our times.

The importance of application manifests the central role played by the virtue of prudence (*phronesis*) or thoughtful reflection which enables one to discover the appropriate means for the circumstances. This must include also the virtue of sagacity (*sunesis*), that is, of understanding or concern for the other. For what is required as a guide for the agent is not only technical knowledge of an abstract ideal, but knowlege that takes account of the agent in relation to other persons. One can assess the situation adequately only inasmuch as one, in a sense, undergoes the situation with the affected parties. Thus, Aristotle rightly describes as "terrible" the one who can make the most of the situation, but without orientation towards moral ends, that is, without concern for the good of others in their situations.

In sum, application is not a subsequent or accidental part of understanding, but co-determines this understanding from the beginning. Moral consciousness must seek to understand the good, not as an ideal to be known and then applied, but rather through discerning the good for concrete persons in their relations with others.

This can contribute to sorting out the human dilemma between an absolutism insensitive to persons in their concrete circumstances and a relativism which leaves the person subject to expediency in public and private life. Indeed, the very statement of the dilemma reflects the deleterious aspect of the Platonic view of ideas. He was right to ground changing and historical being in the unchanging and eternal. This had been Parmenides' first insight in metaphysics and was richly developed in relation to human action through the medievals' notion of an eternal law in the divine mind. But it seems inappropriate to speak directly in these terms regarding human life. In all things individual human persons and humankind as a whole are subject to time, growth and development. As we become increasingly conscious of this the human character of even our abstract ideals becomes manifest and their adapted application in time can be seen, not as their rejection, but as their perfection. In this, justice loses none of its force as an absolute requirement of human action. Rather, the concrete modes of its application in particular circumstances add to what can be articulated in merely abstract and universal terms. A hermeneutic approach directs attention precisely to these unfoldings of the meaning of abstract principles through time. This is not an abandonment of absolutes, but a recognition of the human condition and of the way in which it enriches our knowledge of the principles of human life.

What then should we conclude regarding this sense of the good which mankind has discovered, in which we have been raised, which gives us dominion over our actions, and which enables us to be free and creative? Does it come from God or from man, from eternity or from history? Chakravarti Rajagopalachari of Madras answered:

> Whether the epics and songs of a nation spring from the faith and ideas of the common folk, or whether a nation's faith and ideas are produced by its literature is a question which one is free to answer as one likes. . . . Did clouds rise from the sea or was the sea filled by waters from the sky? All such inquiries take us to the feet of God transcending speech and thought.[18]

HERMENEUTICS

Thusfar we have treated the character and importance of tradition. This bears the long experience of persons interacting with this world, with other persons and with God. It is made up not only of chronological facts, but of insights regarding human perfection which have been forged by human efforts in concrete circumstances, e.g., the Greek notion of democracy and the enlightenment notions of equality and freedom. By their internal value these stand as normative of the aspirations of people's.

Secondly, we have seen the implications of historicity for novelty in the context of tradition, the continually unfolding circumstances of historical development, and the way in which these not merely extend or repeat what went before but constitute an emerging manifestation of the dynamic character of the vision articulated by the art, religion, literature and political structures of a cultural tradition.

It remains for us now to treat the third element in this study of tradition, namely, hermeneutics. How can earlier sources which express the great achievements of human awareness be understood in a way that is relevant, indicative, and directive of our life in present circumstances? In a word, how can we draw out the significance of tradition for present action?

First of all it is necessary to note that only a unity of meaning, that is, an identity, is intelligible.[19] Just as it is not possible to understand a number three if we include but two units rather than three, no act of understanding is possible unless it is directed to an identity or whole of meaning. This brings us to the classic issue in the field, described above as the hermeneutic circle in which knowledge of the whole depends upon knowledge of the parts, and vice versa. How can we make this work for, rather than against us?

The experience of reading a text might help. As we read we construe the meaning of a sentence before grasping all its individual parts. What we construe is dependent upon our expectation of the meaning of the sentence, which we derived from its first words, the prior context, or more likely a combination of the two. In turn, our expectation or construal of the meaning of the text is adjusted according to the requirements of its various parts as we proceed to read through the parts of the sentence, the paragraph, etc., continually reassessing the whole in terms of the parts and the parts in terms of the whole. This basically circular movement continues until all appears to fit and to be clear.

Similarly, as we begin to look into our tradition we develop a prior conception of its content. This anticipation of meaning is not simply of the tradition as an objective or fixed content to which we come; it is rather what we produce as we participate in the evolution of the tradition, and thereby further determine ourselves. This is a creative stance reflecting the content, not only of the past, but of the time in which I stand and of the life project in which I am engaged. It is a creative unveiling of the content of the tradition as this comes progressively and historically into the present and through the present, passes into the future.

In this light time is not a barrier, separation or abyss, but rather a bridge and opportunity for the process of understanding, a fertile ground filled with experience, custom and tradition. The importance of the historical distance it provides is not that it enables the subjective reality of persons to disappear so that the objectivity of the situation can emerge. On the contrary, it makes possibile a more complete meaning of the tradition, less by removing falsifying factors, than by opening new sources of self-understanding which reveal in the tradition unsuspected implications and even new dimensions of meaning.[20]

Of course, not all our acts of understandings are correct, whether they be about the meaning of a text from another culture, a dimension of a shared tradition, a set of goals, or a plan for future action. Hence, it becomes particularly important that they not be adhered to fixedly, but be put at risk in dialogue with others.

In this the basic elements of meaning remains the substances which Aristotle described in terms of autonomy and, by implication, of identity. Hermeneutics would expand this to reflect as well the historical and hermeneutic situation of each person in the dialogue, that is, their horizon or particular possibility for understanding: an horizon is all that can be seen from one's vantage point(s). In reading a text or in a dialogue with others it is necessary to be aware of our horizon as well as that of others. It is precisely when our initial projection of the meaning of a text (which might be another's words or the content of a tradition) will not bear up under the progressive dialogue that we are required to make needed adjustments in our projection of their meaning.

This enabled us to adjust not only our prior understanding of the horizon of the other with whom we are in dialogue, but especially our own horizon. Hence, one need not fear being trapped in one's horizons. They are vantage points of a mind which in principle is open and mobile, capable of being aware of its own horizon and of transcending it through acknowledging the horizons of others. The flow of history implies that we are not bound by our horizons, but move in and out of them. It is in making us aware of our horizons that hermeneutic consciousness accomplishes our liberation.[21]

In this process it is important that we retain a questioning attitude. We must not simply follow through with our previous ideas until a change is forced upon us, but must remain sensitive to new meanings in true openness. This is neither neutrality as regards the meaning of the tradition, nor an extinction of passionate concerns regarding action towards the future. Rather, being aware of our own biases or prejudices and adjusting them in dialogue with others implies rejecting what impedes our understanding of others, of texts or of traditions. Our attitude in approaching dialogue must be one of willingness continually to revise our initial projection or expectation of meaning.

There is then a way out of the hermeneutic cycle. It is not by ignoring or denying our horizons and prejudices, but by recognizing them as inevitable and making them work for us. To do so we must direct our attention to the objective meaning of the text in order to draw out, not its meaning for the author, but its application for the present. Through this process of application we serve as midwife for the historicity of a text, a tradition or a culture and enable it to give birth to the future.[22]

Method of Question and Answer

The effort to draw upon a text or a tradition and in dialogue to discover its meaning for the present supposes authentic openness. The logical structure of this openness is to be found in the exchange of question and answer. The question is required in order to determine just what issue we are engaging-- whether it is this issue or that--in order to give direction to our attention. Without this no meaningful answer can be given or received. As a question, however, it requires that the answer not be settled or determined. In sum, progress or discovery requires an openness which is not simply indeterminancy, but a question which gives specific direction to our attention and enables us to consider significant evidence. (Note that we can proceed not only by means of positive evidence for one of two possible responses, but also through dissolving the counter arguments).

If discovery depends upon the question, then the art of discovery is the art of questioning. Consequently, whether working alone or in conjunction with others, our effort to find the answer should be directed less towards suppressing, than toward reinforcing and unfolding the question. To the degree that its probabilities are built up and intensified it can serve as a searchlight. This is the opposite of both opinion which tends to suppress questions, and of arguing which searches out the weakness in the other's argument. Instead, in conversation as dialogue one enters upon a mutual search to maximize the possibilities of the question, even by speaking at cross purposes. By mutually eliminating errors and working out a common meaning we discover truth.[23]

Further, it should not be presupposed that the text holds the answer to but one question or horizon which must be identified by the reader. On the contrary, the full horizon of the author is never available to the reader, nor can it be expected that there is but one question to which the text or tradition holds an answer. The sense of the text reaches beyond what the author intended. Because of the dynamic character of being as it emerges in time, the horizon is never fixed but continually opens. This constitutes the effective historical element in understanding a text or a tradition. At each step new dimensions of

its potentialities open to understanding; the meaning of a text
or tradition lives with the consciousness and hence the hori-
zons--not of its author, but of persons in history. It is the
broadening of their horizons, resulting from their fusion with
the horizon of a text or a partner in dialogue, that makes it
possible to receive answers which are are ever new.[24]

In this one's personal attitudes and interests are, once
again, most important. If our interest in developing new horizons is simply the promotion of our own understanding then we
could be interested solely in achieving knowledge, and thereby
domination over others. This would lock one into an absolute-
ness of one's prejudices; being fixed or closed in the past they
would disallow new life in the present. In this manner powerful
new insights become with time deadening pre-judgments which
suppress freedom.

In contrast, an attitude of authentic openness appreciates
the nature of one's own finiteness. On this basis it both respects the past and is open to discerning the future. Such openness is a matter, not merely of new information, but of recognizing the historical nature of man. It enables us to escape from
what had deceived us and held us captive, and enables us to
learn from new experiences. For example, recognition of the
limitations of our finite planning enables us to see that the
future is still open.[25]

This suggests that openness consists not so much in sur-
veying others objectively or obeying them in a slavish and un-
questioning manner, but is directed primarily to ourselves. It is
an extension of our ability to listen to others, and to assimilate
the implications of their answers for changes in our own positions. In other words, it is an acknowledgement that the cultural
heritage has something new to say to us. The characteristic
hermeneutic attitude of effective historical consciousness is then
not methodological sureness, but readiness for experience.[26]
Seen in these terms our heritage is not closed, but the basis
for a life that is ever new, more inclusive, and more rich.

CRITICAL HERMENEUTICS: ANTITHESES OF VALUE

As was noted above one major fear arises regarding the
hermeneutic project as described by Gadamer, namely, that recognition of the authority of tradition might undermine the
freedom of those to whom the tradition is mediated. This could
be the result of a romantic attitude towards the past as having
had a complete grasp of the meaning of human life and of the
structures for its realization. In that case the past would rule
the present: text would become dogma.

H.G. Gadamer's response focuses rather upon new and unique applications of the tradition for the present and future. It is neither desirable, nor even possible, to attempt simply to reconstruct the text objectively according to its original horizon. Instead, from its perspective the text challenges us to live up to its insights and values in our own circumstances, while from our perspective we question it in order to draw from it new implications for our life. Gadamer considers this questioning to be a matter of understanding, and the type of fore- or pre-understanding of meaning it implies to be an essentially contemplative act. Thus, it is the task of the human sciences (*Geisteswissenshaften*) to correct any misunderstanding.

In contrast, critical hermeneutics focuses upon the material conditions which causally shape our awareness. It is concerned, not with understanding and hence judgments and prejudices, but with interests and ideologies, and their correction through the social sciences. Its task is to identify the material causes and thereby to make possible action to remove or adjust those material factors which by impeding the proper flow of dialogue and communication give rise to misunderstanding and conflict.[27]

There is real continuity between the hermeneutic efforts of Gadamer and critical hermeneutics. Both are directed ultimately towards understanding, both search for theoretical truth, and both oppose dogmatic acceptance of the "text." However, where Gadamer seeks this through understanding, critical hermeneutics seeks it through an explanation of the conditions for misunderstanding and their correction. Yet, even in this, the positions are still not as far apart as at first they might seem for, if today's interests lie less in the materials for production than in the techniques thereof, it is not so much material possessions as knowledge and its implementation that now hold the keys to power.

The roots of critical concern lie deep within the development of modern vision, and indeed within the nature of intellectual knowledge. As reflexive, the person had been understood classically to be self-aware and hence capable of reasoning, language and self-responsibility. This self-consciousness was not undermined by the distinction between subject and object as long as, with Aristotle, in the act of knowledge the subject was understood to become the object and all was received according to the mode of the receiver.

With Descartes, however, the object of knowledge came to be seen as ideas rather than things. Conditions of knowledge, which previously had been within consciousness but were not distinctly attended to, did not figure in his clear and distinct ideas of natures. In this situation it became crucial to know these conditions of knowledge, that is, to have critical knowledge.

Kant thematized as categories factors which had been actually, but only implicitly, in knowledge. Hegel articulated them in a developmental pattern through which the subject is progressively realized in and for itself and for us. He saw this as taking place, not through pure theoretical reason or practical reason acting in separation, but in the lived process of the socialization of the person in the universal history of mankind.

In search of a real, rather than an ideal, basis for his dialectic, Marx turned to labor in interaction with others-- social labor--as the mechanism for the evolution of the human species through history. This works by creating the conditions for the reproduction of social life. Indeed the very identity of the social subject is altered with the scope of his or her power of technical control. This, in turn, determines the epistemological order by constituting the conditions for apprehending the world.[28]

In this way Marx was able to integrate much in his understanding of history. By adding to the forces of production the institutional framework or relations of production his analysis encompassed both material activity and a critique of ideologies, both instrumental action and revolutionary practice, both labor and reflection.

Unfortunately, in increasingly focusing upon work alone as the self-generative act of the species, he lost the ability to understand his own mode of procedure. Though he did not eliminate the structure of symbolic interaction and the role of cultural tradition, they were not part of his philosophical frame of reference for they did not coincide with instrumental action. Yet, it is only in these terms that power and ideology can be comprehended and dissolved by a mode of reflection to which Marx applied the Kantina term "critique."[29]

Since instrumental action by the forces of production responds only to external stimuli, communicative action is required for liberation from the suppression of man's nature by the institutional framework of socially imposed labor and socially determined rewards. For when progress renders this work no longer objectively necessary for the common good, in continuing to demand the state reflects only the private interests of the class in power.[30]

THE SYNTHESIS OF TRADITION AND CRITIQUE

We are then in an essentially dialectical situation which reflects the hermeneutic circle. On the one hand, the pattern of interests can be evaluated only in the context of a tradition and its sense of human life and meaning. On the other hand, tradition must continually be critically examined in order to avoid, by mechanical repetition, becoming an instrument of repression rather than of liberation. As both tradition and critique are required and both are interrelated, it becomes important to look more closely into this dialectic. There are two ways in which tradition must draw upon critique if it is to respond to what Habermas refers to as an "interest in emancipation" which surpasses technical or instrumental and practical interests. First, Gadamer's hermeneutics concerns the application of our cultural heritage in the present by a renewal and reinterpretation of tradition in order to draw out its new implications. The means for this are especially the humanities in which the tradition--through texts in their literary form, and as values and ideals--is articulated. Here, the emphasis is upon appropriating the tradition, identifying with it, and acknowledging its presence as fore-understanding in our every question.

In social critique the sciences must not only describe regularities as do the merely empirical sciences, but must identify also the controlling relations of dependence at a deeper level which have become fixed ideologically. Self-reflection, governed by an interest in emancipation, subjects these to a critique which, in turn, allows the real implications of the tradition to emerge.

There are roots in Gadamer's thought for recognition of the importance of this critical element, for he sees historical distance and a consequent new horizon for questioning as a prerequisite for drawing out new implications of the meaning of the text or tradition. This, in turn, reflects the importance of distinguishing the text from the intention of its author(s), for the text transcends the author's psychological and sociological context. This emancipation of the text--its psycho- and socio-cultural decontextualization--is a fundamental condition for hermeneutic interpretation: "distanciation now belongs to the mediation itself."[31]

This is reflected both on the essential or structural level and on the existential level. In the former it becomes necessary to go beyond Gadamer's description of discourse as a spontaneous conversation of question and answer and to begin to consider discourse as a product of praxis by which it is crafted from smaller units. Here meaning takes place in structures: "the *matter* of the text is not what naive reading of the text reveals, but what the formal arrangement of the text mediates."[32] Hence, structural analysis is required in order to understand the *depth semantics* of the text as a condition for grasping its matter.

If the sense of the work is its internal organization, the reference of the text is the way in which being unfolds *in front*, as it were, of the text. This is the existential reality of being emerging as temporal and historical--as the power to be. In sharp contrast to a deadening repetition of the past frozen in a fixed ideology, the creative space opened by reference to the "power to be" makes a critique of ideology.

This implies not merely a liberation from the structures of our environment, but a liberation of the self as well. Hermeneutic understanding is not an imposition of the reader upon the text; rather, the text provides an interlocuter which enables the reader consciously to examine his or her own subjectivity. By making possible imaginative variations of one's ego, one can achieve the distance required for a first critique of his/her own illusions and false consciousness, and of the ideology in which he/she has been reared.[33]

Critical distance is then an essential element for hermeneutics. It requires an analysis by the social sciences of the historical social structures as a basis for liberation from internal determination by, and dependence upon, unjust interests. The concrete pyscho- and socio-pathology deriving from such dependencies and the corresponding steps toward liberation therefrom are the subject of the chapters by J. Loiacono and H. Ferrand de Piazzia below. Critical distance also has an existential dimension which is made possible by the temporality of being and man's projection toward the historical future (see the chapters of O. Pegoraro and M. Dy also in this volume.) Together these open up the possibility of a liberation of the subject.

Dependence of Critique upon Tradition

The relation between hermeneutics and social critique being dialectical, just as the distancing characteristic of the critical social sciences can make possible some dimensions of awareness essential for emancipation in a world of increasingly technical and convoluted structures, so also tradition provides other dimensions of awareness essential for the critique to which these sciences contribute. Paul Ricoeur has attempted to codify these contributions in his article, "Hermeneutics and the Critique of Ideology."[34]

First, a critique must recognize that it is carried out in the context of interests which establish a frame of meaning. The sequence of technical, practical and emancipating interests reflect the emergence of man out of nature and correspond to the developmental phases of moral sensitivity. Habermas studies Kohlberg closely on this and employs his work. But to the question of the basis of these interests no adequate answer is provided. They are not empirically justifiable or they would be found only at the level of technical interests. Neither do they constitute a theory as a network of working hypotheses for then they would be justified at most by the interest in emancipation, which in turn would fall into a vicious circle.

The only proper description of these interests as truly all-embracing must lie in Heidegger's existentials, which are hidden only in being so present as to be in need of being unveiled by hermeneutic method. Thus Gadamer's hermeneutic project on the clarification of prejudices and Habermas's suggestion of critical work on interests through the social sciences--though not identical--share common ground.

Secondly, critiques of ideologies appear in the end to share characteristics common to those of the historical hermeneutic sciences. Both focus upon the ability to develop the communicative action of free persons. Their common effort is against a reduction of all human communication to instrumental action and institutionalization, for it is here that manipulation takes place. Hence, success or failure in extending the critique of interests beyond instrumental action determines whether the community will promote or destroy its members.

Ricoeur moves from this concern regarding the general horizon of social critique to the observation that it is unlikely ever to be successful if we have no experience of communication with our own cultural heritage. This can be required in a dialogue, for the effective basis for any real consensus must be not only an empty ideal or regulative idea, but one that has been experienced, lived and shared. "He who is unable to interpret his past may also be incapable of projecting concretely his interest in emancipation."[35]

Thirdly, today communicative action needs more than a model to suggest what might otherwise not occur to our minds, for the rationalization of human life has become such that all of its aspects are controlled pervasively in terms of instrumental action. Whereas Marx could refer in his day to surplus value as the motive of production, this is true no longer. Instead, the system itself of technology has become the key to productivity and all is coordinated toward the support and promotion of this system; this is the ideology of our day. As a result the distinction between communicative action and instrumental action has been overridden and control no longer can be expected from communicative action.

This raises a new type of question, namely, how can the interest in emancipation be kept alive. Undoubtedly, communicative action must be reawakened and made to live if we are not to be simply subjects--indeed 'slaves'--of the technological machine. But how is this to be done; whence can this life be derived if the present situation is pervasively occupied and shaped by science and technology as the new, and now all-encompassing, master? The answer of Ricoeur and Gadamer is that it can be done only by drawing upon our heritage in the manner suggested by Heidegger. We need--now as never before--to reach back into our heritage in order to retrieve contents which were present seminally, but never developed. These are the resources of our traditiion, which can give rise to the radically new visions needed for the emancipation of mankind living in an age of increasing domination and manipulation, not primarily of economy and politics, but of minds and hearts.

Finally, there is a still more fundamental sense in which critique, rather than being opposed to tradition or taking a questioning attitude thereto, is itself an appeal to tradition. Criticism appeals unabashedly to the heritage of emancipation as an ideal inherited from the Enlightenment. But this tradition has longer roots which reach back to the liberating acts of the Exodus and the Resurrection. "Perhaps" writes Ricoeur "there would be no more interest in emancipation, no more anticipation of freedom, if the Exodus and the Resurrection were effaced from the memory of mankind."[36]

According to the proper norms of communicative action, these historical acts should be taken also in their symbolic sense according to which liberation and emancipation express the root interest basic to traditional cultures. In this manner they point to fundamental dimensions of being, indeed to Being Itself as the unique existence in whom the alienated can be reunited, to the logos which founds subjectivity without an estranging selfishness, and to the spirit through whom human freedom can be creative in history. Remembrance and celebration of this heritage provides needed inspiration and direction both for any in power who might be indifferent to the needs of the poor and alienated and for the alienated poor themselves. It enables both to reach out in mutual comprehension, reconciliation and concern to form a social unity marked by emancipation and peace.

The Catholic University of America
Washington, D.C.

NOTES

1. Richard E. Palmer, *Hermeneutics* (Evanston: Northwestern Univ. Press, 1969), pp. 12-29.
2. Ivor Leclerc, "The Metaphysics of the Good," *Review of Metaphysics*, 35 (1981), 3-5. See also *Vocabulaire technique et critique de la philosophie,* ed. André Lalande (Paris: PUF, 1956), pp. 1182-1186.

3. J. Mehta, *Martin Heidegger; The Way and the Vision* (Honolulu: Univ. of Hawaii Press, 1967), pp. 90-91.

4. Hesiod, *Theogony* trans. H.G. Everland-White (Loeb Classical Library; Cambridge, Mass.: Harvard Univ. Press, 1964), p. 85.

5. Aristotle, *Metaphysics,*I, 2.

6. R. Carnap, *Vienna Manifesto*, trans. A. Blumberg in G. Kreyche and J. Mann, *Perspectives on Reality* (New York: Harcourt, Brace and World, 1966), p. 485.

7. R. Descartes, *Discourse on Method*, I.

8. H.G. Gadamer, *Truth and Method* (New York: Crossroads, 1975), pp. 240, 246-247, 305-310.

9. John Dewey, *Existence as Precarious and Stable,* see J. Mann & G. Kreyche, *Perspectives on Reality* (New York: Harcourt, Brace and World, 1966), p. 379.

10. Gadamer, pp. 248, 250-251.

11. *Ibid.*, pp. 252-253.

12. *Ibid.*, p. 254.

13. See n. 4 above along with Ch. III by S. Samay, "Affectivity: The Power Base of Moral Behavior," pp. 71-114.

14. Gadamer, p. 258.

15. *Ibid.*, pp. 281-286.

16. *Ibid.*, pp. 278-279.

17. *Ibid.*, pp. 281-286.

18. *Ramayana* (Bombay: Bharatiya Vidya Bhavan, 1976), p. 312.

19. Gadamer, p. 262.

20. *Ibid.*, pp. 263-264.

21. *Ibid.*, pp. 235-242, 267-271.

22. *Ibid.*, pp. 235-332.

23. *Ibid.*, pp. 225-332.

24. *Ibid.*, pp. 336-340.

25. *Ibid.*, pp. 327-324.

26. *Ibid.*, pp. 324-325.

27. J. Bleiker, *Contemporary Hermeneutics: Hermeneutics as Method, Philosophy and Critique* (London: Routledge & Kegan Paul, 1980), pp. 143-151.

28. J. Habermas, *Knowledge and Human Interests* (Boston: Beacon, 1971), 28-35.

29. *Ibid.*, p. 42.

30. For a more extended treatment of the character of the critical hermeneutics of J. Habermas see G. McLean, "Cultural Heritage, Social Critique and Future Construction" in R. Molina, T. Readdy and G. McLean, eds., *Culture, Human Rights and Peace in Central America* (Washington: Council for Research in Values and Philosophy and The University Press of America,

1988), ch. I.

31. "Hermeneutics as the Critique of Ideology," *Hermeneutics and the Human Sciences*, ed., J.B. Thompson (New York: Cambridge, 1981), pp. 81.

32. *Ibid.*, pp. 93.

33. *Ibid.*, pp. 93-95.

34. *Hermeneutics and the Human Sciences*, J.B. Thompson, ed. (New York: Cambridge, 1981), pp. 82-91

35. *Ibid.*, pp. 97.

36. *Ibid.*. pp. 99-100.

CHAPTER III

VALUES IN AN HISTORICAL, SOCIO-CULTURAL CONTEXT

HORTENSIA FERRAND DE PIAZZA

THE SOCIO-CULTURAL DYNAMICS

The concept of moral agent is the focal point of a perspective based upon two considerations: (a) that values come into being in an historical process and (b) that human persons living and acting according to values, which have roots in their cultural heritage, shape this historical process. This calls for a conceptualization derived mainly from phenomenology. This seems a preferable approach to the issue of historicity for it offers a broad perspective in terms of an open movement in which the present is but an instant that meaningfully articulates the past toward the future. This conceptualization was developed in chapter I above. Here I would like only to call attention to the fact that the meaning or value content of this process is given by persons acting and interacting historically. From this derives the concept of the moral agent inasmuch as one's historical action is directed to the promotion of the fullness of being with its personal and communitary connotations.

From a more sociological point of view, the moral agent can be conceived in terms of Alain Touraine's "historical subject." Touraine begins from what he considers a main human endeavor: "the need present virtually in every agent to realize a work endowed with one's own social experience, and to maintain or regain control over this work, in sum to overcome alienation. . . . Work is the social experience which best expresses this creative tension of production and its appropriation."[1]

Thus, Touraine develops a "Sociology of Action" theoretically and methodologically oriented to understanding man's efforts to realize socially meaningful "work," and to maintain or recover his control over this work. He uses the term "work" in the very open and inclusive sense of culture:

> But sociology of action is not only a sociology of work. It must be extended to all experiences or relations with one's neighbor and with nature, that is, with the life of the body which are marked by this double movement of creation of the object and of regaining control over the object created by the at gent.[2]

It is here, at the heart of the double movement of the creation of an object (in a very wide sense) and of the maintenance or recovery by the agent of the control over the object created, that Touraine places the "historical subject," creator of culture and main actor of his *Sociology of Action.* Historical subjects should not be misinterpreted as super or supra-beings, but conceived simply as persons interacting among themselves and together in a certain direction.

Touraine's accent is therefore upon the constituting forces which Lourau would call the constituting (*l'instituant*), rather than upon the cultural systems of values and norms already constituted which Lourau would call the 'constituted' (*l'institué*).[3]

> The sociology of action rejects focusing on systems of cultural values and already constituted social norms, to study their coherence, modification and transmission. Its object is to understand not how society functions, but how it is created and how men realize their history.[4]

I will not follow here the methodology worked out by Touraine in his *Sociology of Action,* which offers an alternative theory and methodology for studying how the social is historically constructed. However, I do want to call attention to the difference he notes between, on the one hand, the cultural values and social norms already constituted and, on the other hand, his main concern, namely, how people invent society, how they make their history. Each of these two processes has its own dynamics which later will have to be taken into consideration.

Touraine has an hermeneutic intention; he wants to discover and reconstruct the meaning, direction or sense of social action: "to discover and reconstruct the sense of a system of relations, . . . to investigate the nature of a debate, conflict or movement."[5] Touraine calls for a sociology able to include the value oriented and creative thrust of man--for a study of the spirit and social systems which should contribute to the formation of a vast anthropology.

> Sociology should focus upon the very heart of social action in order to contribute to the formation of an integral anthropology which is already a study both of the spirit and of social systems, and which should as well be the study of creative action. It should not remain at the periphery of action, heavily describing relations between types of conduct and society as if these could be defined as a state of things, when in

reality they are movement, contradiction and creation that is an affirmation of values. . . . No sociological analysis can dispense itself from taking account of the most fundamental character of social action, namely, its normative orientation.[6]

Touraine does not conceal, but consciously assumes a value content orientation. He does not shun responsible evaluation of situations and conduct, and is concerned mainly with reflection upon the dynamics of reality as a means of clearly evaluating situations in view of correct action. He thus urges us to "avoid laying down from the beginning a system constituted of values, and to find in action itself--in its double movement of objectivation, which in turn calls for reflection upon the constituted work--the principle for evaluating situations and conduct."[7]

Thus, Touraine hopes that his position will be understood best by those who search for the best ends or goals and the appropriate means for their fulfillment amidst confused, conflictual situations, rather than by those concerned with the organization of means.

The call for a sociology of action probably will not have its best response in established societies where the organization of means is more important than the conflictual elaboration of goals. Rather, this call can be understood whenever the social order or personal life is lacerated, when the individual or collective agent must impose a new meaning on a social field modified under his initiative, every time one takes up the fight for the formation of a new society, new social relations, or new feelings and tastes. . . . At the heart of the industrial civilization sociology is above all a study of the formation and transformation of social experience.[8]

I have taken Touraine as my starting point because his overall perspective is similar to ours, though from a more sociological point of view. For understanding values from an historical, socio-cultural viewpoint it offers very helpful analytical categories within a sound theoretical context. His concept of the historical subject enables us to give a more sociological meaning to the concept of moral agent. The historical subject can be seen as a collective creator of culture, struggling to express itself through the constitution of institutions which express the deeply rooted values of its culture while responding creatively to the challenge of an ever-changing historical condition.

In creating these institutions the historical subject is really institutionalizing certain forms of relationship in order to produce, and eventually reproduce, certain socio-cultural forms.[9] In a wide sense of cultural creation the action of the historical subject is thus grounded in the human effort to constitute a socially meaningful work and to maintain its control. The consideration of this positive process, on the one hand, and of alienation as the loss of this capability, on the other, enables us to explain the double movement of creation/control and alienation.

Alienation is conceived as the escape of man's creation from his own hands. For there is a tendency for one's creation to cease to reflect what it had of oneself or of human relations and to become a thing in itself, no longer under his control. The relation could even be reversed, with man being controlled by the forces he created. It is not that his creation really controls him, but rather that man makes an "idol" of that which he has created. His creation having become "reified," man turns to adore it as if it were a "being" or a good in itself, rather than a means for him. He thus loses control of it.

From the economic point of view, for example, in terms of a socially meaningful product and one's control over it, there is a great difference between an artist producing and selling his/her own work of art and the automobile worker who assembles the same piece on many cars. The latter would never recognize this as a product of his personal creation, and it really is not. Furthermore, these cars will be sold by someone else; the worker loses all control of the product of his work which is subject to economic forces beyond himself. In this light the type of industrialization spreading over the world poses a great problem and calls for a more humanizing solution.

Furthermore, these products no longer reflect that they are products of man's creative work and human relations. Reified as they are, they turn out to be like "idols" and reverse their relation with man. Instead of means for the promotion of his full being, they turn one into a consumer of goods without clear purpose (except perhaps for those who induce him to buy): they turn one from "being" to "having." Instead of man really possessing things, things possess him. Something similar might tragically be happening with the development of nuclear power. Man could lose control of himself and of his relations with others through adoring the idols he has created.

It is in the religious dimension that alienation takes on its clearest meaning of idolatry, through the fabrication of a god which alienates man from his essential relation to the divine and to others. The type for this is found in Moses's coming down from the mountain with the tablets containing the essence of man's relation with God and kin, only to find his people adoring the golden idol, Baal. The idol created by man, being adored as if it were God, alienated the people from a profound, vital relation with God and others. "You will no longer adore the work of your hands."[10]

The dynamics of the process of alienation can be further clarified by developing the concepts of institutionalization and ideology. To do this I will refer to the above-mentioned distinction between:

1) a constituting (instituant) human impetus by which the "historical subject" invents society, that is, men make their history through the conflictual elaboration of goals and the appropriate means to achieve them, and

2) a constituted (institué) system of cultural values and social norms, characteristic of stabilized societies, which centers upon the disposition of means (and, I would add, sometimes leaves no time to stop and think of ends or goals).

Let us begin from the first moment, that of constituting. The constituting force is that of the historical subject in its drive to express itself through the creation of institutions which might best respond to the historical situation. Historical subjects, starting from and recreating their deeply rooted cultural values, would be open also to the assimilation of new ones. Persons would be creating institutions that could best promote the fullest expression of their cultural identity, or "self," through their way of responding to the historical conditions of that moment. This is the moment of the "utopia" or the ideal that inspires action.

But the ideal world exists only in our minds as a parameter, as something for which to fight, live and die. When ideals take form, they cease to be the ideal and begin to reflect it only to a limited degree. If people continue to think of reality as if it functioned just as does the ideal model, their thinking becomes ideological; they are no longer aware of what is happening in reality, of how much it is diverging from the ideal model. The beneficiaries of the system promote this type of unconsciousness since it best fits their interests; indeed, in many cases they themselves would not be conscious of it, being themselves ideologically constituted.

This is precisely what happens in the process of institutionalization, through which "the constituting" becomes "the constituted." The process of institutionalization takes place between the moment when the "historical subject" is elaborating its ends and creating institutions as appropriate means for these ends, and the moment when the system is comfortably instituted with its systems of cultural values and social norms well established. At that point society is devoted to promoting means and each member is dedicated to his role or way of developing a certain means, no thought is given then to the ends.

Putting their ideals to work men create institutions. When facing a certain historical challenge they elaborate their goals and the ways and means to achieve them--in which are expressed their values. That is, they create ways of response in which their values inspire goals and particular forms of interaction to achieve them. Stabilizing these patterns of relations they create institutions. With the passing of time, however, institutions created as means begin to acquire a sort of life or drive for self-preservation. The new interests created during the process of institutionalization contribute to this transformation of the institution from a means to an end in itself, since they are interested in its conservation. A suspicion of power thus always hovers over the process of institutionalization. Through it men, having created institutions as means, not only lose control of them as they become structures--stabilized patterns of relations which persist through time and acquire certain historical weight--but are finally dominated through them. The individuals and groups who are favored by these structures and interested in maintaining them promote their reproduction and thereby the continuation of the system through which they maintain their dominant position.

Turning once again to ideology--in the sense of dominant ideology[11]--this type of alienation, like others, takes form during the process of institutionalization. As new interests are created, people interested in maintaining the institutions or the system of institutions which favors their interests, and this both for their own benefit and for that of their descendants. There are many ways of doing this. Mainly, it is through economic and political power. But there is another, less obvious way--since if it were obvious it would no longer work--namely, the ideological reproduction of the system. How does this work?

Ideology is a form of alienation and works through mechanisms similar to other forms of alienation. Men create their ideals, put them to work, create institutions, and then adore them as "idols." Such idols take the place of reality: the ideal model takes the place of the existential context and conceals what there is of real inter-human relations at the concrete level.

Passing from the macro to the micro consideration of the way ideology works, it should be noted first that it strongly favors those who believe in it and impose their belief on others. The sense that the system favors the interest of all gives them the needed psychological reassurances that they are working for the benefit of all and not mainly for their own interest. And as it really does work, business and political leaders can be quite honest in their idealism and work hard for what they believe is the best for all. Remaining unaware that they themselves are ideologically constituted, they contribute to the ideological re-production of the system by reproducing the ideal interpretation of reality and the corresponding forms of inter-relations.

For the broader population this works as a psychological soporific. The ideological rationalization of the system, which makes its positive aspects stand out, gives reassurance through a sense of participation or belonging to the best of worlds. I will not take up here the socio-psychological question of how these ideological patterns are internalized in personality structures. In terms of present dominant rationality, however, we can look for the ways in which such very complex motivational patterns are introduced into one's personality through socialization practices considered as functional imperatives.

From an epistemological perspective ideology proceeds mainly by the abstraction from reality of certain ideal entities which become absolutized in a partial, static, ideal model. This model, which symbolizes the social reality, is constructed on the basis of three fundamental processes:

- naturalization of historical laws,
- universalizing abstractions, and
- mystification of social relations.

The abstract rationalization thus constructed, detached from its real context, constitutes the model from which reality is interpreted. When applied to reality, which is much more complex than the model, only the variables or categories con-tained in the model are perceived for they are the only ones consciously or unconsciously selected. This leaves out of the picture a very considerable portion of reality.

All that has been said in this introduction concerning alienation, institutionalization, structures and ideology might give the impression that we are concentrating on the "tail" in-stead of the "head"--on the institutionalized, instead of on the positive side of the creative moral agent--thus losing sight of Touraine's emphasis upon the "historical subject." But without this side of the coin we would not be able to understand the positive movement of the historical subject as the moral agent takes hold of him/herself. That aspect will appear in the last part of this paper dedicated to the presentation of the pos-sibility of a new synthesis. It will draw particularly from the resources of traditional culture, for which I will use as an example the case of Latin America focusing, on the seeming constitution of an historical subject of Andean roots.

WESTERN CULTURAL HERITAGE

The development of western culture is marked by the tension within it between Christianity's sense of totality, rooted in its traditional hebraic origins, and the reduction and partialization brought about by the development and absolutization of some categories assimilated from Greek thought.

Origins: Hebraic and Greek Visions of Man and Reality

This analysis begins from Heidegger's idea of historical consciousness which directs our attention to the fact that each culture has its own consciousness. The problem is that when one discovers or becomes "conscious" of some aspect and clarifies his/her ideas about it one tends to concentrate upon this and to forget other aspects. This happened with Western Christian civilization when it centered on some discoveries made by the Greeks and became less sensitive to the traditional Hebrew sense of reality and existence. In so doing, it lost the concrete sense of life, as lived in the family, the tribe and through the covenant.

Hebrew consciousness was vital, existential, and historical: it had a profound sense of unity in relation to God and with others. Through the covenant, their relation to the Holy gave them a sense of both holiness and wholeness, of the possession of an intelligence of truth and of a relation with others manifested in kinship. This inter-personal relationship is typical of family and tribe; it is still alive in traditional cultures. As historical, the covenant led to liberation in history. This Hebrew thought was centered upon life and action to promote life; it did not develop abstract forms as did the Greeks.

The Greeks developed philosophy and science as means for understanding reality. To do so, from reality they abstracted ideal entities and searched for relations between them, thereby developing systematic thinking. This laid the foundation for the subsequent flourishing of Western scientific culture centered upon a new type of consciousness whose importance cannot be overstressed. This has not been without its price. Beginning from the Greeks, Western culture progressively lost the sense of real human existence in its totality, being concentrated upon developing systems of abstract thought in science and philosophy. "Unfortunately, the progress made in the conceptual clarification of the variety of nature was accompanied by a corresponding loss of sensitivity to the power and activity of nature, that is, to its existential reality."[12]

While acknowledging the magnificent contribution of Greek thinkers to posterity, it is important to note how this was achieved through the development of universalizing abstraction.

This was related to Socrates' and Plato's search for virtues, ideas and ideals as a safeguard for a Greece in crisis, whose institutions were being questioned by an absolute relativism. In these circumstances the philosophers focused upon truth that would be "essential," absolute, unquestionable. In so doing, however, their thought was void of a sense of historicity, and thus was conducive to a mystification of social relations and to laying the foundations for ideological constructions.

Following Heidegger we might trace this reduction to Socrates and Plato. Attempting to provide an ontological basis for Socrates' endeavour and to provide essential definitions, Plato located truth in the realm of the "ideas" or the eternal, immutable "essences" of things. Conversely this implied a reduction of the concept of "physis" to the sensible, devalued in favor of the realm of "ideas." Thus, the "eidetic" or ideal became the real, conceived as permanent or eternal; this was to be found in the intelligible spirit or rationality of man.

According to Heidegger, the primordial or pre-Socratic notion of "physis" was a "totality of beings," or even "Being itself": physis was comprehensive, all inclusive. Moreover, "physis" was self-emerging or self-emergence; and this, in turn, implies as its origin that which is hidden and from which manifestation is possible. Thus, "being" contains in itself both manifestation at the level of that which is manifest, as well as being manifesting itself. In such a perspective, truth, in its pre-Socratic sense is the truth of being, self-emerging, and thus manifesting itself.

Plato himself did not abjure completely the primordial sense of *physis*, for he retained the sense of *aletheia* as "unveiling." Nevertheless, he directed his attention to that which is manifest, and placed truth in that which is consistent or invariable as the "essence" of that which is present or manifest in time. This could be only the "ideas" or essences of that which is manifest as these are accessible to the mind. Thus he interpreted Being in its essential sense of *physis* as "idea," thus "transforming the meaning of truth from the self-unconcealing of primal Being (the manner in which 'physis' brings itself to appearance) to a notion of truth as the 'correctness of seeing'."[13] With Plato, "truth became correct seeing, and thinking became a matter of placing an idea before the mind's eye, that is, it became the proper manipulation of ideas."[14] Truth and reason would thus be put at the service of the will.

This location of truth in the essence of things led to a subsequent reduction in medieval thinking when essence was linked to, and interpreted as, "efficient cause." The primordial sense of *physis* though was not "a question of an emerging or coming to appearance as the result of having been caused. Rather, if we may so express the matter, self-emerging in the manner of *physis* is self-caused, i.e., a self-rising."[15] Later, especially in the modern elaborations of Descartes and his heirs, truth would be considered to be no longer in beings manifesting themselves, but in man, the philosopher. Truth concerns knowledge, or the relation between man and that which is present; it is no longer the truth of being, but of the knowledge of being.

This was the ground for the modern subjective conception of truth and its "forgetfulness of being" in the Cartesian sense of

> the person as the knowing 'subject' around the pivotal point called consciousness or self-consciousness. . . . From a Heideggerian standpoint, a philosophy of subjectivity is one which pretends that 'Being' is the result ensuing from the subjective activity called 'thinking' in the sense of *Vorstellen* or acting, that is, manipulation, in the way of *Bestellen*. Thus, on this view 'Being' would end up to be the mere produce of the subjective dimension.[16]

Thus the Platonic conception of "idea" provided two of the roots of modern rationality, Descartes and essentialism.

> The Platonic 'idea' suggests another direction which itself is two-dimensional: the 'idea' and its correlate *idein* laid the ground for the Cartesian 'representedness' (*Vorgestelltheit*) or 'representing' and secondly, the 'idea', insofar as it is considered as the 'Whatbeing' (*Wassein*) of beings, clears the way for the 'Essentia' of 'School' Philosophy.[17]

The alienating form of modern rationality is divorced from totality and hence from reality. On the one hand, in the search for greater accuracy or more "correctness of seeing" man constructs abstract models which become ever more partial. These models are then projected upon reality, which they reduce to partial analytic categories, thereby mutilating reality. On the other hand, we have the search for fixed essences of reality, often coming from the models themselves and thus tending to legitimate the "reality" contained in the model. It is not necessary to elaborate on the way in which these rationalizing constructions lay the basis and provide the tools for the construction of modern ideologies.

Scientific-technological Rationality: Development and Domination

Scientific-Technological rationality is the collective consciousness which undergirds the development of capitalism. On the basis of this consciousness the bourgeoisie, as the historical subject, elaborated the new social relations which made capitalism possible. This rationality was later raised to the status of "the truth" by the bourgeoisie, who institutionalized its power and promoted this model of development and its corresponding social relations as "rational." They did this in terms of this model of scientific-technological rationality, thereby justifying their dominant position within the system of social relations.

At present, the development of the systems based on this specific type of rationality appears to be exhausting its possibilities. It is producing dissatisfaction, even among the beneficiaries of the systems in industrialized countries, where there is a progressive consciousness of the limitations it imposes upon persons. Namely, it replaces a view of the whole with a view that is partial, elevating what should be a means in the service of mankind to the position of an absolute end in itself to which persons are subjected and by which they are thereby alienated.

The distinctive context and implications of this problematic in the countries of the Third World will be considered later. At that time we shall consider the possibility of reconstituting historical subjects on the basis of their traditional roots which confer diverse value orientations upon their own distinctive historical projects. These will take form through efforts directed at institutionalizing the relations corresponding to these values within the ever conflictual elaboration presupposed by the affirmation of the self.

In a general way the roots of modern scientific-technological rationality can be traced first to Galileo. His epistemological revolution consisted precisely in considering as real and concrete what in fact was abstract, namely, the mathematical form of interpreting reality. This was a step beyond Plato, for whom reality consisted in a world of ideas of which the sensible or perceivable world was but a disfigured reflection. For Galileo reality is in the concrete, but he considers this only in abstract mathematical terms.

> The concrete, the sign of the ontological weight or reality of things, is properly the abstract mathematical configuration which is the sign of productive nature. For this reason sense experience is for Galileo a second step and can be understood only as integral to the sequence of rational discourse, whose norm is constituted by mathematics.[18]

Descartes adapted philosophy to the scientific-epistemological revolution whose philosophical characteristics had been set by Galileo.[19] For Descartes the subject (mind or "res cogitans") could know the object (matter or "res extensa") only in terms of the physical properties of the object. This promoted an analytical dissection of reality into successive levels of categorization and mathematization, ruled by principles of cause and effect. Such a mechanistic conception, required for the development of machines, was the basis of Newtonian physics which constituted the model for classical scientific thought.

Auguste Comte first articulated scientific positivism which, in contrast to the more theoretical tendencies, was to be predominant in the technological era in both the natural and the social sciences. For him all valid knowledge was positive knowledge which, in turn, was identified with "science" and then with "truth." "Positive" knowledge was that in which the "subject" could objectively and directly know reality, which, in turn, was identified with its quantifiable properties. This knowledge was based on the impressions received at a given moment--ecstatic vision--through which are encountered the causal relations which explain how phenomena take place.

This type of rationality--proper to scientific knowledge--is necessary for instrumental action which permits man to act and survive. However, by rejecting other types of knowledge as true it gave "science," understood positivistically, an absolute character. This provided man with a sense of security sustained by the increasing and impressive scientific and technological developments; it provided science with its sacred "patina" and made possible its assumption for the throne vacated by the gods.

Historical Development of Scientific Technological Rationality Within the Context of Capitalism.

Scientific technological rationality developed historically as the collective consciousness of capitalism, which was constructed and reproduced as a system through the following process.

(a) The concentration of capital in the hands of the bourgeoisie, who, by channeling it into industrial production, constituted itself as the dynamic center of the development of productive forces which became the central axis of the whole historical project achieved thereby.

(b) The development of the sciences and of a scientific mentality which, through the strong emphasis put on its task of dominating nature, led to its technological orientation.

(c) The development of a mentality of efficiency and saving among the bourgeoisie which was inculcated in the working class. This made it possible to increase productivity and contribute to the ideological reproduction of the system.

(d) At the inter-personal level, the shift to functional relations between abstract individuals and relations--between roles, not persons-- favored the ideological delusion by making oppression less visible because indirect, diffuse and generalized.

(e) The institutionalization, at the political level, of a liberal democratic system as the form of government based upon formal equality, participation and liberty permitted free circulation of capital and labor and the freedom of contact required for the economic system to function.

The bourgeoisie strove to secure the prerequisites for the continued existence of the system of relations necessary for the capitalist productive process to develop. Toward this end it concentrated its efforts upon building up a state apparatus to institutionalize these structures. This process was sustained, in turn, by the liberal model's function as a utopia which permitted the bourgeoisie to promote its goals through a system of supposed free competition. In this way the bourgeoisie played a dynamic role in developing the possibilities of the new model, and in some areas this resulted in optimizing productivity within the frame of consumer society.

While this model was postulated as being convenient for everyone in terms of an ideal of generalized equality, it contains elements which negate this on the concrete level. The model favors the bourgeoisie and can function only on the basis of real inequality. Though it is proposed in terms of an ideal of equality and of free competition and "freedom of compacts" between individuals who are supposed to be free and equal, it is obvious that a capitalist and a worker meet in very unequal conditions in negotiating a contract.

As its off-spring, scientific technological rationality was developed within this process. Its manipulative mentality regarding reality is manifest in its emphasis upon the efficiency expected both of the results of the application of the sciences as well as of the functional actuation of persons. As the fundamental mentality of the bourgeois project of development scientific technological rationality has constituted the collective consciousness of capitalism from its beginning. It is the dominant ideology in the recent most technological phase of capitalism, where it has become an absolute, extending beyond the area of instrumental action to all spheres of human life. The system is justified on the basis of its surprising technological advances. By seeming to function on the basis of technical decisions, it hides the political or economic origins of its fundamental decisions.

Absolutization and Ideologization of
  Scientific Technological Rationality

Scientific technological rationality implies a manipulatory

attitude; ultimately it requires technology in order for this manipulation to be as efficient as possible. Thus, there develops a
type of instrumental mentality which Habermas describes as
"purposive-rational action" in reference to the organization of
means or the choice between alternatives. Planning consists in
the progressive establishment of systems and sub-systems of this
"purposive-rational action."

Acting within these systems and sub-systems, in which
success demands efficiency, individuals increasingly internalize
the rationality of means. They interrelate in functional terms;
they suppress possibilities of intersubjective and symbolic
communication which appear disfunctional in relation to the
goals of the institution. As producers require efficient cooperation from the areas of education, health, transport, etc., instrumental rationality increasingly penetrates all areas of human
life. In the family, the ultimate bastion of intersubjectivity,
members are pressured by the demands of the system which
force them to struggle to be efficient, to strive to relate in
functional terms and thereby progressively to reduce the ways
of protecting and of loving one another which are possible only
on those levels which are repressed and thus negated in favor
of instrumental relationality. Regarding the scientific mathematical bases of this rationality, Marcuse notes:

> Nature (including man) is scientifically rational only
> in terms of the general laws of movement: physical,
> chemical and biological. . . . Values can have a high-
> er dignity (moral and spiritual), but they are not real
> and thus count less in the real business of life, the
> more these values are elevated.[20]

This progressive rationalization of society is tied to the
institutionalization of scientific technological development and
the ideological position this assumes. Historically the definitive
elevation of scientific technological rationality to an ideological
position took place in the second World War. Then the United
States consolidated its hegemony through its technological progress in the development of productive forces. The same happened in the Soviet Union, other state capitalist countries, and
subsequently in such countries as Japan, Germany, etc.

The bourgeois ideology, which had always presented a
facade of autonomy for technology, politics and economics as
independent areas, could now claim that the decisions were
taken on the basis of scientific technological criteria, obscuring
in this manner the political or economic interests which com-
manded these decisions. The great prestige which science and
technology had acquired through its advances endowed it with a

special aura characteristic of the sacred and the absolute, thus promoting its ideological character.

At the level of purposive-rational action, this ideology operates at an abstractive level according to its own achieved social interests by keeping everybody busy trying to be most efficient in the prosecution of his/her immediate goals. This removes from public consciousness the framework of interests from which these same goals derive.

> Because this sort of rationality extends to the correct choice among strategies, the appropriate application of technologies, and the efficient establishment of systems (with presupposed aims in given situations), it removes the total social framework of interests in which strategies are chosen, technologies applied, and systems established, from the scope of reflection and rational reconstruction. Moreover, this rationality extends only to relations of possible technical control and therefore requires a type of action that implies domination, whether of nature or of society. By virtue of its structure, purposive-rational action is the exercise of control. That is why, in accordance with this rationality, the "rationalization" of the conditions of life is synonymous with the institutionalization of a form of domination whose political character becomes unrecognizable: the technical reason of a social system of purposive rational action does not lose its political content.[21]

In the highly industrialized capitalist countries, class relations--established on the basis of the social relations of production--reproduce themselves through the impetus of the whole apparatus to reproduce itself. They are legitimated by being postulated as technically rational: "The existing relations of production present themselves as the technically necessary organizational form of a rationalized society."[22] Domination, nevertheless, tends to lose its exploitative character and direct oppression diffuses throughout the whole society to which everyone is subjected as pieces of the great machine. Political domination does not disappear while the oppression appears "rational" inasmuch as it seems necessary for the reproductive capacity of the system as a whole. The system, in turn, legitimizes itself on the basis of the growth of the productive forces through its impressive scientific-technological progress, although, at the same time, these conquests make the limitations and burdens suffered by individuals appear at each step more unnecessary and irrational. Habermas notes that:

In Marcuse's judgment, the objectively superfluous repression can be recognized in the 'intensified subjection of individuals to the enormous apparatus of production and distribution, in the deprivatization of free time, in the almost indistinguishable fusion of constructive and destructive social labor.' Paradoxically, however, this repression can disappear from the consciousness of the population because the legitimation of domination has assumed a new character: it refers to the 'constantly increasing productivity and domination of nature which keeps individuals . . . living in increasing comfort'.[23]

Following Habermas we can see how the capitalist project, centering on the development of productive forces and its concomitant scientific technological rationality, has absolutized what in other cultures pertained only to the sphere of instrumental action, thus reducing man to a partial dimension. Man progressively has become alienated as the part has taken the place of the whole. Habermas remarks that what has been forgotten by this concentration upon the technological sphere is the sphere of communication, which he calls the practical.[24] Practical interest refers to free communication and intersubjectivity.

The new ideology consequently violates an interest, grounded in one of the two fundamental conditions of our cultural existence: in language or, more precisely, in the form of socialization and individuation determined by communication in ordinary language. This interest extends to the maintenance of intersubjectivity of mutual understanding as well as to the creation of communication without domination. Technocratic consciousness makes this practical interest disappear behind the interest in the expansion of our power of technical control. Thus the reflection that the new ideology calls for must penetrate beyond the level of particular class interests to disclose the fundamental interests of mankind as such engaged in the process of self-constitution.[25]

Thus, the only way to reverse this progressively alienating technologically-centered process would be to recover free communication liberating the medium of symbolic interaction.

. . . two concepts of rationalization must be distinguished. At the level of subsystems of purposive-rational action, scientific-technical progress has already compelled the reorganization of social institutions and sectors, and necessitates it on an even larger scale than heretofore. But this process of the development of the productive forces can be a potential for liberation if and only if it does not replace rationalization on another level. Rationalization at the level of the institutional framework can occur only in the medium of symbolic interaction itself, that is, through removing restrictions on communication. Public, unrestricted discussion, free from domination, of the suitability and desirability of action-orienting principles and norms in the light of the socio-cultural repercussions of developing sub-systems of purposive-rational action--such communication at all levels of political and prepolitized decision-making processes is the only medium in which anything like "rationalization" is possible.

In such a process of generalized reflection institutions would alter their specific composition, going beyond the limit of a mere change in legitimation.[26]

TRADITIONAL CULTURES AND THE POSSIBILITY OF A NEW SYNTHESIS

The scientific-technological rationality which was described previously as characteristic of highly urbanized and industrialized societies, in third world countries is superimposed and variously mixed with traditional cultures. The values of these cultures either disappear as those who carry them are absorbed by the dominant social system and culture, or are expressed through the creation of new cultural forms or social relations responding to the difficult challenge imposed by the historical situation. In this latter case we could speak of historical subjects expressing their cultural values through the creation of new forms of relationship which, if successful in becoming institutionalized, eventually could reproduce a new model of social integration.

To pretend to predict the outcome of such a social process would be precisely to negate the possibility of the existence of an historical subject. Nevertheless, I would like to pose, as a possibility, the following question: Do some traditional cultures maintain their cultural roots so as to be able to assimilate important achievements of the dominant culture, while, at the same time realizing forgotten human dimensions within a revitalized dynamic and total vision which could restore the capacity for a more fraternal and fuller life?

To attempt an affirmative answer, in the spirit of hope, I

would recall first the importance given by Habermas to communicative action as the medium for recreating meaning and as the motor for social evolution. Thus, the constitution of historical subjects would be linked to communicative competence and to symbolic interaction between people. In contrast to industrialized countries, people in the third world, not having been incorporated into the technological development and its concomitant rationality, may be able to maintain within the following context their communicative ability.

In third world countries, not only do many of the most fundamental needs of the people remain unsatisfied, but as people are incorporated into the system under conditions of subordination and exploitation, they are negated as social persons. This has obliged them to create new forms of response in which they maintain their traditional values as a means of resistance and of recreating their identity. This form of resistance, grounded in the maintenance of one's identity, has been possible by keeping alive symbolic recreation and free communication. The existence of myths founded upon the background of a lost harmony and manifesting themselves as an utopic projection indicates the historical dimension of this recreation of identity. Diverse traditional cultures thus have remained vigorous without being fragmented by the fractioning and reductionism endemic to occidental rationalism; they maintain a conception of totality in which the relationship of persons between themselves and with nature is recreated and embedded within an integral experience with profound religious roots.

Returning now to Habermas, let us see how it is precisely through the mediation of communicative action--which in order to flourish requires a lack of constraint and symbolic interaction--that new normative structures take shape. These, in turn, and within the dynamics of social movements, eventually institutionalize new forms of social integration.

> Rationality structures are embodied not only in amplifications of purposive-rational action--that is, in technologies, strategies, organizations, and qualifications--but also in mediations of communicative action in the mechanisms for regulating conflict, in world views, and in identity formations. I would even defend the thesis that the development of these normative structures is the pacemaker of social evolution, for new principles of social organization mean new forms of social integration; and the latter, in turn, first make it possible to implement available productive forces or to generate new ones, as well as making possible a heightening of social complexity.[27]

In industrialized countries purposive-rational action represses intersubjective communication, and the global system tends to make individuals merely receptive and thereby impedes real and free inter-communication. In contrast, in many Third World countries with living traditional cultures communication between people remains very lively. Through spontaneous and rich communicative action they recreate their own identity. This, in turn, is the source from which their values inspire original ways of solving the problems for which the institutional framework has no answer. These solutions imply new forms of social relationship which, to the extent to which they could succeed in becoming institutionalized, would change the prevailing sociocultural model.

The Case of Andean Culture in Peru Today

Conscious of the fact that concrete universality, as Hegel would say, passes through singularity, and precisely in opposition to the abstract and superficial universality of generalizations, the following analysis will focus upon Peru and its Andean cultural roots as one instance of a vigorous historical subject reflecting the capacity for free communication and symbolic interaction described above. This is not to say that Peru is necessarily the most representative case, but it has been the cradle of important and perduring cultures.

Historical Context. When the Europeans invaded America they found in the Andes a highly developed culture and a complex, efficient social organization. The Incas ruled an Empire built by conquering and unifying cultures whose remains--particularly its fine textiles, jewelry and ceramics, as well as its achievements in such fields as medicine, astronomy, architecture, etc.--are still amazing. They found a people who, in contrast to the Europeans, did not know of the atrocious consequences of famine since, in addition to their wise utilization of the various ecological habitats, they reserved grain in silos throughout their territory for difficult times.

Within this system economic, political and social activity took its meaning from a sacralized vision which unified the natural with the transcendent in a dynamic and cyclic manner. This can still be observed in rites, depicted particularly in pottery, which witness the annual repetition of life and death cycles, corresponding to their ritualized calendar of life.

The worldview which integrated the diverse aspects of the relationship among men, with nature and with the divine was structured upon a spatio-temporal axis whose terms were simultaneously opposed and mutually dependent: "To preserve both (parts), to maintain the equilibrium, was indispensable so that all could function. Heaven would require of earth as much as men of the divinities."[28] This basic bipartition, combined with a tri-partition and the decimal system was reproduced within increasingly extended patterns so that the smaller was included in the wider hierarchical order. Thus, according to a division which was both social and geographical, a town would pertain to hierarchically wider regions which finally would be unified with others under the whole Empire. This was divided in two halves, which in turn were divided in two, forming four quarters, whose center was Cusco, the capital. To this socio-geographic division corresponded a political one, with the representatives of the four regions forming the Great Council, presided over by the Inca.

In the temporal dimension, the annual calendar, with its ritualized socio-economic activities, also contained two halves, each of which was divided in two. This whole annual cycle was inserted in longer cycles which would later give birth to such millenarian beliefs as the utopias of the return of the lost order, or the reconstitution or resurrection of the Inca.

Upon the arrival of the Spaniards, this division in worlds and sub-worlds could have facilitated their incorporation into a broader, more powerful world, with an extended hierarchy in which the King of Spain would be the new apex. This might also be the case for the popular religiosity which still survives and in which Mother Earth and the gods of mountains and lakes are indisolubly tied up with Christ, the Cross and the saints. This synthesis could be explained the same way: more powerful gods being superimposed upon a politheistic world. Nevertheless, in the Andean iconography of today one observes that the sun is often placed above the Cross and other Christian symbols, which could reflect the return of an Inca utopia.

The Spaniards who conquered the Inca Empire found there serious internal difficulties which contributed to its succumbing to the Spanish domination. The extension of the Empire, even to latitudes in which the ritual agricultural calendar would no longer be functional, made it difficult to keep all under control. The greatest internal weakness was the division of the Empire by a civil war between two royal clans, headed by two Incas who disputed power over the whole. The Spaniards made good use of this rivalry for their own benefit.

Additionally, some nations helped the Spaniards for, although the imperial system had benefitted them in some ways, "the Incas were seen by many of the Andean people as conquerors and invaders, against whom rebellion was legitimate."[29] Perhaps they discovered their error too late for the Inca domination would later be shown to be far less oppressive than that of the Spaniards--to such a point that the Inca Empire later and even today has been idealized.

From of old, Andean culture had based its organization in the "ayllus" or communities. Although these have been altered by the influence of Spanish colonial institutions, they still preserve traits of their original organization. The new synthesis is expressed in the gradual assumption of tasks by all the male members of the community, starting from the least important jobs and gradually assuming those of more responsibility. The participation of all adults, men and women, in assemblies--reinforced by the Spanish "cabildo"--to decide all issues of importance for the community traces its history to pre-Inca times. During the Inca Empire decisions taken in these assemblies guided the action of the "Curaca" (later called "Cacique" by the Spaniards), who was the chief of the "ayllu" and its direct representative to the Inca.

The 'ayllu' constituted the nucleus of the diverse cultures which flourished at these latitudes prior to Inca times and which subsist today in modified form. Its organization was structured around the principles of reciprocity and redistribution, not only at the level of circulation and consumption, but also and fundamentally within the process of production. These two principles--which despite everything are still alive--began to function improperly at the distributive level when restructured under Inca domination. Within this system they kept working with the double function of allowing the system to operate while playing an ideological role. Not having lost their operating capacity, the principles could disguise how imperfectly they were actually functioning and the growing disparity of their terms. The development of the productive forces attained by the Inca organization had permitted maintaining the members of the ayllus in a decent condition while at the same time increasing the transfer of goods to the Inca and the privileged class. Thus, the Inca system was able to maintain, though twisted, the principles of reciprocity and redistribution which were able to function while simultaneously playing an ideological function.

These principles, still deeply internalized in the Andean mentality, were broken as regards distribution through the system imposed by the Spaniards, in which they began to function in only one direction and turned into mere exploitation. Nathan Wachtel describes it in the following way:

> while reciprocity had given way to a flow of goods (though ficticious and uneven) among the ayllu, Curaca and Inca, Spanish domination produces an unidirectional flow of goods from the Indians to the Spaniards, without a counterpart. . . . The Spaniard has

taken the place of the Inca and inherited his central-
izing function without maintaining the redistribution
of riches for the benefit of all. While the Inca tribute
worked through a circular, balanced structure, Spanish
tribute was characterized by an unbalanced, one-way
structure:

INCA TRIBUTE   *SPANISH TRIBUTE (30)*

One cannot forget what Spanish domination, with its deadly
abuses, oppression, etc., brought upon the Andean people. Nevertheless, to take account of the real dimensions of the disaster
as a total collapse of the their worldview, we ought to remember the intimate liaison of the economic with their whole conception of reality, their entire life, which thus disintegrated: "If
the fact that the economic system of the Inca Empire had religious and cosmological dimensions, which gave it its meaning, is
taken into consideration, then the depth of the colonial rupture
can be grasped."[31]

The Spaniards from the first moment utilized the Curacas
as intermediaries in their exploitation of the Indians. Nevertheless, they finally shortened internal social distances as well as
inter-ethnic rivalries, by organizing their laws on the basis of
the distinction between the "Republic of the Spaniards" and the
"Republic of the Indians." With this division they contributed to
the development of an Indian identity profile. Besides, the Spaniards, having to deal with several native languages, promoted a
wider spread of "quechua," the language of the Incas. The harsh
campaign against indigenous religions, the so-called "extirpation
of idolatries," was another factor which contributed to the development of an Andean identity.

Once dominated, the Indians had to develop adaptative and
resistive mechanisms. Nevertheless, they never ceased to fight,
nor did they lose faith and hope, acquiring the ". . . conviction
that the Inca will return so that everything will be better."[32]
The history of their struggle is the other side of a history
which has never ended. Of its many episodes the most important
was the rebellion of Tupac Amaru II, Curaca (Cacique for the
Spaniards) from a region of Cusco, who appeared as legitimate
successor of the Incas, restorer and redeemer, at the end of the

eighteenth century.

Within this context, the image of the Curacas, traditionally regarded as having sold out to the Spaniards, is being reconsidered. Today, it seems rather that they had no alternative to assuming the role imposed on them--while benefitting from it, of course--but that they surreptitiously protected the Indians and permitted cultural practices prohibited by the Spaniards.

Political independence from Spain brought no major changes in the system, aside from adaptation to a new type of domination--this time exercised by England as the new hegemonic axis of world power. The new type of domination, structured upon economic mechanisms, allowed a relative and formal independence from the new hegemonic metropolis: "New times made it possible for neo-colonialism to result from an interplay of essentially economic processes and mechanisms, without the need for a formal political bond with the metropolis."[33]

The Republic brought no significant change in the life of the Andean person from what it had been in Colonial times. The most significant process was, indeed, the greedy expansion of the landowners' possessions at the expense of the communities, which were reduced to the poorest lands. The "Republic of the Indians" having been abolished, the Andean person--though still treated as a member of a separate and inferior world--had lost the legal protection he possessed under that Republic. They became private subjects under the new principle of freedom of contract. This conversion into abstract entities gave them the freedom to be easily plundered.

The landowners, nevertheless, had to face the fight by the communities in defense of their lands. The process was a double one for the communities: on the one hand, it was a struggle for survival, on the other, the fight had a cohesive effect.

With the turn of the century, the process began--which continues till today--of more direct domination by the United States as the new hegemonic power. Joined with a constellation of power exercising a financial-monopolist imperialism, this process fundamentally aims to control the price of raw materials and broaden the market for its products. Market relations penetrate rural areas and are expressed through market prices, market labor and the assimilation of some consumer needs.

This penetration, however, does not constitute a real alternative to the rural economy, which continues to be based in non-market relations and maintains the principle of reciprocity. Through this the means of production are obtained without the mediation of money due to an exchange of labor for labor as well as, for example, tools or seeds. To some extent, barter of commodities is also maintained and many goods still are produced by family units.

> The production of exchange goods for the general
> market thus has a previous condition: the production
> of use commodities and the non-market barter of
> commodities and services.
> Thus, interchange in the community does not
> belong exclusively to the sphere of exchange created
> by the process established in the general market, but
> it also participates of another sphere of interchange
> based in a system of values whose nature differs from
> that of the general market. The two spheres of inter-
> change are far from being autonomous for both coex-
> ist within a single structure.[34]

The fact that capitalism has not penetrated rural areas
even at the market level, has permitted the survival of fundamental dimensions of the Andean cultural tradition, always
exteriorly bowing before power while inwardly keeping what is
its own. In community life the principles of reciprocity and
redistribution have remained operative, as has the Andean
worldview with its conception of totality tightly linked to the
still functional ritual-agricultural calendar. Consequently, Andean
communities have continued to live in a consistent sacralized
world expressed in its political organization with its respective
duties, as well as in communitary work marked by a sense of
reciprocity, redistribution and maximum utilization of scarce
means to solve common basic needs. It is a ritualized life, in
which symbolic-communicative medium the group relives its
identity which is based in memory and recreates its culture,
constantly incorporating new elements and giving them a distinctive content and significance.

The greatest challenge for the survival of the Andean
culture is, however, the ever-growing urban-rural interpenetration and the massive migration from country to city. During the
last decades this has turned Peru from a rural into an urban
country. This is the crucial phenomenon upon which we will
have to focus in order to understand the present dynamic of
Peru and its future possibilities.

Today's Challenge. The Latin American world is a melting
pot in which diverse cultures with traditional roots converge.
These constitute a counter force to the homogenizing assault
from dominant capitalism. It is

> a tense coexistence of indigenous forces: Andean,
> Afro-American, mestizo, middle-class, natives of the
> Amazoneon forests, all of which, along with their

particularities, have a common horizon in their opposition to Western capitalism.[35]

Among these cultures in the majestic Andean Cordillera the fact that cultural roots remain alive and strong could constitute a unifying factor and generate a new mode of social integration.

> This is the force, the roots, in their Andean region. . . . The truth is that there are vigorous roots, which hold real promise. I would consider traditions to be the source for new human coexistence: roots in conflict with the parameters of occidental progress.[36]

The issue sketched above raises important questions and hopes in the midst of the confusion precipitated by the recent massive migrations which have turned our countries from rural to urban. In the case of Peru:

> In the period from 1940 to 1981 the urban population grew almost five times (from 2.4 million to 11.6) while the rural one grew by only a third (from 4.7 to 6.2 million). Thus, while in 1940 the rural constituted 65% of the total population and the urban 35%, by 1981 these percentages were reversed; in 1940 two out of every three Peruvians lived in the country while in 1981 two of three lived in cities.[37]

More specifically in the capital, Lima, "this increase is significantly greater: it has grown 7.6 times in this period: from 8.6% of the country's population it has grown to 26% of the population."[38]

Why do people migrate to the cities; what are the main causes of this phenomenon? First, they were practically expelled from the country by such factors as the crisis in agriculture around the middle of this century and recently the situation created by subversion in the south of Peru. Among the comparative advantages or incentives the city offers and which seem to have weighed most are the availability of better services such as health and especially education, as well as the possibility of higher wages. One must take account also of the attraction exerted by the city as opening new worlds of discovery, progress and liberty.

All migrants--whether they search for new opportunities or are fleeing from unbearable situations--arrive with great hopes, with an enormous will to begin a new life. What they find is a daunting challenge. The city does not greet them; it has other owners who do not wish to share with them. How are they to face a hostile world that has no place for them, does not take them into consideration and even denies them? How are they to survive; what are they to do?

To better understand their response, let us look into a newly occupied area in the outskirts of Lima and follow the creation of a whole life which, by struggle, succeeds in overcoming adversity. This includes opening a new geographical space, imprinting upon it a new countenance and making life possible through the weaving of a copious network of interpersonal relationships.

Due to the growing penetration of capitalism in rural areas, the migrants have already had the experience of combining with their strong cultural roots, powers of adaptation and coping with dominant structures. Those who have had more of this diversified experience will have a greater chance to succeed at the social as well as at the personal level, and will respond in original ways to the difficult situation they face. These creative modes of response have communal roots in the deep and strong sense of organization, solidarity, collaboration, reciprocity and maximum utilization of scarce means for the satisfaction of the basic needs of all--values which are sustained in solid interpersonal relationships.

At the risk of simplifying a much more complex panorama, the situation in which the lives of these immigrants evolves might be sketched as follows.

The migrant who comes today--in contrast to what occurred with the pioneers--usually arrives at a relative's house. Sometimes this relative can put him in contact with someone through whom he/she can obtain some sort of job. In general, however, he has to look out for himself and learn to solve his own survival problems. This is especially so when one begins one's own family, if one has not arrived with one.

As urban development has not considered the need for low-cost housing, there is no alternative for migrants but to search for their own solutions. They organize themselves and invade generally barren lands in the deserts surrounding Lima. These lack any type of service or urban substructure; they are distant from everything: everything has to be started from zero. Life seems impossible and the human cost of having to choose this precarious mode of survival is enormous.

Sometimes they must even defend with their lives their right to a home. Arguedas compares the fight for urban property with the historical one for community lands. In the city, as well as in the country, the authorities will have to face the ordeal of either killing those who thus fight for their right to live or permitting a fissure in the established order. Thus, regarding one of the first settlements in which the invaded deserts were legally recognized as the property of a neighboring landowner,

Arguedas relates:

> The political authorities of the Capital of the Republic
> face an identical alternative in the invasions by mi-
> grant masses. Though they are not invasions of large
> highland haciendas, the unused pieces of desert sur-
> rounding Lima did turn out to belong legally to neigh-
> boring estates. In lightning invasions and a sole night
> migrants construct there, in the midst of the desert,
> illegal slum settlements. In one of the most recent
> ones--on a small hill and "Angel's Fall" plain--the
> leader of the invasion notified the official who com-
> manded the troup sent to dislodge them: "Sir, all we
> want is either this little piece of land to live upon or
> that you kill us all." They killed only one.[39]

Having set up during the first night some very flimsy huts
--which they will later improve little by little--the next step is
to strive for the most basic services, for there are no sanitary
conditions. It might take up to 10 or 15 years of petitions before a water supply and sewage system are installed, during
which time they live in conditions of misery. As the price of
the water transported in trucks is exorbitant, they have to do
with the minimum indispensable for the most urgent needs. This
scarcity of water, plus the problem of refuse, the lack of sewage and problems of nutrition, bring catastrophic consequences,
particularly upon the children.

There is no need to expand upon the miserable conditions
these settlers must undergo. It is more helpful for our purpose
to see the ways in which they organize in order to respond to
the severe challenges and to survive. Their new settlement is
not chaotic or random, but grows as planned neighborhood development. From the very first moment of the process of urban
settlement they are organized by blocks, committees and sectors.
This structure enables them to respond to a variety of everyday neighborhood problems. From this they move to solving
urgent needs of some of the settlers such as obtaining money
for those who are sick, for a funeral, or for hospitalization. If
the mother if hospitalized a spirit of solidarity is manifest in
the way in which neighbors care for and feed her children. This
is particularly significant in view of the precarious conditions in
which all live.

The women organize into clubs and common kitchens
which, even if supported by external institutions, reflect their
effort to make the best communal use of scarce means in response to their needs. Due to the lack of legal and police protection, the migrants usually develop ways of solving internal

disputes and organize neighborhood watches in order to defend themselves, for example, from burglars or drug vendors.

The migrant has to undergo a *via crucis* to find a job. Employment in industry is quite difficult to find because of the precarious state of its development due to the dependant situation of the Peruvian economy. Even if one manages to find a job in industry, due to the recent economic crisis, one would be very poorly remunerated and would need somehow to complement this income. Furthermore, as employment is so unstable, one continually needs to change jobs.

Thus, since the established productive apparatus does not resolve the migrant's problems, they must search out such answers as workshops, services and street vending. In all these the logic or organization differs from that which is proper to a capitalistic enterprise. Several members of the family, including children, elders and relatives, are employed; sometimes a few wage earners also participate in the enterprise. All work and all live, but no one necessarily profits or saves. This, however, is no reason to close the enterprise; they will keep on working and living.

Thus in the workshops the division between capital and labor which is typical of capitalism does not obtain. Those who at times participate in the productive process at other times sell their products, while also alternating--particularly in the case of the women--with household jobs: home and shop share the same roof.

Starting from street vending, they implement original forms of survival which reflect great versitility in the way of responding to market demands as well as creating new avenues for earning. Furthermore, the relationships do not acquire the abstract character which the market imprints, but are predominantly personal.

> These activities, in addition to being ruled by the market obey other rules: loyalty and solidarity between small merchants who skillfully compete with the big ones, interpersonal dealings with purchasers whom they attract with wisdom and cleverness. In sum, "informal" commerce offers guidelines for a more humanizing interchange of goods and services than that of the capitalist order.[40]

Thus, we see that the immigrants, faced with the problem of lack of employment, develop alternatives which reveal a synthesis between their own culture and the dominant structure.

> The activities connected with independent work (such as those performed in workshops and by street ven-

dors) pick up and often reinforce elements of their traditional culture, coexisting with those proper to the dominant model. That is why this sector of the subordinate classes moves between apathy and resistance, individual endeavour and the rescue of the collective, disunion and cohesion. Its history thus appears as fragmented, episodic and spontaneous; but transcending this first impression, we find a constant creation of bonds, coherence and continuity between them.[41]

One of the main examples of how the principle of reciprocity works can be found in home construction. Usually, relatives and other relations come on the weekends to work. They are provided with food and drink and will be helped when their turn comes to have their homes constructed. The close relation between feast and work is also reflected here, for on the day of the topping, when the house is completed, a cross is placed over the door and everybody participates in a feast.

Some organizations are based on the place of origin. In these, original bonds and feasts (*fiestas*)--the communal rites-- are celebrated. In these associations, which are the place of greatest interchange, the principle of reciprocity clearly functions. One who takes part in the feasts and activities of his native town and remains united with his fellow townsmen will be helped enthusiastically should he fall into need. Mainly through these associations, strong bonds with their mother community are maintained, and from Lima these nuclei promote improvements in their home towns.

On weekends in the popular quarters surrounding Lima there are processions of those who were not able to go to their home town to celebrate the feast of its patron saint. But, why are there so many feasts; what is their meaning? Irarrazaval answers this:

> We can all perceive that celebration is joy, surprise, gratuity, but we cannot so easily detect its symbolism. How to explain the quality and quantity of feasts? Just for the sake of having fun? No. They symbolize the roots and progress of the indigenous Andean population.[42]

Here we reach the heartbeat of the Andes. In these feasts Andean persons live communitarily their cultural values, recreate their identity, and elaborate their own myth. This, in turn, poses the question of the historical subject.

The Possibility of the Constitution of an Historical Subject of Andean Roots. Here the issue concerns what the outcome of this process will be. We cannot know, for otherwise we would be denying the dynamic character of the historical subject. All we can do is postulate a hope, but we have already provided some grounds to sustain this hope.

I am among those who, like the anthropologist and novelist, Jose Maria Arguedas, believe in the possibility of the constitution of an historical subject with Andean roots. This historical subject would be capable of giving birth to a new historical project as long as he sustains himself in his sacred, mythical character and on that basis is able to overcome the reductive project now being imposed on him. Pedro Trigo, analyzing what several specialists in the work of Arguedas say with respect to his novel, *All Bloods*, notes:

> Subsequently, Cornejo concludes his study asserting that the new world he imagines blossoming from the death of the *comunero* (member of the community, in the novel) is, basically, the Indian world of fraternity among men and with nature. This is the only destiny that Arguedas accepts for Peru. Not, certainly, the elimination of the Western contribution, but undoubtedly the constitution of a modern world . . . ruled by Quechuan values. Forgues enumerates the principal ones: throughout the whole novel, he says, we see the progressive eruption of the formidable potency of Indian strength, made of courage and discipline, of a spirit of solidarity and abnegation, of dignity and respect. . . . Marin, on his part, refers to the beliefs and rites which operate, he says, as real cultural substrata. . . . There is a keen sense of dignity and firmness as well as a profound lived religiosity where the Inca and Christian mingle and the Indian pantheistic sense turns visible in multiple attitudes, rites and happenings. It is noticeable how the Inca and the Christian blend into each other with no possibility of subsequent division . . . thus giving birth to a new cultural form resulting from the process of transculturation. Marin sums up saying that the deep roots of Peru . . . are grounded in the sacred.[43]

This anchoring in the sacred leads us to what Arguedas seems to be saying throughout his entire work, that the roots of the Andean historical subject lie in its mythical-sacred character.

There remains another question:

Will this mythical man be confined to traditional

societies, so that the process of modernization will automatically lead to his extinction? Or will he be able to plunge into this process assimilating his opponent's qualities and thereby vanquish him? . . . If he can assimilate technology, would not this automatically lead to the destruction of the mythical man? Would this mean for him not merely assimilating the achievements of the other, but becoming like him?[44]

In regard to this crucial question Arguedas insists upon the fact that the mythical does not imply stagnation, alienation, idealism, or irrationality. On the contrary, it is a live historical reconstruction, and hence capable of incorporating the dominant rationality, which indeed has always been partially incorporated in traditional cultures. Thus, Trigo notes with respect to the novel, *Deep Rivers*:

The life world is no longer that of the native or of automatic adaptation to the environment; it is a construction. It is the subject who, through memory, rite and acts of social solidarity, makes of himself a mythical man. But if myth is the result of a choice, then it is not 'primitive', a prior elemental stage characterized by lack of conscience and individuality. In *Deep Rivers* the mythical is rather a port or harbour, a goal attained through long, strenuous combat against individualism and the typical devaluations by modernity. It is not that some traumatic contact with modernity causes regression as a pathological reaction. The sensation of solitude and culpability is not annulled by the negation of the subject; on the contrary, the subject constitutes itself precisely through responsibly overcoming these situations. Hence, in *Deep Rivers* the mythic as overcoming modernity is a modern possibility. Because the mythic is "religation" (from *re-ligare* or bind back as in the term "religion") it cannot be maintained at an idealistic level without degenerating into nostalgia. That is why the mythical as the construction of a subject demands the social constitution of the mythical space.[45]

Regarding *All Bloods* Trigo notes:

The mythical as monstrous resistance has no future. The mythical as life-world can only maintain itself if, going on the attack, it conquers the historical project of modernity. For this, it needs to assimilate its achievements. The mythical is thus similar to an orchestration in which some elements fall and others remain, but everything is transformed. This means that the mythical has a dynamic complex structure and hence integrates that planning which is typical of modernity.[46]

Hence, a new synthesis is not necessarily probable, but remains possible as long as the Andean cultural roots remain vigorous. Critical reason constitutes a "second act," whereas the mythical subject expressing itself in ritual communion constitutes the "first act." In this first act meaning is recreated in communion which is lived at the symbolic-intersubjective level. In a second moment, rational elements are incorporated at an operative level and reelaborated in order to be adapted to the values of the relational structure expressed and lived communitarily at the ritual level.

Therefore, the possibility exists that as long as he keeps living the relational structure of his mythical religious world the historical subject with Andean roots can, in a second moment, incorporate the modern rational-operative way of thinking, without totally yielding to it. He would thus be exercising the planning capability which purposive rational action implies as a necessary means for men. Means-end rationality would thus find its place in the operative sphere within a more holistic conception. This could overcome the reductionism inherent in occidental rationalism, taken to an extreme in the totalizing instrumentalization of our present-day "developed" worlds.

Nevertheless, I wish to reiterate that the example of Peru and its Andean roots is just one case. It would acquire greater significance to the degree that it were representative of the possible constitution of historical subjects with traditional roots in other places. Starting from their diverse identity recreation processes, these could generate important new historical configurations.

Universidad de Lima
  Lima, Peru

NOTES

1. Alain Touraine, *Sociología de la Acción* (Barcelona: Ariel, 1969, pp. 13-14.

2. *Ibid.*

3. Cf. René Lourau, *El analisis institucional* (Buenos Aires: Amorrortu, 1970).

4. Alain Touraine, *op. cit.*, p. 14.

5. *Ibid.*, p. 15.

6. *Ibid.*

7. *Ibid.*, p. 16.

8. *Ibid.*

9. Cf. René Lourau, *Les analyseurs de l'Eglise; Analyse institutionelle en milieu chretien* (Paris: Anthropos, 1972), p. 72.

10. *Mic.* 5:13.

11. The term "ideology" has many meanings, starting from the rather positive connotation of the German "Weltanshauung," as an organized system of notions, images and values, by means of which a collectivity or an individual organizes its diverse experiences in an acceptable manner. Here we shall use "ideology" in the sense of dominant ideology, which is a type of alienation. This is the case when a dominant group imposes its ideological view of reality and justifies it as most convenient for all, concealing the fact that it favors mainly the interests of that dominant group.

12. George McLean, *Plenitude and Participation: The Unity of Man in God* (Madras: Univ. of Madras, 1978), p. 7.

13. John Loscerbo, *Being and Technology: A Study in the Philosophy of Martin Heidegger* (The Hague: Martinus Nijhoff Publishers, 1981), p. 5.

14. *Ibid.*

15. *Ibid.*, p. 43.

16. Richard E. Palmer, *Hermeneutics: Interpretation Theory in Schleiermacher, Dilthey, Heidegger and Gadamer* (Evanston: Northwestern University Press, 1969), p. 142.

17. John Loscerbo, *op. cit.*, p. 44.

18. Jean Toussaint De Santi, "Galileo y la nueva concepción de la Naturaleza," *Historia de la Filosofía* (Madrid: Espasa Calpe, 1976), p. 82.

19. Cf. Alexandre Koyre, *Etudes Galiliennes* (Paris: Herman, 1940).

20. Herbert Marcuse, *El hombre unidimensional* (Barcelona: Ariel, 1981), p. 174.

21. Jurgen Habermas, *Toward a Rational Society* (Boston: Beacon Press, 1971), p. 82.

22. *Ibid.*, p. 83.

23. *Ibid.*

24. See Chapter VIII below.

25. Jurgen Habermas, *op. cit.*, p. 113.

26. *Ibid.*, pp. 118-119.

27. Jurgen Habermas, *Communication and the Evolution of Society* (Boston: Beacon Press, 1979), p. 120.

28. Alberto Flores Galindo, *Europa y el pais de los Incas: La utopia Andina,* (Lina: Instituto de Apoyo Agrario, 1986), p. 43.

29. Pablo Macera, *Vision historica del Peru* (Lima: Ed. Milla Batres, 1978).

30. Nathan Wachtel, *Sociedad e ideologia: ensayos de historia y antropologia Andinas* (Lima: Instituto de Estudios Peruanos, 1973).

31. *Ibid.*, p. 83.

32. Jan Szeminski, *La utopia Tupamarista* (Lima: Fondo Editorial de la Pontificia Universidad Catolica del Peru, 1984).

33. Heraclio Bonilla and Karen Spÿalding, "La independencia en el Peru: las palabras y los hechos," *La independencia en el Peru* (Lima: Instituto de Estudios Peruanos, 1981), p. 106.

34. Jürgen Golte and Marisol de la Cadena, *La codeterminacion de la organizacion social Andina* (Lima: Instituto de Estudios Peruanos, 1986), p. 6.

35. Diego Irarrazaval, "Potencialidad Indigena-Andina," *Paginas*, No. 74 (Lima: Centro de Estudios y Publicaciones, 1985), pp. 4-5.

36. *Ibid.*, p. 5.

37. Hernando de Soto, *El otro sendero* (Lima: El Barranco, 1986), p. 7.

38. *Ibid.*, p. 8.

39. Jose Maria Arguedas, *Indios, mestizos y senores* (Lima: Horizonte, 1985), p. 22.

40. Diego Irarrazaval, *op. cit.*, p. 9.

41. Romeo Grompone, *Talleristas y verdedores ambulantes en Lima* (Lima: DESCO, 1986), p. 228.

42. Diego Irarrazaval, *op. cit.*, p. 10.

43. Pedro Trigo, *Arguedas, mito, historia y religion* (Lima: Centro de Estudios y Publicaciones, 1982), pp. 161-162.

44. *Ibid.*, pp. 33-34.

45. *Ibid.*, pp. 197-198.

46. *Ibid.*, p. 198.

CHAPTER IV

LIBERATION AS
AUTONOMY AND RESPONSIBILITY:
Habermas and the Psychoanalytic Method in
the Analysis and Critique of Values and Tradition

JAMES LOIACONO, O.M.I.

INTRODUCTION: VALUES AND TRADITION

Liberation is the transformative elimination of unjust and oppressive structures. This takes place through an on-going process of critique of the values and traditions of a given "culture-subject," that is, of a culture as well as the persons and communities who live in its terms. Values and traditions provide the articulated morphological and syntactical matrix from which societal and cultural structures are evolved and through which they are transmitted. As warp and woof of the fabric of societal structures, they are the objects of the liberating critique.

The Frankfort School of critical theory has offered several analytical and methodological approaches to the critique of values and tradition. This chapter will examine the analysis and methodology of one member of this School, Jurgen Habermas,[1] as a means (a) of liberation from what is oppressive, and (b) of growth in self-understanding. This is directed toward continued development in autonomy and responsibility within those specific values and traditions which constitute the grammar of one's self-understanding and one's cultural-societal structures.

Cultural Self-Identity

As both constitutive and dispositive factors in the culture-subject's self-understanding, values and tradition are central to its identity and integrity. They articulate the self-constitution of one culture-subject's[2] identity as distinct from another's, as well as the channels through which various systems within that culture-subject interact. They maintain its integrity through the transmission of a common or shared grammar to all individuals within the group, who, in turn, identify with, use and pass on this self-constitutive articulation of their values and tradition.

The linguistic anthropologist, Edward G. Hall, sees this as a mechanism of evolution through advanced development of the cortex, to adapt and preserve the human species from negative biological selection, i.e. from extinction.[3] In terms of semiotics humans are effected through symbols or signs at a triadic level of true communication, rather than through a mere signal or stimuli-response dyadic type of biological interaction. While Jurgen Habermas agrees with the idea of evolutionary adaptation rooted in biological origins, he rejects a purely positivist notion of human knowledge or a biologically determined self-constitution of the human species. Instead, Habermas emphasizes the transcendental quality of knowing, self-reflection and communication.[5] From the perspective of semiotics, one can say that the human species transcends the mere external dyadic relationships of biological determinism and adds a third or intentional dimension by becoming self-reflective. Human persons know that they know. They think, will and have a self-constituting interior life. In this there are meaning, values and love, and from this also there flows work, language, politics, history and tradition.

Seen in a more favorable perspective than that of Habermas, values and tradition are this self-constituting wisdom achieved as the culture-subject determines its own history. It progresses not only technologically, but in constant interaction with the natural and social environment. Advancing in its understanding of nature and self, it writes its own history, and thereby progressively frees itself from its biological constraints. For Habermas, in this process the culture subject, by liberating itself from oppressive and exploitive social constraints, achieves autonomy and responsibility (*Mundigkeit*).

The culture-subject's linguistic nature is its ability to symbolize in word and action this understanding of self and nature. Linguistic transmission of knowledge, values, and tradition is, in turn, always social, for language can occur only when there is a symbol-giver and a symbol receiver. In fact, beginning from one's intra-uterine developmental till one's death, the human person is always interacting with others in the social environment: the person is never outside a social milieu. This sociality is radical to the human person, who is therefore essentially both a symbol-giver and a symbol receiver. Both constitute the basis for language and, in turn, make possible the constitutive and dispositive self-understanding and self-formation of the culture-subject. Values and tradition are the linguistic and ritualistic symbols or expressionsof this. They maintain the identity and integrity of persons in their linguistic and productive interaction with others. By this interaction culture is constituted in all aspects.

If then the person and the culture articulate who and what they are specifically through values and tradition, the effect of these is autonomy and resistance to loss of cultural identity and self-determination. At the dyadic level of signal interaction and stimulus/response a species is continually confronted with the possibility of biological selection and struggles to maintain its existence and to propagate its species. Similarly at the triadic level of symbolic interaction the culture-subject is continually confronted with the possibility of extinction and must struggle to maintain its identity, integrity and autonomy in the face of oppressive and exploitative forces. As this takes place through time and reflects the cumulative free acts of individuals and social groups, the values and traditions of a culture-subject are marked by historicity.

Further, it is through intense linguistic interaction in loving and positive relatedness to one another that persons acquire their self-identity or self-understanding. This is done in terms of the wisdom of the community, as this has been developed in time and passed on as the values and tradition of a culture. All individuals of the culture group are thus bound in sociality, which is the solidarity rooted in each person's intrinsic inclination to relatedness in love. This sustains the group in its identity, integrity, and self-understanding, while preserving it from historical negative selection at the hands of a more dominant, exploitative, oppressive cultural group. This can be seen practically in the Aymara culture's preservation of its identity during Inca-Quechua domination and, in turn, the Inca-Quechua culture's maintenance of its identity under Spanish dominance. The tenacious cohesiveness within the group generates fierce resistance to the imposition of values by a dominant group which would threaten it with loss of both identity and integrity, resulting in total or near total cultural-historical extinction.

Much as the chromosomes, through the particular and unique genetic code bequeathed by one's ancestors, carry the biological identity of the person, values and traditions constitute the linguistic-cultural genetic material from cultural history which bequeath a specific identity to the culture-subject. As the body fiercely rejects the intrusion of a foreign genetic code, so the culture-subject rejects the intrusion of forced values and tradition from an imposing group. Yet these very values and traditions, which are the morphological and syntactical warp and woof of the linguistic fabric of the culture-subject's self-understanding, are also vulnerable to being used for the exploitation and manipulation of the group as a whole or in its parts. It will be necessary, Habermas suggests, to discover the locus of any such debilitating and oppressive factors which limit the function and progress of the subject. The specific purpose of this chapter is to scrutinize the psychoanalytic dimension of the methodology developed by Habermas for discovering debilitating flaws in a culture's linguistically and ritualistically articulated "genetic" code. We shall attempt to protect the project from doing violence to the identity and hence to the self-understanding of the culture-subject. This is a point on which Habermas seems less--though increasingly--concerned.

The Psycho-Social Problematic

Habermas stresses that the transmission of this cultural ('genetic') code of values and tradition occurs through symbols which are linguistic or, one might add, ritualistic in nature.[6] He understands this to be rooted in the historicity of the culture-subject. He sees three profound similarities between the way in which, seen psychologically, values form the individual's superego (ego ideal and conscience) and the manner in which values and tradition comprise the self-understanding of the culture-subject. First, just as the individual identifies with the symbolic content of the ego ideal and conscience, so the culture-subject identifies with its own values and tradition. Second, the superego may be flawed through reception of defective values or some other symbolic distortion, leading to neurotic behavior whose origin and activity are not comprehended by the individual. Similarly a culture-subject may receive from its past or from significant power groups within itself values and traditions which distort self-identity, self-understanding and self-formation. Third, Freudian psychoanalysis self-reflectively critiques the symbols both of the superego, in order to correct the linguistic and historical distortions of the ego ideal, and of the conscience, in order to cure the neurosis and its behavioral manifestations. Similarly, Habermas would critique the values and tradition of the culture-subject in order to correct the symbolic distortions of rigidified abstractions. This suggests that psychoanalytic insights might provide means both for liberation from linguistically encoded material that is oppressive, exploitative, and stultifying, and for the goal of cultural autonomy and responsibility, that is, for liberation.[7] This responds to the fundamental problem of how to achieve liberation understood as autonomy and responsibility by restoring or enabling an "authentic" self-identity. More classically it is the issue of how to achieve the truth that makes one free.

In terms of the Marxist notion of rigidified abstractions, Habermas sees a danger within values and tradition. That is, having developed in the historical self-formative process of the community to meet the exigencies of the commonweal at one historical moment, one's values and traditions may become reified and be carried into successive historical sequences to which they no longer apply, thereby becoming stultifying and oppressive.[8] Historically, as the culture-subject progresses in the sciences of nature and advances technologically toward greater instrumental action for the exploitation of natural resources, small power-elites have tended to maintain control over virtually every aspect of the culture. This is especially true of the means of production and of political-economic structures, both at home and abroad, through forms of colonialism and modern-day neo--colonialism. Thus, values and traditions, developed originally in response to given exigencies, subsequently maintain a *status quo* which divides the culture-subject's self-understanding between power-elite and common people, managerial caste and working caste, imperial power and colony.[9]

As in Freudian psychoanalytic theory where the individual identifies with parental figures and significant others during the formation of the superego (ego ideal and conscience), so the culture-subject identifies with the values and tradition which, in turn, articulate its self-understanding.[10] Thus, though these subsequently may have become oppressive, there is a very vigorous tendency to maintain them in spite of their social and cultural inequities or contradictions.

As noted, one reason for this is that values and tradition maintain the identity and integrity of the culture-subject, preserving it from historical selection. They are the skeletal structure to which the culture-subject adheres in developing its unique self-formative history with its linguistic-anthropological, socio-psychological, philosophical-religious, creative-artistic, and economic-political elements. This overall historical fabric constitutes not only the unfathomable wealth of each group in its special values, but also its limitations in its self-understanding. It typically fails to exceed these categories in perceiving, ordering and evaluating reality; these are the parameters of its self-understanding and of its understanding of others.

Another reason for maintaining values and tradition, even after they have become rigidified abstractions, is the particular self-interest of the power elite. Because any contradictions which arise must be critiqued by the very mechanism of values and tradition which caused them; the very understanding of the problem is confused and biased. Thus, the oppressor-exploiter is able to maintain the linguistic structure of self-understanding and self-formation which preserves the contradictions.[11] Ironically, even those oppressed and exploited, having identified so completely with these categories of self-understanding as the only linguistic structure in which they can operate, identify in solidarity with the very structure that serves them neither equally nor justly. Freud calls this: "identification with the aggressor."[12] Prior to the elimination or correction of such contradiction the values and traditions of the culture-subject usually are vigorously defended and the contradictions rationalized, much as the neurotic defends inapporpriate behavior through a complex of defense mechanisms and rationalization.[13]

Thus, values and tradition, while positive in the sense of maintaining identity and integrity and preventing negative historical selection by oppressive outside cultural forces, can constitute an obstacle to liberation from within. As categories of self-understanding they can limit perception by those who suffer; because ultimately self-serving, they can result in lack of sensitivity to oppression by those who profit.[14] In Freudian terms, which will be elaborated later, being the core personal structure of self-understanding, identity and integrity, they provide all in the culture-subject--both exploiter and exploited--with a sense of security, regardless of how true or false that security might be. As a result, any attempt to alter or eliminate these core or linguistic structures (values and tradition) is seen as a threat, thereby causing anxiety in the culture-subject and generating resistance as defense mechanisms.[15] The power-elite in whose interest it is to maintain these values and traditions are the least likely to cooperate in dismantling the system; ironically they may find a ready ally in the very group whose interest is not well served.

For this reason, liberation is a complex matter which requires a sophisticated methodology for analysis and response. In these major steps this chapter will attempt to identify the historic hermeneutic method elaborated by Habermas. First it will survey the scientific insights he draws from Marx, Peirce and Freud, noting in each case both the way in which he assimilates those ideas and the way in which he adds his own correctives. Secondly, the chapter will analyze the method constructed by Habermas focusing especially on the role of abduction, hermeneutic and interest. Thirdly, it will review the clarifying critiques he makes of positivism in order to clarify elements of his method which are especially important. This paper will also examine and critique Marcuse's position on liberation. The conclusion will suggest a way of understanding the place of value and tradition in our hermeneutics of liberation.

SCIENTIFIC METHODS: RESOURCES AND LIMITATIONS

Marx's Social Analysis

Where Marx speaks of surplus value and Marcuse develops his idea of 'surplus repression,' Habermas moves to values and tradition as the reservoir of contradiction.[16] Let us follow in greater detail this sequence in relation to the thought of Habermas. Marx considered two major factors in the analysis of the Capitalist culture subject to be: (a) surplus value, which pertains to the accumulation of wealth and profit in the hands of those who control the means of production, and (b) continued growth in the knowledge of nature (cognitive progress) with concomitant growth in technology (instrumental action). These two factors combined with certain self-defeating mechanisms in the capitalist system were to bring about a negation in the organic relationships in the culture-subject, specifically between the proletariat and the capitalist power structure leading to revolutionary activity and change. Habermas considers this view severely limited precisely because it does not address itself to the self-constituting and self-formative process of self-reflection and critique.[17] The Marxist view, not unlike the positivist approach, is geared to a reductionistic and hence to a deterministic understanding of the culture-subject which has no room for an interior life, and hence no metaphysics of the person or epistemology in the sense of a study of the origin of meaning. In contrast, Habermas insists that the culture-subject--contrary to being bereft of self-reflection and freedom--is a creature of historicity who, through transcendental linguistic structures and processes, writes its own destiny and thereby freely constitutes and forms itself toward ever increasing autonomy and responsibility.[18]

As the transcendental linguistic structure of this self-formation, tradition and values are the means by which the culture-subject evolves in continually expanding freedom beyond the biological and historical constraints imposed upon other species of our planet. On the basis of its essential character as persons existing and acting with others through time, that is, its sociality and historicity as expressed linguistically in word and ritual, the culture-subject strives to realize its total potential. Values and traditions which express the nature of the culture-subject must be seen also as constitutive of, and dispositive toward, continual cognitive progress in understanding nature and the constant development of technology for greater distribution of goods to the members of the group. Thus, the Marxist emphasis upon 'surplus value' as the ostensible locus of contradiction arising from the capitalist abuse of cognitive progress and instrumental action must be replaced by a focus upon that of which surplus value is a mere epiphenomenon, namely, upon distortions in values and tradition; this is the true locus of the contradictions.

In this way, Habermas moves from biological and historical determinism, expressed as advancement in productive technology for meeting the physical necessities of the culture-subject, to self-determination and self-formation, manifested in historicity. This is found at the transcendental level of language through a process of self-reflection and critique of values and tradition as a means for the continuous self-constitution of the culture-subject.[19]

At this point, one must extend the notion of surplus value beyond the positivist framework of excess capital in order to include its source in the not so obvious concept of values and tradition. Power is accumulated and maintained by an elite in the values and tradition of all levels of the culture-subject. It is here that linguistic distortion takes place in the form of rigidified abstractions which have been reified for the maintenance of the status quo. As these rigidified abstractions are the linguistic categories of self-understanding and self-interpretation, as well as of interpreting the natural environment, they determine and distort all perception for the exploitation and manipulation of the group as a whole or in part.[20]

In order to correct these rigidified abstractions and distortions present in the culture-subject's values and tradition, Habermas seeks a means of self-reflection for achieving autonomy and responsibility as an ongoing process of self-determined liberation. The problem he encounters in the Marxist and positivist approaches is their objectivism, which reduces all historical hermeneutic sciences to an empirical-analytic status both in methodology and interpretation. Habermas notes that within Marx's materialist re-development of the Hegelian system which had abolished epistemology, he failed to grasp the moment in his metacritique of Hegel to develop a radicalized epistemology.

In the Marxist perspective, truth is the consciousness which nature achieves in the human species as determined by production and its modes.[21] In the positivist perspective, truth is obtained methodologically through linking empirically obtained data into general laws. Both systems treat the science of the human person with the empirical-analytical method of the science of nature, and thereby fall into the trap of the illusory logic of what I shall term an objectivist cognitive loop. As a result they are not able to critique the ongoing process into which the culture-subject becomes hopelessly enmeshed. For both the Marxist and the the positivist, the very question of the human person, of nature, and of truth is grossly reduced to questions of production, while the question 'why', in the sense of meaning or significance, becomes absurd and is therefore ignored.[22] This lamentable development carries with it an even more peculiar consequence for Marx, namely, the reduction of the historic-hermeneutic sciences of the human person to the methodology and interpretation of the empirical-analytic sciences. Thus, every time the issue of critique arises with its question of meaning or significance it is reduced to a methodological approach which is incapable of such analysis, and indeed annihilates the very question altogether. Upon asking the question of critique the culture-subject finds itself on the twisted track of an objectivist loop which can only bring it back to the same point. Not only is it frustrated in its effort, but it is unable to grasp the very means by which the loop can be transcended and the logical knot in the process can be untied. Thus, the culture-subject is forced to move along a track without critiquing the reason for the method and direction taken.

The 'objectivist illusion' among the Marxists and the positivists is the matrix from which flow the demands for the exclusive use of the positivist, empirical, scientific method for all aspects of nature and the human person. Moreover, in the positivist, empirical, scientific method, this 'objectivist illusion' is articulated linguistically in the form of values and tradition as 'surplus value' and the control of the power elite. It constitutes the semantic structure of rigidified abstractions, which have been reified and become the constitutive and dispositive means of the self-understanding and formation of the culture-subject. Its result is the conservation of the status quo and of the ancillary self-interests of the power structure.

In a certain sense, Kant feared most the collapse of human understanding into the objectivist-positivist mode of empirical-analytic science; the need to avoid this gave impetus to his examination of pure and practical reason and judgment. This objectivist reduction would deprive the human person of freedom and, therefore, of moral action by subjecting the interpretation of human behavior to the same parameters as the physical and biological universe. In fact, without the transcendence of autonomous thought and action such a being would be neither person nor human. Habermas notes emphatically that, whatever the faults of the Kantian critique, it was central to the establishment of a basis for freedom and autonomy. Kant did this through his epistemological analysis of thinking. To establish the fact that the human person is free and autonomous in thinking, judgment, decision, and action, Kant asked how one can know this with the same certitude as a scientific or mathematical postulate. The statement, "the human person is free and autonomous," is an *a priori* synthetic statement without correlative phenomenological experience; it is postulated in praxis, that is, in action dependant upon pure practical reason. Hence, Kant analyzed knowing itself as a transcendental function of the human person.[23]

This is the precise point that Habermas wishes to pursue, albeit in a different manner and direction. He rejects the Hegelian-Marxist and positivist subjection of the culture-subject to biological determinism and objectivism precisely because, without freedom, autonomy and responsibility would be unattainable, liberation an essentially meaningless term, and the critique of values, tradition and society an exercise in futility.

As noted above, with the elimination of personal interiority and meaning in the Marxist and positivist schools and their completely objectivist thrust, one can only explore thinking and learning as a physiological function, devoid of any transcendental significance. Yet, Marx predicates the activity of labor only of the human species precisely as conscious and purposive. The culture-subject is completely subsumed into an empirical-analytic scientific mode of self-analysis which is mechanistic and determined by the laws of the bio-physical universe. Without a transcendental level of freedom and self-understanding, and reduced to an empirical-analytic scientific determinism, the culture-subject cannot engage in the process of self-reflection to critique values and tradition and to correct exploitative, oppressive factors in the cultural environment. Self-reflection is then impossible and critique irrelevant because the culture-subject is carried by inexorable laws and determined by factors which not only are beyond the culture-subject's control, but to which the culture-subject is subjected in all dimensions and modes of existence.

Thus, the culture-subject is thrust into a dyadic mode of existence on a par with any atom, molecule, or biological species, namely, one of action/reaction, stimulus/response, or of signal; it is trapped in a biological-historical determinism. At a dyadic level of simple non-transcendental interaction, such as stimulus and response, the culture-subject cannot ask why because the process of learning and thinking has been reduced to a tautological cognitive loop. This can be illustrated by the following series of questions and answers, in which each loop finally repeats an earlier question:

Q. 1. What is the culture-subject doing?
A. 1. The culture-subject is nature acquiring knowledge of itself?
Q. 2. Why?
A. 2. To realize itself.
Q. 3. How?
A. 3. Through production.

Loop 1
Qa. 4. How?
Aa. 4. By acquiring knowledge of itself.
Q. 2. Why? (i.e., returns to Q. 2 above)

Loop 2
Qb. 4. Why?
Ab. 4. To realize itself.
Q. 3. How? (i.e., returns to Q. 3 above)

Loop 3
Qc. 4. What if there is error in direction or aim?
Ac. 4. The question is without sense as the culture-subject is nature acquiring knowledge of itself.
Q. 2. Why? (i.e., returns to A. 2 above)

In the attempt to critique itself and its direction, the culture subject finds itself linguistically and logically on a track which loops around and reconnects one end with the other, endlessly bringing the inquiry back to the same point. In order to resolve the loops, the culture-subject must move to the transcendental level of self-reflection. This means that epistemology must be reappropriated in order to re-examine the question of freedom toward ever-greater autonomy and responsibility.[24] First, the culture-subject must be able to ask the question why it is doing something in a particular way in order for it to be able to change or modify its direction and write its own history--unlike other animal species which are completely fixed genetically, with no possibility of self-determination. This can be achieved only by transcending the positivist objectivist understanding of the empirical-analytical scientific method in order to be free of the cognitive loop at that level. Secondly, if all were determined, critique would be a waste of time better spent in cognitive progress and instrumental action directed toward production.

But, if this be true, then humanity's experience of afflicting suffering upon itself is not an avoidable tragedy, but an inevitable destiny. The concern over colonialism or neo-colonialism; slavery, discrimination or apartheid; right or left-wing dictatorships; first and second world imperial expansionism; the imposition of satellite status on weaker nations and the denial of the right of self-determination to peoples; censorship and religious persecution; lack of respect or wanton disregard for the human person from the womb to the tomb, from abortion to euthanasia; total control of the means of production and of the distribution of the goods by the power-elite of capitalist and communist countries, placing capital and production over the human person; the maintenance and preservation at all costs of socio-economic or political systems which deny work, food, shelter, education, medical care, or full participation in all its dimensions; the use of capital and resources for the nuclear and conventional arms race, rather than for the betterment of the world condition: in effect, any concern over these or other situations is rendered an inane and pathetic exercise in futility if the deterministic objectivist-positivist understanding of the science of the human person be adequate. For then the process of human life could be nothing but one of inevitable evolution-- possibly toward oblivion or extinction. Because critique is not possible the culture-subject would be caught in a cognitive loop which makes epistemology either impossible or not necessary, or both. Under such conditions values and tradition would be meaningless, atavistic manifestations which should and will be eliminated altogether. As will be explained below, this would bring the culture-subject into total antithesis and render it vulnerable to negative historical selection and extinction. It would subject the culture-subject to a juggernaut of conditions before which, as biologically and/or historically determined, it would lie helpless.

Peirce's Transcendental Logic

Like Kant, Jurgen Habermas seeks to reestablish an epistemology in order to reappropriate freedom and take account of autonomy and responsibility.[25] He therefore endeavors to refute the deterministic mode of thinking, to uncover its objectivist illusion, and to unravel the cognitive loop. In this last task he finds help in Charles Sanders Peirce's philosophy of pragmatism where knowledge is critiqued, not by dogmatism or by the interest of a particular party or power elite, but by consensual acknowledgement developed through a process of analysis and experimentation. The questions of how knowledge is acquired and truth is distinguished from error become issues in pragmatism as it undertakes its epistemological inquiry.[26]

Peirce's study of the nature of deduction, induction, and abduction brings into focus the question of the very mechanism of cognition and learning. He asks how cognitive progress is possible and can be communicated, and how error in cognitive content can be corrected. He sees this as a critique of knowledge and error by the members of the culture-subject. One can say that this is done in a linguistic mode which moves the level of semantic interaction from the dyadic to the triadic, and achieves thereby a certain transcendence. By breaking free from the cognitive loop of the objectivist-positivist mode of thought this makes possible a critique of the stated process, its content, and results.[27] Let us examine this in greater detail.

In the logical process of human thinking there is a step which defies the positivist-objectivist assertion of mechanical thought restricted to the dyadic level, and breaks beyond or transcends this in a most peculiar leap: knowledge is acquired by a flash of insight, as it were, which later is the basis of an hypothesis to be tested experimentally and validated by subsequent repetition and consensus.[28] Ostensibly, it is the purpose of science to acquire new knowledge, to make cognitive progress; this is especially the realm of inductive and abductive reasoning.

Deduction, in contrast, appears to add nothing new; it merely draws out and makes explicit what had been included in the major and minor premises. In the deductive syllogistic form *"Barbara"* (AAA-1):

All mammals are warm-blooded.
All cats are mammals.
Therefore, all cats are warm-blooded.

As such, deduction does not lead to cognitive progress, for it merely states in the conclusion the logical implications of what is already contained in the first two premises.

In contrast, the process of abduction does add new knowledge. Its contribution is the formulation of new generalizations, new statistical hypotheses. However, as the process has very little probative force, these generalizations require independent verification.[29] In the abductive syllogism AAA-2:

All cats are warm-blooded.
All mammals are warm-blooded.
Therefore, all cats are mammals.

The conclusion, though correct, links the terms of the major and minor premises in a way which is not legitimated under the normal rules of logic. Such a conclusion must be tested and verified by repeated experimentation, exploration and consensus since, under the conditions of abduction, it can be argued with equal force:

All cats are warm-blooded.
All birds (as a classification) are warm-blooded.
Therefore, all cats are birds.

Though this method obviously defies the principles and rules of positivism and determinism by its rather free-wheeling manner, Habermas insists that the abductive method, rather thatn deduction, is the way of science and cognitive progress.

Yet, as noted, assurance of the truth of the generalization can come only from continued correction through a given experimental procedure. Peirce likens this to a reflex-arc whereby the organism tests its environment to achieve a desired goal. If it should fail to achieve this goal through some specific method, it continues its efforts in different ways until another method succeeds. Thus, the perception of some desired goal sets into motion a specific behavioral pattern. If the behavioral pattern is incorrect or ineffective it will receive stimuli to this effect and pull back, once again attempting another behavioral pattern. This cycle of action will repeat itself until the results of the effort are positive. The crux is correction; the model is the reflex-arc; its nature is that of feed-back controlled instrumental action.

Peirce's theory of inquiry tends to an analogy between the reflex-arc and cognitive progress in the sciences using the inductive and abductive method. Unlike the assurance of the correct conclusion in deductive reasoning, it offers no certainty of reaching the desired conclusion. But it does require that the goal of inquiry be achieved through a precisely communicated set of rules and procedures which clearly specify the methodology for approaching the goal. If failure results, the experimental procedure is redesigned and the goal is attempted once more. This process continues until it is so articulated that others might duplicate the same procedure and achieve identical results. Peirce speculates that induction and abduction as methods of logical inquiry may be rooted in the process of evolution as a quantum advancement in learning enabling one to know and master the environment and its resources for survival, growth, and reproduction of the species.[30] He speculates further that these methods of inquiry may be a quantum cortical advancement of the reflex-arc made possible by the achievement of a transcendental level of language. This enables the process of logical inquiry to be structured and communicated linguistically by the one who signifies or symbolizes.[31]

On the sub-human species level there is merely feed-back controlled instrumental action: the negative or positive stimuli received by the organism is fed back to the sensory and nervous systems for subsequent correction in order to modifying its continuous instrumental action until the goal is achieved. Moreover, the human species, by its evolutionary and advanced cortex and its transcendental linguistic ability, is able to be purposive and rational. Thus, cognitive and technological progress are achieved through a method of inquiry which is structured linguistically as an abductive process and results in purposive, rational, feed-back controlled, instrumental action.

Habermas is acutely interested in Peirce's analysis precisely because of its epistemological critique of cognitive progress and instrumental action as transcendental-linguistic processes which are specifically communicated, validated, and critiqued by others. It is of the utmost importance, first, that there be absolute freedom from any dogmatism so that this is never restricted to a power-elite but open to all who wish to duplicate the experiment or the problem under investigation; second, that the results must be experienced tangibly, that is, that they not only be predictable from the procedure but make a difference; and third, that this truth be consensual, that is, that it be linguistically articulated in concepts which can be "tested" by others for their validation and "truthfulness." This is able to produce consensus within the group insofar as all must achieve the same results as stated by the theorist.[32] Through this communicative effort cognition itself is critiqued; this is what makes it possible to transcend the cognitive loop.

Habermas laments that in the end Peirce succumbed to the objectivist positivist fallacy, though like Marx he was essentially on the right track.[33] Hence, Habermas continues to develop this process, shifting from a critique of science to a critique of culture, distinguishing from the empirical-analytic sciences to the historical-hermeneutic sciences. His work centers increasingly upon an analysis of language and meaning (i.e., hermeneutics) and of history as the constitutive elements in the self-understanding and self-formation of the culture-subject. We will apply the abductive method of logical inquiry put forth in pragmatism, not on the dyadic empirical-analytic level, but as an historical-hermeneutic method within which the Freudian psychoanalytic technique can be of service.

Peirce himself had stated that the linguistic apparatus of beliefs and judgements determines the direction of cognitive progress.[34] As noted at the beginning of this chapter, the culture-subject identified itself with a linguistic structure that articulates its own self-understanding and the understanding of nature. This self-understanding can be seen as beliefs and judgments in Peirce's sense or as values and tradition in the sense of this chapter. But, whichever is chosen, there is a general agreement in the fallibility of these beliefs/judgments or value-traditions which determine self-understanding and the scientific processes of inquiry. This error must be discerned through a critique at the transcendental linguistic level in an on-going process of continued liberation from error. In the empirical-analytic sciences this process is utilized as a "liberation" from error in the science of nature. Habermas sees it as able to be applied to the liberation of the culture-subject from the oppression and exploitation inhering in the linguistic structures in which it articulates its self-understanding and self-formation. In this process the Freudian psychoanalytic method can serve to correct these "errors" and open the way toward greater autonomy and responsibility. As this must take place on a transcendental, triadic level it cannot be carried out within a deterministic supposition, but requires reflection on an epistemological and, beyond Habermas, a metaphysical level.

Freudian Psychoanalytic Method

Peirce's transcendental method of inquiry at the triadic level of communication is consistent with Habermas' insistence that the culture-subject is not subject to biological determinism, but is a creature of self-reflective and self-formative historicity. This rejects a deterministic understanding of the culture-subject in favor of freedom or self-determination. Thus, Habermas critiques not merely the "what and how," but opens to the possibility of examining the meaning of the values and traditions of a culture. He develops his method of cultural critique by interpreting Freud's psychoanalytic theory in historico-analytic terms. His intent is to avoid the objectivist fallacy while enabling the restoration of a self-determined thrust toward autonomy and responsibility in a process which can be called liberation.[35]

Individual Analysis. As noted above, the manner in which an individual identifies with the values of significant others is analogous to the manner in which the culture-subject identifies with its acquired values and tradition. In the first case, under the exigency of reward and punishment or pleasure and pain, the value system and acceptable or desirable modes of behavior are inculcated into the individual at an early age--precisely when the person is both totally dependent and defenseless.[36] Through parents and other significant persons, society teaches the child to suppress the primitive impulses of the "id," which seek instant gratification of all needs, in favor of a reduction of all tension, both psychological and physiological.[37] Driven by libidinous energy, the impulses of the id if unchecked would disrupt the commonweal. Hence, through such powerful agents as parents and significant others, the society rewards "appropriate" behavior and punishes "inappropriate" behavior.

Thus commences the development of the superego, which consists of the ego-ideal (the "do's" which bring rewards) and the conscience (the "don'ts" which call down punishments.) As the id makes demands for gratification, the superego insists that these demands be met according to the dictates of the ego-ideal and the conscience. The resulting elaboration of the id, known as the ego, mediates between the impulsive id and the restraining superego.[38] In this tri-partite Freudian personality the id and the superego are the non-rational elements and the ego is the rational element. This can be likened to a triptych in which the center painting which is seen by the public is the ego, while the id and the superego are attached to either side but turned back and hidden from public viewing. One's personality, which emerges in development and expression through linguistic and ritualistic symbolization or signification within the matrix of social communications, is the constitutive and dispositive element of self-understanding, self-formation, and the individual's *Weltanschauung*.[39] The linguistic structure of personality is the cultural-historical genetic code which is transmitted to the individual, constitutes his/her self-understanding and disposes one to a certain self-formation and interpretation of the world. Thus, the psychological, linguistic structure is the very lens through which one views self, other and nature.

In an analogous manner the culture-subject receives its values and traditions under the exigency of survival. In this regard, the threat is negative selection by a potentially hostile environment; the reward is the goods produced through growing control over natural resources by means of cognitive progress and improved instrumental action.[40] In whatever environment, to satisfy the basic needs of growth and reproduction and to avoid the risk of negative selection, the culture-subject develops a 'superego' which expresses the 'ego-ideal' and 'conscience' as values and tradition. In this process the natural and cultural environments "teach" the culture-subject by imposing a terrible price for failure to cope effectively with the surrounding risks. The negative consequences are meted out by nature or another culture-subject.

In time, the culture-subject acquires an accumulated body of understanding in order to avoid such natural and historical or cultural selection, while increasing its ability to exploit nature's resources for the distribution of goods.[41] As in the case of the superego this is articulated as values and tradition and transmitted through symbolization in language and ritual.[42] These values and traditions are developed through a system of reward and punishment, concretized as survival and threat. They are the constitutive and dispositive elements of self-understanding and self-formation, as well as the lenses which form the culture-subject's world view. It is the cultural historical genetic code which linguistically symbolizes the specific culture-subject.

In Freudian psychoanalytic theory, the id, which is the most primitive part of the personality, seeks pleasure and avoids pain; this is appropriately known as the pleasure principle.[43] Yet, because the id is both autistic and impulsive, it is governed by automatic reflexes and--more importantly in this consideration--by the primary process of wish-fulfillment through images of the object which would satisfy the need. Because the id does not recognize the outside world per se, but only the immediacy of its needs and the drive to satisfy them by seeking pleasure and reducing tension,[44] any object, whether imaginary or real, will do.

As in our elaboration of the id, it is the ego that seeks the appropriate object at the appropriate time. Neither fantasy nor an inappropriate object will bring the desired satisfaction; indeed seeking satisfaction at an inappropriate time or manner will bring punishment through greatly increased tension and its resulting discomfort and pain.[45] For this reason, the ego is said to operate on the reality principle, as opposed to the id's pleasure principle; and by means of a secondary process, in distinction to the id's autistic and primary process. It tests reality, altering instrumental action until success is achieved. In this it is akin to Peirce's reflex-arc model described above as "purposive, rational, feed-back controlled, instrumental action."[46] Yet as the person can learn to get what he/she wants without regard to the commonweal, such testing could be in the service of sociopathology. Freud was under no illusion that the person, untouched by social values, might be the "noble savage" fancied by Jean Jacques Rousseau. He did not believe in an innately beautiful and balanced human nature which was distorted by society and religion. Freud saw the person as a libidinous beast which had to be controlled for the weal and advancement of society and civilization. This control was effected by identification with, and subsequent internalization of, society and religion as values and tradition. The superego is precisely this inculcation of values and tradition as ego-ideal and conscience. These internalized linguistic structures direct the individual regarding what is socially appropriate and acceptable or inappropriate and unacceptable--in fine, what is good and what is bad.

This point and the following bear heavily on the culture-subject's development of values and tradition, for in the superego, the child does not imitate his/her parents but actually identifies with them.[47] The child *becomes* the parents and significant others and identifies with their values, which then become the child's linguistic structure of self-understanding and interaction. Because these values are articulated by the parents at a time of utter dependence and defenselessness, and are transmitted symbolically with reward (pleasure) and punishment (pain), the child begins to feel anxiety (tension/fear of punishment/pain) if he/she acts contrary to the superego, in spite of the demands of the id. It is up to the ego to find the means to negotiate realistically between the demands of the id and the restraints of the superego.

Similarly, faulty superego development is germane to Habermas' critique of rigidified abstractions or erroneous content within values and tradition. Because the superego is irrational, the person's self-understanding and formation can be oppressive and distorted, rendering their relations with others psychodynamically disturbed and without recourse to correction by reason. In understanding this problem, the Freudian concept of "anxiety" plays a most significant role. First, Freud theorized, the person's libidinous impulses originating in the id had to be controlled for the weal and advancement of society and civilization. This was effected through the internalization of religious and social values.[48] Nonetheless, psychodynamic difficulties in the form of neurotic manifestations arise from severe overcontrol of the libido by an overbearing and equally non-rational superego. This prevents the ego from carrying out its mediating function so that the person cannot achieve reasonable release of necessary libidinous tensions.

The 'healthy' individual has a balanced and properly controlled libido, inasmuch as its tensions are suppressed in a conscious and healthy manner rather than repressed in an unconscious manner leading to neurotic manifestations. As a result libidinous tension is sublimated to a higher and more noble goal of working for the good of humanity.[49] As Freud considered this to be a vital and necessary role of religion--which remained a fanciful superstition--he did not envision a quick demise of religion through science, but felt that it would perdure for ages as socially necessary for channelling otherwise destructive impulses.

Habermas examines the development of neurotic impulses arising from distorted over-control by the superego. He studies this in conjunction with the faulty content of the linguistic structure of the superego which oppresses and exploits. Freud's psychoanalytic technique is essentially a critique of the neurotic's language and behavior which manifests the symbolic, linguistic structure of its superego. By examining its historical distortions, one can reveal the problematic content in the development of the superego. By appropriating the reconstructed historical correction the person would be liberated from the oppressive elements of the superego and function with greater psychological freedom and health. In the light of Peirce's pragmatism, Habermas develops this methodological approach into a linguistic critique through seeking truth in consensus. By examining the oppressive elements in the culture-subject's "superego," it achieves liberation from rigidified abstractions and moves toward greater autonomy and responsibility.[50]

Freud believed that no individual escapes all distortion in the development of his/her superego, and Habermas asserts the same as regards the culture-subject. This can be illustrated by an examination of the three types of anxiety in this distortion: 1) reality anxiety, which originates from real danger within the natural environment; 2) neurotic anxiety, which originates in fear of punishment from a significant other due to instinctual gratification; and 3) moral fear, which originates in the fear of punishment from the superego, i.e., the conscience rendering the person guilt ridden. All three manifestations of anxiety raise tensions which the ego seeks to reduce to a homeostatic level of quiescence by escape and/or avoidance, but the last is the most important because it is the person's own system of self-identity which causes the tension.

The first two forms, reality and neurotic anxiety, are external to the person who seeks ways of achieving gratification by delay until the danger passes, by some other means of gaining access to the desired goal, or by substitution. Inasmuch as the restraint is external, gratification will be achieved in time through a specific object-cathexis, i.e., the desired object through which the need is met. Thus, reduction of tension can occur in reality and neurotic anxiety when either: 1) the source of external threat disappears or is eliminated, or 2) the object-cathexis is achieved and thereby satisfies the need.[51]

Moral anxiety is far more central to Freud's psychoanalysis and Habermas' critique of the culture-subject's self-understanding and self-formation. For, if the threat has its genesis in the very superego of the person, i.e. within the individual's own psychic system, there is no escape; the punitive agent is one's very self. Moral anxiety may reduce or mask libidinous tension temporarily, but soon the id will reassert its demands for the reduction of the drive through an object-cathexis. If, for example, the object-cathexis is altogether or even largely prohibited, i.e. becomes an anticathexis, the ego will seek a substitute object to diminish the tension in a process called displacement. A critical concept in the Freudian construct, displacement is the mechanism by which libidinous energy is trapped through suppression of the instinctual drive and stored within the psyche of the individual to be used appropriately and constructively for the advancement of culture and civilization.[52]

Thus, the utopian illusion plays a critical and valuable role in challenging the libido and is not to be confused with delusions since it is based on human wishes that are realizable. Moreover, Habermas notes that religion has symbolized a utopian notion into which the culture-subject invests much energy and behavior to realize the goal, not only of the self, but for the common good. It is precisely the illusion--symbolized verbally, and ritually becoming the linguistic articulation of the superego--which constitutes the goal of the ego ideal and conscience.

These, in turn, constitute the self-understanding and self-formation of the individual. The person invests his/her store of libidinous energy towards various object-cathexes which are seen as appropriate and socially acceptable inasmuch as they are components of the Utopian ideal or illusion. Because this is done in terms of an ideology which legitimizes the power structure or status quo and thereby, removes the institutional reality from criticism, however, it is a linguistic distortion.[53]

Socio-Economic Analysis. Freud sets up a permanent antagonism between the individual and group ideals, even though the person identifies completely with them. Though the id always demands gratification through the primary object-cathexis, it is compelled by the superego, through the agency of the ego, to settle for secondary or tertiary object-cathexes which do not directly satisfy the id. This results in constant frustration within the person. The residual energy not used lingers within the system and manifests itself as restlessness. Society has effectively incorporated controls into the person in order to check destructive, self-centered impulsive gratification of the id. Instead, through the mechanism of displacement, the energy is cathected to such higher, civilized goals as science, art, music, literature, and general altruistic behavior.[54]

Moral anxiety drives this mechanism of displacement. It is the source of that tension which persons seek to reduce by shunting their libidinous energy, originating in the id, through the channels of displacement. This transforms 'eros' into altruism, motivating the individual to work towards the continual advancement of civilization. Without this moral anxiety and displacement, the individual would remain at the primary-cathexes level, completely and impulsively discharging libidinous energy. The result would be socially disruptive, destructive behavior; for lack of motivation for altruistic development it would result in the collapse of civilization. While this antagonism remains between the needs of the individual's id and the socially incorporated superego there exists the threat that the id will override the superego's control and wreak havoc on the social structure.

In moving from the individual to the society Freud sees a conflict between the impulses of the individual's id and the social constraints which continually frustrate the pleasure principle. He also gloomily concluded that the death wish, 'thanatos,' was stronger than love or the life principle, 'eros'--both of which are critical, genetically encoded elements which direct the behavior of the individual.[55] He had experienced the irrationality of antisemitism, other forms of national prejudices, and the massive destruction wrought by the delusions of national grandeur in two world wars. All discovery, interaction and progress have been mixed blessings for humanity, whose history is written in ink mixed with tears and blood--a history of savage wars, senseless persecutions, heartless genocides, brutal oppression and exploitation. All of this, Freud conjectured emanated from the selfish, autistic, egotistical impulses of the id and was directed by 'thanatos'.

Habermas does not agree that the relationship between the person and society is one of basic antagonism and, though not overly optimistic, he cautions against Freud's absolutist understanding in this regard. One is compelled by the positive relational quality of sociality found in the nature of the individual. The person is not an isolate in a group of isolates, but a creature of relationships whose very being from the time of conception develops in kinship with others. Freud's positivist frame of reference resulted in a reductionism which separated person from person, and in a deterministic conception of human nature. Habermas, in contrast, sees more clearly the positive relationship and communication within the community through his appreciation of the culture-subject as a creature of symbolization, with a potential for greater autonomy and responsibility based upon emancipatory interest. Though predicated upon human communication as it emerges in a self-reflective critique, this emancipatory activity realizes itself in the praxis of production and interaction.[56] This attribute of the human person radically distinguishes him/her from other living species by adding positive relationship to, and sharing with, other symbol-givers and symbol-receivers.

This marks the person with the quality of transcendence in terms of which one can speak of love, a quality to which Habermas does not advert in the texts considered. The transcendental ability to signify, symbolize and articulate the understanding of self, to reflect upon the self and to grow in understanding and appreciation of others differentiates the community of persons from any other group of animals, which do no more than signal. Where animals live with a crowd, humans live in community; animals are totally determined genetically, whereas people are self-determined and write their own history in a self-reflective labor process. The distance between the two is infinite and beyond description, and Habermas strongly rejects the positivist-objectivist-reductionist attempt to reduce the human reality to the dimensions of other creatures.

Reaching beyond Habermas, while incorporating his thought, we can say that communication in language through sign and ritual, rather than mere signal, makes sense only in a community which is built upon positive bonds of love with one another.

Freud correctly saw as problematic the destructive and impulsively selfish tendency which requires an inculcation of virtues in the growing child through discipline and constraint. But it must be noted also that children identify with, and learn from, those they love and admire. Whether this be due to a wish to gain the affections of the admired person or a fear of loss of love, it reflects a strong desire to be related to and loved by the other. This is not to see the individual as merely epiphenomenal in relation to the group, but to note that, despite the negative and perverse elements in behavior and interaction, there exists also a positive mutuality. This manifests itself among members of the culture-subject inasmuch as they realize themselves through communication and work which is self-determined, articulated symbolically and rooted in love. Sociality and historicity are dimensions of this mutual symbolizing through which learning is shared through either verbal or ritualistic expression. Values and tradition are then the articulated morphological and syntactical matrix from which societal and cultural structures are evolved and through which they are transmitted.

Thus, for Freud antagonism is irrevocably encoded in the individual from the beginning, and history is written by events determined by specific biological and psychological causal factors over which the individual has no control. For Habermas, in contrast, the culture-subject is a creature of historicity, yet not completely independent of behavior and activity rooted in biological necessity. Though not a disembodied spirit, the culture-subject is free, choosing to write its own history through self reflective positive relations and communication among its members in non-antagonistic, nonexploitive production and interaction. The implication of these views for critical social theory needs more extended attention.

In Freud's view the distribution of natural resources in a way that would benefit all members and reduce selfishness is directed by the general mechanism which determines both the development and behavior of the person. Two specific factors shape this process: 1) a lack or insufficiency in the amount of goods to be distributed, and 2) the basically antagonistic, antisocial nature of the id. Together they lead to a social antagonism in regard to the distribution of goods and power which of itself would engender struggle. However, the utopian illusion of reward and punishment induces persons: 1) to act in a way that will bring future reward, rather than punishment; and 2) to channel libidinous energy toward the utopian object-cathexis through the mechanism of displacement for the good of the social group.[57] Therefore, from the Freudian perspective, individuals within the cultural group are not free to determine their future development. Rather, their formation is governed by the environmental factor of available resources, the intra-psychic factors of the antagonistic, pleasure-seeking, antisocial id, and the values of the superego which act as a harness to control and direct libidinal energy. Since all three factors are non-rational but critical determinants of human behavior the individual is not free and autonomous and the term responsibility is rendered ambiguous.

The individual is compelled to self-denial by the intrapsychic mechanism of moral anxiety. Thus, there is a twofold source of tension: 1) the need which demands the reduction of tension through gratification as directed by the id, and 2) the fear of punishment through guilt deriving from the superego. Under the pleasure principle of the id the tensions must be reduced, but under the reality principle of the ego they must be addressed: (1) in a way that avoids punishment, and (2) through a process of displacement which provides an object-cathexis which is both gratifying and appropriate.

The person can flee from neither the id nor conscience; and, as the needs constantly recur in what Freud calls a repetition compulsion,[58] the threat of punishment is incessant. This reflects the lament in Book IV of Milton's *Paradise Lost* as Satan realizes that he carries the process of his torment and perversion within his very being, forever and without respite.

> Horror and doubt distract
> His troubl'd thoughts, and from the bottom stirr
> *The hell within him*, for within him Hell
> He brings, and round about him, nor from Hell
> One step no more then from himself can fly
> By change of place: Now conscience wakes despair
> That slumbered, wakes the bitter memorie
> Of what he was, what is, and what must be
> Worse; of worse deeds worse sufferings must ensue.
> Sometimes towards Eden which now in his view
> Lay pleasant, his grieved look he fixes sad,
> Sometimes towards Heav'n and the full-blazing sun,
> Which now sat high in his Meridian Towre:
> Then much revolving, thus in sighs began.[59]

When persons experience fierce id impulses from which they cannot flee and to which they cannot admit for fear of conscience, they repress what threatens to bring retribution.[60] Moreover, if the impulses are so strong as to constitute a threat of breaching control, bizarre behavior may arise in the form of defense mechanisms to mask the real situation as a defense against self and others. This manifests itself idiosyncratically as regression, projection, denial, fixation or reaction formation.

Not being able to admit either the existence of the impulse from which it cannot flee, nor the desired, primary object-cathexis for fear of punishment and ostracism, the person reconstructs its content linguistically. This is done by imposing linguistic structures or categories which constitute the superego as ego-ideal and conscience upon the impulses and the desired object-cathexes. This distorts the information in such manner as to make the truth fit the categories. In fact the behavior is bizarre, neurotic as it were--with the impulses periodically surfacing to near visibility in spite of the defense mechanisms. This break through the surface of conscious behavior may manifest itself in a dream whose content is highly symbolic or in a *lapsus linguae* which embarrasses the person at an appropriately inappropriate moment.[61]

A similar mechanism is in operation when a child desires a forbidden object-cathexis, but fears punishment or retaliation by those upon whom the child is totally dependent and before whom it is without any defense. Here anxiety becomes so overwhelming as to surrender the child into total denial of the object desired, i.e., self-denial.[62] If the parents have reacted with sufficient violence and irrationality to terrorize and bewilder the child, the historical symbolic content of the forbidden desire, and even the actions of the parents, may be plunged into the obscurity of intra-psychic structures--in this case the unconscious--where it is repressed to such an extent that it cannot be remembered. The person has effected a self-imposed amnesia. In fact, so virulent an anti-cathexis is formed that even the memory or slightest hint of the true content brings fierce anxiety and trauma, eliciting within the person psychic barriers or defense mechanisms which act as a buffer to the critical process of self-reflection.[63]

At some point, when the individual is in a circumstance which threatens to surface the impulse/memory, he/she becomes anxious and befuddled. Either the person will forever flee such situations or bizarre contradictory behavior will emerge. The individual, in both cases, has been given a linguistic structure which does not match the reality or truth of the impulse/object-cathexis: the symbolic structure of the linguistic or ritualistic action has a hidden or obfuscated referent because the ego-ideal and conscience, which are the values and traditions, have become rigidified abstractions. In a sense, psychic surplus value, in the form of ucathected or unreleased psychic energy, is being stored and/or utilized inappropriately by the oppressive or exploitative force which has been introjected through 'identification with an aggressor' rather than with the person's own intra-psychic structure.[64]

This applies specifically to that repressive training which not only establishes the constraints necessary to construct and preserve a just and loving community, but either renders the person incapable of being a value and joy to self and others or savagely enslaves the person to manipulation and exploitation by others. The liberative process of self-reflection, which would have been the means for a critique of the problem, is avoided for it threatens to surface the material which elicits the unwanted anxiety. As shall be seen further on, it would be useless to remove any and all constraints upon the id, as these must be controlled for the positive development of the person and the community.

Because of total identification with the values and traditions linguistically introjected as the superego structure, the person's self-understanding is the linguistically articulated structure of history. This constitutes a cognitive loop from which the person cannot easily escape: ever returning to the same point, one repeats the same bizarre behavior. In listening to the dreams, the lapses of tongue, the distorted, fragmented history and in observing, the behavior the psychoanalyst is dealing in symbolic material and must analyze its content and discern its meaning. This is matched against the verbal content of the patient who is speaking under the constraint of repressed material and filtering the content through the defense mechanism. In the instance where the person is rendered helpless or damaged by the repression manifested as neurosis, psychoanalysis endeavors to help the individual critique the symbolic content of linguistic and ritualistic behavior so as to reconstruct the history which is articulated in a broken, distorted or perverse manner through defense mechanisms. In this way, the psychoanalyst takes the individual above the cognitive loop to critique the problem.[65]

HABERMAS' HISTORICO-HERMENEUTIC AS A PROCESS OF LIBERATION

Analysis and Abduction

Habermas sees this as an abductive process of inquiry, not in an empirical-analytic scientific sense, but as an historic-hermeneutic science; that is, it deals not only with what is but with what it means. Many have charged that the psychoanalytic method is not scientific because it is not repeatable for verification and consensus. Habermas responds that it is as legitimate a method of science as is, for example, a bio-chemical experiment utilizing an empirical-analytic model. The problem is the positivist-objectivist illusion which reduces the person and the culture-subject to an objective fact. Certainly beyond a positivist, tautological transformation of a mere signal or sign, a symbol cannot be reduced to the dyadic level of interaction but transcends to the triadic level of communication. Thus, the psychoanalyst asks not only what this linguistic and ritualistic behavior is, but also what it means, for the psychoanalyst must critique meaning by transcending the level of the cognitive loop which would run the inquirer through endless twisting circuits only to return to the same point.

Hence, Habermas sees the positivist's demand for repeatability, which is a desirable characteristic of the empirical-analytic sciences, as in no wise applying to the historical-hermeneutic sciences. This is true especially of the psychoanalytic method where change in linguistic-ritualistic behavior as attested to consensually by the psychoanalyst, the patient, and others is the observable proof of success, but always in the context of, and in reference to, the self-formative process. Repetition would be an absurd attempt to subject the inquiry to an empirical-analytic scientific standard based upon a reductionist understanding which does not, and should not, apply.

Instead, Habermas perceives a relationship between the psychoanalytic method and the reflex-arc model of purposive, rational, feed-back controlled, instrumental action. The psychoanalyst matches the content of the dreams, the lapses of speech (*lapsus linguae*) and the observed behaviorism against the distorted or fragmented history as remembered by the patient. He/she does this to interpret the symbolic (linguistic and ritualistic) content and discover its meaning. This is compared to the history which issues through the filter of repressive defense mechanisms and is a linguistic construct of defense mechanisms, manifesting itself in distortion and broken fragments. As the history does not match the meaning of the dream content and neurotic behavior, it is really akin to a rigidified abstraction which indicates to the analyst the past, i.e., what was repressed, why it was repressed, and how it was repressed. This truth--too painful to be admitted for fear of punishment--is imprisoned in the dungeon of the unconscious and kept under strict censorship and beyond the realm of articulation. The psychoanalyst reconstructs the history from the broken, distorted fragments, correcting them from insight into the intention of the dreams, lapses of tongue, and behavior. He thereby gives linguistic content to the unspeakable which, up to this point, lay hidden in the unconscious.[66]

This is an historical-hermeneutic methodological approach not reducible to empirical-analytic inquiry. What the psychoanalyst reconstructs is not necessarily correct, nor does it follow in a deductive sense. Through abduction the psychoanalyst reconstructs history and challenges the patient's inconsistencies in history and behavior. The patient must then appropriate or "own up to" the reconstructed history. If it is a correct reconstruction and defenses are breached, the unconscious material has been given linguistic structure at the conscious level. The meaning can now be analyzed and understood, thereby adding to the self-understanding of the person and his/her subsequent self-formation. In a sense, this is reflexively simultaneous with self-knowledge, because the subject is engaged in self-production through a communicative process of self-reflection. Here the psychoanalyst is midwife to the birth of the newly liberated transcendental process of self-reflection which can now proceed under the terms of a linguistically corrected self-understanding. Accordingly, 'a catharsis' or 'abreaction' should occur once the censorship has been lifted, releasing the dammed up energy. There should be an observable change in the person's behavior towards 'healthier' and more creative activity. This may be perceived as a difference by the psychoanalyst, the patient and others, but must be confirmed or negated within the context of the process of self-formation.[67] How the abductive process actually works in achieving truth is largely speculative. That this is the case, however, is born out by scientific success in both the empirical-analytic and the historical-hermeneutic sciences which continually grow and advance through greater accuracy by means of further experimentation and correction.

The possibility of achieving truth through the abductive method is confirmed by science, on the one hand, and by the survival of the human species, on the other, for certainly negative selection would have overtaken the species were it otherwise. Furthermore, for the patient, this process is not mere dyadic signal change as in mere mechanical interaction of an empirical-analytic experiment, but a triadic symbolic change which adds to the symbol giver and the symbol receiver the dimension of meaning in an historical hermeneutic inquiry. It cannot be reduced to mere determinism as in positivism, including that of Freud himself--as noted by Habermas, it transcends the categories of biological or historical determinism. His patients decide freely to examine and change their situation in a process of self-reflection catalyzed by the psychoanalyst, to critique their very self in order to be liberated from the problematic elements of their personality.[68] Thus, they selfdetermine their historical process by critiquing oppressive elements within their psychic system with the intent of continual growth in autonomy and responsibility. This breaks through determination by an outside force.

Should the psychoanalyst be incorrect in his/her abductive insight no change will occur; the investigative, abductive process must start over, much like the reflex-arc model of the organism in the environment mentioned above. The psychoanalyst must continue to alter the variables, i.e. the linguistic content of the material, until the history is sufficiently corrected to effect the desired change. Moreover, the patient's defense mechanism must be breached as this resists threatening material from entering consciousness. At times, the patient may accept an historical reconstruction by the psychoanalist precisely because it is incorrect and, therefore, preserves the neurotic *status quo*. Nonetheless, at the transcendental linguistic level of meaning, the psychoanalyst proceeds to correct and maneuver towards the desired results which are observed in a positive change within the context of the self-formative process.[69] In this way, analysis is a process of purposive, rational, feed-back controlled instrumental action.

Relating to autonomy and responsibility, this process cannot be based on a biologically or historically deterministic perspective. As an act of self-determination, a transcendental leap above the cognitive loop of self-understanding through self reflection, psychoanalysis defies reduction to a positivistic, deterministic model. Only in freedom could the person desire to undergo the excruciating and anxiety-inducing process of self--reflection and self-correction which results in partial selfreformation. Were the person totally determined, the pleasure principle would short-circuit the process by forcing the person to flee the tension induced by the analysis and/or to resist the process itself. To the contrary, the person decides a change is necessary in spite of the tension-anxiety. By critiquing his/herself-understanding, the person loosens the bonds of self-understanding in the form of a rigidified abstraction that induced oppression in order to be liberated for greater autonomy (self-determination) and responsibility.

Historico-hermeneutic and Cultural Pathology.

Habermas considers this self-reflective process of self--determined reformation to be possible for the culture-subject.[70] Like the patient, the culture-subject has inculcated an articulated structure of values and traditions with which it identifies. Just as Freud insists that no person is spared the conflicts mentioned above, Habermas sees this same problematic in the structure of the values which have been passed on, namely, the traditions. Hence, rather than conceive an analysis of the culture-subject through the empirical-analytic method, Habermas envisions an analogous use of Freud's psychoanalytic method for culture analysis. Thus, just as the psychoanalytic method is used in a transcendental process of self-reflection to critique the person, an analogous method is applied to analyze the linguistic structure of the self-understanding of the culture-subject as articulated in historically distorted values and traditions.

The culture-subject identifies with values and traditions as the linguistic and ritualistic articulation of its self-understanding and formation. Like the superego, it maintains not only controls which are beneficial for the commonweal, but, at the same time, a status quo which contains historical distortions and oppressive elements. In the process of analysis and self-reflection the culture-subject critiques the unhealthy elements, whether contradictory, disruptive, oppressive or exploitative. Inasmuch as one's values and traditions are one's self-identity, this distorted linguistic structure operates as perverse self-formation.

This may have developed under certain historical exigencies as the culture-subject experienced a lack of natural resources due to the limitations of the knowledge and technical skills at hand. In this case values and traditions fulfill the superego's function in the culture-subject by maintaining control of the distribution of goods and the preservation of the power structure. Values and traditions developed in those straightened circumstances would probably contain unjust elements; projected into the present, they may no longer apply but have become rigidified abstractions which, along with the unjust elements themselves, must be critiqued and corrected. Thus, an analysis of the culture-subject's behavior and a reconstruction of the linguistic structure of its history are steps in the attempt by the culturesubject to perceive and appropriate its own inconsistencies in order to correct them. As in the psychological order, the defense mechanisms which preserve the self-understanding of the culture-subject must be breached before a proper abreactive catharsis can release and channel more creatively and positively the "neurotically" blocked energies.

This must be done by an abductive analysis which jumps the cognitive loop in which the positive-reductionist perspective traps the culture-subject--a trap which is mentioned also in the Marxist analysis. The analysis is abductive inasmuch as it begins at the conclusion of the syllogistically structured inquiry where the middle term which links the two premises is apprehended and tested against the pragmatic consensual scheme of observable change in the behavior of the culture-subject. The reflex-arc model applies in like manner, constantly adjusting the historical reconstruction until success is achieved through a linguistic, purposive, rational, feed-back controlled instrumental action.

It is useless to subject this process to the demands of the empirical analytic method for it is a search for meaning effected only through a transcendental process of critique as self-reflection--the meaning expressed in a utopian illusion. Moreover, the abductive inquiry is transcendental inasmuch as the middle term in the investigative syllogism is not implied in the starting point, namely, the conclusion of the syllogism, much as in the Kantian synthetic a priori. The arrival at the abductive insight has no obvious determined cause of which it is an effect; its truth is attested through a methodological consensus.

The process has notable similarities to the psychoanalysis of the individual person. First, the culture-subject reasserts its autonomy and responsibility through achieving a greater control over the process of historicity by correcting in the self-reflective process that which distorts, oppresses, and exploits. Second, there is resistance due to the desire to maintain control, and hence to enforce the status quo. Thirdly, like the person, it is the very self-identity which is under analysis and, therefore, under attack. This identity is constituted of the accumulated cultural wisdom which has been developed in order to survive both biological and historical negative selection.

Positivist approaches had subjected the need for investigating values and tradition to the objectivist fallacy that the observer must conduct the inquiry free of interest or passion. Yet, subjecting values and tradition to this perspective would deprive them of meaning, the very quality of their ability to symbolize or signify. To reduce values and tradition to empirical-analytic inquiry is to reduce symbol or sign to signal and thereby to render it altogether meaningless and, hence, useless.

This reductionist tendency of the positivist objectivism of empirical-analytic sciences has been questioned also by Heisenberg's Indeterminacy Principle. The investigations of Niels Bohr and Werner Heisenberg regarding the speed and position of high velocity, sub-atomic particles demonstrates that the observer's instrument of observation effects the field of observation in such wise that the object observed is itself effected and, therefore, restricted to certain parameters of bias and probability regarding what can be known and predicted.[71] This renders calculation and prediction merely probable, By implying also that there are limits to our knowledge due to the very nature of the knower this has renewed interest in the reexamination of epistemological issues.

As mentioned above, Peirce also suspects that the cognitive categories of the investigator biased the perception, analysis, and conclusion of the investigation. For this reason he considered consensus to be imperative in the validation of the results.[72] Only thus is it possible to correct for, and avoid, the dogmatism of the statements which derive from and support an ideological stance based upon an interest unscrutinized interest and reified in rigidified abstractions.

Phenomenology recognizes that the object of consciousness cannot be assumed to be other than effected and altered by the specific consciousness. Nevertheless the danger of a solipsistic dead end and skepticism can be defended against by the pragmatic method's notion of consensus achieved through continued cognitive progress which integrates the technological advances in instrumental action. Kant's *Critique of Pure Reason*, Werner Heisenberg's Indeterminacy Principle, and Kurt Godel's Incompleteness Theorem, in raising questions of uncertainty in metaphysics, science and mathematics respectively, are based upon the same dynamic. From all three it might be suggested that the problem rests less with the object than with the subject of knowing, and that it points to the need for a more ample philosophical anthropology, metaphysics and epistemology to integrate the dynamics of historicity, distortion and liberation in the emergence of truth.

Interest and Liberation.

This deeper question of the role of interest in effecting human knowledge retains the critical issue, for, if in the empirical-analytic sciences the observer effects and biases what is observed this will be no less true in the historical-hermeneutic sciences. Freud insisted that interest was the driving mechanism in directing the person towards the object-cathexis, for as an object of desire the object-cathexis does not leave the person in a state of indifference. Vital interest, predicated upon the desire to release the tension of the libidinous energy through the mechanism of displacement from the primary object-cathexis to the secondary and tertiary, is the impetus that drives the person to learn and advance in the arts and sciences. The innate bias or interest towards learning is specified by conditioning, for indifference plays no part in learning.

The ego channels the energy of the id towards the utopian illusion of the superego, the ultimate object-cathexis.[73] The engine of science is not a process of cold, detached observation of acts, but interest that is fundamentally rooted in biology and in the superego. This is linguistically structured as values, i.e., as what is meaningful, important, and desirable to the person. Marx, himself, attributes the formal traits of reason to needs, linking the two conceptually so that need becomes the reason for interest in cognititve progress and instrumental action. This is intrinsic to the person as informed by sociality; it always transcends biological and historical determinism.

Habermas notes Nietzsche's insistence that whatever is done is done in self-interest. Knowledge, as unbiased, objective, and disinterested is an inane illusion, foreign to the Dionysian passion according to which the person desires to learn in a continual process of transcendence. What does not serve this end is neither of use nor of interest; passion informs human knowledge, rendering the idea of objective observation and knowledge meaningless.[74]

Interest centered upon maintaining a continuous self-identity as a means of avoiding and preventing historical selection, while undergoing corrective critique in order to evolve greater autonomy and responsibility, has many manifestations. The desire to survive both biologically and historically motivates the culturesubject towards both the empirical-analytic and the historicalhermeneutic sciences. One finds this manifest first in the desire for progress in the sciences of nature and technology in order to acquire more adequate resources, to explore them productively and to achieve a greater distribution of goods. A second manifestation of interest is found in the manipulation and exploitation of this process of learning and production in order to enhance both the position of the power elite and the status quo. Beyond Habermas' explicit categories, one might add a third manifestation of interest, namely, the positive and loving relationships within the culture-subject which give impetus to acquiring and communicating knowledge and to technological progress in solidarity and for the commonweal.

With Habermas it can be said that values and tradition are the articulation of the interest which motivates learning as a self-formative process within self-understanding. More than Habermas, however, it is necessary to stress the fundamental fact that the purpose of analysis, critique, and correction is neither to ignore nor to destroy values and tradition, but to change only those elements which are problematic. Earlier in this chapter, values and traditions were characterized as a cultural, "genetic" code; i.e. the culture-subject's self-identity. Neither biologically nor historically determined--though indeed conditioned--they are transmitted in time as the culture-subject's own self-written history; as its self-identity, they constitute its self-understanding and formation. If one were to consider this in terms of an evolutionary model on the biological level--albeit self-determined in a rational and purposive way-- values and traditions would be the historical genetic code which identifies the culture-subject. One would not change the genetic defect of color blindness through the elimination of all genes pertaining to vision thereby eliminating vision, or by altering the genes in such wise that the individual is no longer the person he was before. One seeks the defective gene and alters it in such a way that the person now has what he/she was previously lacking. As one does not eliminate that which constitutes the identity of the person, evolutionary development takes place by accumulating, not rejecting, positive, biological wisdom. Hence, one eliminates or circumvents that which is perverse and debilitating in the structure while preserving continuity and identity so that the result is not a new entity, but a healed person.

Similarly, the identity of the culture-subject must remain continuous through the process of correction. In psychoanalytic and cultural critiques, as processes of self-analysis or self-reflection, the aim is not to eliminate the person's superego or ego identity or the cultural-subject's identity in its values and traditions. That, in itself, would constitute an oppressive act of historical selection; in the case of the culture-subject it would be cultural genocide. The attempt radically to alter the superego of the person or the values and traditions of the cultural-subject, to make over the specific reality so that the identity is no longer continuous, has been exemplified in vastly varying degrees by the Pol Pot regime in Kampuchea (Cambodia) and by processes of attempted anglicization of immigrant populations in North America. Any such case amounts to tampering with the cultural genetic code in such wise as critically to alter the historical linguistic identity. This changes the self-identity--and subsequent self-understanding and self-formation--which it has uniquely become through the accumulated wisdom of the historical experience communicated linguistically and ritualistically through symbolic articulation.

Resistance to the historical, selective process can be observed in such examples as the maintenance of the Quechua (Inca) language and culture under Spanish linguistic and cultural domination; the persistence of the Aymara language and culture under both Quechua and Spanish rule; the affirmation of Mexican identity in its native American racial and cultural roots; the maintenance of a distinct African identity in the Americas under the particularly severe and historically selective processes of slavery. Overall, the culture-subject tends relentlessly to resist attempts to destroy or alter its self-identity. For this is a linguistic articulation of its self-understanding and self-formation, maintained through the relationships of love and concern of its constitutive members united in the bonds of sociality.

This is not to say the culture-subject is without problematic values and traditions. Freud notes that all individuals have some quirks within their intrapsychic structure,[75] and the same is true of all culture-subjects. However, rather than destroy its identity, within a value or tradition one critiques the linguistic distortion of its self-understanding in a manner analogous in psychoanalysis to targeting the locus of the problem contained in the superego. In this way, the integral self-identity of the culture-subject under critique is preserved through being corrected in a way that promotes creative and positive self-understanding in a process of self-reflection. This, in turn, is the self-formative, emancipatory process.

Freud expressed this point specifically in *The Future of an Illusion*. The utopian illusion allows for the introjection of mores and folkways in the development of the superego through identification with societal values and traditions. Without this development, predicated upon the introjection of linguistically and ritualistically articulated values and traditions, the person could not develop the anti-cathexes necessary for the displacement of libidinous energy from the primary object-cathexes in order to contribute to the higher pursuits of a well-disciplined, creative civilization realized through the arts and sciences.[76]

In a similar way, for the culture-subject the destruction of values and tradition would destroy the channels of creativity by dissipating energies in idiosyncratic directions. It would become a question of 'why,' 'for whom,' and 'for what' with no answer, because all 'meaning' would have been removed from self-understanding. The loss of meaning would then reduce the culture-subject and its constitutive members to a dyadic level where there would be mere signal interaction rather than sign or symbol communication. One could state what a thing is, but not what it means. This would soon degenerate into a destructive cynicism, a materialism with little concern for the altruistic values and traditions necessary for interpersonal relationships and the preservation of the culture-subject. The result would be cultural despair or disorientation due to ambiguity in self-understanding.

The loss of values and tradition, which articulate meaning, would deprive the culture-subject of its 'reason' to be, precipitating destructive struggles within the culture-subject as the constitutive members seek ever-increasing self-interest in lieu of ways to be for others. Sociality would be muted due to a failure to articulate its self-identity and self-understanding. As a result self-formation would be carried out in terms of radical individualism, while altruistic acts, having no motivating force, would begin to appear as peculiar manifestations of a neurotic mind *a propos* of nothing in particular. Eventually, the culture-subject would become terminal, for due to the loss of meaning successive generations would know little or nothing of their historical self-identity or unique wisdom.

CLARIFYING CRITIQUES

Positivism

The specific mistake of the positivist-objectivist perspective in understanding values and traditions merely as arbitrary manifestations of various culture-subjects can be noted within the field of sociology and, to a lesser extent, in the field of cultural anthropology. This perspective holds critical sway even within the area of contemporary revisionist psychoanalysis, as was noted by Eric Fromm. It is a great irony that Habermas seems to be trapped by this positivistic reductionism through inadequately adverting to the significance of values and tradition for the critical work of preserving self-identity from the most destructive forms of oppression.[77]

In reality, a profound wisdom has been engendered and accumulated through a transcendental process which cannot be subjected to an empirical-analytic methodology or, failing this, categorized as irrelevant or essentially meaningless. This wisdom, articulated in values and tradition, has been largely abductively acquired and tested in a pragmatic manner through the reflex-arc model of linguistic, purposive, rational, feed-back controlled instrumental action and attested to in its validity through the cultural consensus typified in the culture-subject's survival of the biological and historical selective process. Positivist analysis can no more account for this phenomenon than it can for the transcendental process of abductive inquiry which in both the empirical-analytic and the historical-hermeneutic sciences.[78]

Applied to social change, the positivist-objectivist perspective finds it impossible to assert the validity of any values and traditions. It is compelled to call upon the force of a new power elite to inaugurate another arbitrary status quo, to enforce stability and to prevent chaos from ensuing, while remaining always vulnerable to an even more powerful element ready to assert its will. Nothing proceeds without interest as the basis for meaningful behavior and action. At the level of the culture-subject, therefore, in circumstances bereft of meaning radically individualistic self-interest among the constitutive members forms the basis of meaning for knowledge and instrumental action as its constitutive members seek only self-gratification and interact only at a diadic level. They are devoid of the ideals which should constitute and dispose the self-understanding and self-formation of the culture-subject as a cultural group united in solidarity, rooted in sociality and self-determined in common historicity.

Eventually, however, sociality should begin to reassert itself in the most primitive and rudimentary way after a ruthless process of selection irrevocably has destroyed the unique beauty, dignity and wisdom of the past, and, therefore, its self-identity. In the inter-regnum between the collapse and the reestablishment of values and tradition, however, reason and truth, based upon the fundamental elements of sociality and love, would be largely suppressed in favor of cunning and force. Where they existed, they would be applied to stark necessity and survival under stressful conditions, for the culture-subject's control over its self-formation for any length of time would be tenuous at best.

Eventually, the nature of sociality in the culture-subject would reassert itself with enough positive force to overtake the force of self-interested knowledge and action. Through linguistic and ritualistic articulation the tartan of self-identifying values and traditions of the culture-subject would be rewoven-- differently perhaps, but nevertheless inevitably--and the warp and woof of the culture-subject's fabric of self-understanding and self-formation would reappear. Such a long, costly and at best questionable process could have been better accomplished at the transcendental level of self-reflection, leaving the self-identity intact while correcting the problem. This process would be impossible within a positivist-objectivist approach and perspective.

Yet to avoid certain problems which accompany a positivist-objectivist approach, Habermas seeks greater autonomy and responsibility through 'communicative action or interaction' for the creation of conditions for an unrestricted discussion and democratic resolution of practical issues. This must be seen as a process of communicative self-reflection by the culture-subject at the transcendental level of critique. Because this avoids restricting the process to the limits of a positivist-objectivist perspective, his method of critique can include and account for self-understanding or self-formation based on meaning which is rooted in the values and tradition which articulate the culture-subject's identity as a creature of self determined historicity.[79] Caught in the objectivist cognitive loop of its limitation, while unable to grasp the principle and more profound problem of triadic communication, the positivist-objectivist perspective remains at the dyadic level of interaction.

For Habermas, the overriding concern is to examine cognition-guiding-interest in an intersubjective, coercion-free communication or dialogue which would exclude no member of the culture-subject. Such a communication must be coercion-free to allow the truthful examination of the interests guiding the direction and momentum of the culture-subject to facilitate real consensus among all members. In this way norms and ethical principles can be established by which to direct the action of the culture-subject in all its dimensions, at all its levels, and for every member. This is the foundation of the methodological approach for examining the oppressive factors, i.e., the perverse and distorted linguistic and ritualistic elements found within values and tradition. Interest must be admitted and understood as being the fundamental force of all action, including scientific action. It is therefore imperative that these values be surfaced in truthful intersubjective, coercion-free communication so that they not become hidden unspoken factors of oppression which are utilized manipulatively by a power-elite or status quo. Rather, it is the exposition of these interests and the explicitation of the interest of all members of the culture-subject which are to be examined and decided upon consensually.

Marcuse

To clarify the limitations of such an analysis in applying Freudian theory to social critique it is helpful to follow Eric Fromm's criticism of Marcuse who rejects the displacement of libidinous energy to the socially approved object cathexes.[80] Though it is not our intent to discuss Marcuse at length, it is germane to this discussion to see how the superficial character of his approach ultimately misses the mark of critique, results in oppression and exploitation rather than autonomy and responsibility, and becomes thereby, as Fromm observes, anti-revolutionary rather than revolutionary.

Marcuse writes of the exploitation of 'eros' by oppressive power structures in the human society and develops a theory of the liberation of libido. He reasons that severe social repression of libidinal energy at its primary pleasure seeking level allows for exploitation through the subversion and distortion of primary drives into anomalous forms, thereby enabling the individual voluntarily to live under oppressive and exploitative systems of depersonalization and alienation.[81] Realizing a systemic imbalance but unable to articulate the problem, one is in bondage to manipulative forces. Moreover, so internalized do these structures and their destructive values become that such an individual diverts and displaces his/her libidinal energy in the service of a conservative, truncated 'eros'--really more 'thanatos'--to one's own detriment, rather than creatively employing it for the construction of a just and loving society. The libidinous energy is sublimated from self-gratification in terms of the pleasure principle to the socially productive reality principle which Marcuse calls the 'performance principle.' This energy is trapped in a common pool for the use of an oppressive and exploitative power structure toward maintaining the status quo. This displaces for its own selfish use all inquiry, knowledge, technological advances, production, and capital. This reservoir of libidinous energy is referred to by Marcuse as 'surplus repression' which he deescribes as:

'required' for the maintenance of a society, or the need for systematic manipulation and control of tendencies, forces which can be identified by an analysis of the existing society and which assert themselves even if the policy makers are not aware of them. They express the requirements of the established apparatus of production, distribution, and consumption--economic, technical, political, mental requirements which have to be fulfilled in order to assure the continuing functioning of the apparatus on which the population depends, and the continuing function of the social relationships derived from the organization of the apparatus . . . . They generate common, superindividual needs and goals in the different social classes, pressure groups, and parties.[82]

The means of liberation for Marcuse is regression from the reality or performance principle to the narcissistic, pleasure seeking, self-gratifying pleasure principle, that is, a regression to the primary level of gratification as Orphic-Narcissistic Eros.[83] Since Orpheus is associated with homosexuality and Narcissus with erotic self-centeredness, both are seen by Marcuse to embody the revolt against repressive, procreative, genital sexuality which lead to conservative control of libidinous energy for purposes of production and consumption by an oppressive, exploitative social order. Thus released from social bondage this libidinous energy becomes the means of liberation. Through easing and eliminating surplus repression, and thereby releasing the libidinal energies of the id as a revolutionary force, the power structure is overwhelmed and the system collapses.

Though in Marcuse's construct there are some extraordinary interpretations of Freudian psychoanalytic theory, much as Fromm notes, for our purposes the issue is that of the ultimately negative effects of the impulses of an unbridled id. The positivist-objectivist perspective traps one in an objectivist cognitive loop which renders critique superficial at best and indeed virtually impossible. Habermas' analysis ultimately misses the point of the transcendental level of communication on which values and tradition must be considered, thereby eliminating the possibility of self-reflection and self-identity as articulated in the very values and traditions which are disparaged. As is the case with Marcuse, no attempt is made to discriminate between the positive and negative in the self-identifying values and tradition of the culture-subject. Rather than revolutionary, this is anti-revolutionary and regressive, resulting in cultural, historical selection through the elimination of self-identifying values and traditions.

Moreover, because the superego is seen to be the enemy of the revolution--counter-revolutionary, as it were--it is disparaged and ignored as the spokesperson of the exploitative, oppressive structure of the culture-subject. The validity of this conclusion is ruthlessly correct in its insight, but logic also dictates the disastrous results of leaving the autistic, non-rational, self-centered id as the locus of authority. Beyond this, if true authority is based on truth, the id can by no means measure up, for its only interest is not truth, goodness, justice, love and peace, but its own immediate needs according to the pleasure principle. Thus, the id would discriminate between positive and negative values only in terms of their providing immediate access to primary and immediate gratification. If not, they would be subsumed under the category of obstacles to be ignored or eliminated. Reason would now be placed at the service of, and as spokesperson for, the id--which Freud considered an irascible tyrant. This is perhaps the result of collapsing reason into need, placing far greater trust in this dynamism than either Freud would allow or history has witnessed. Predicated upon Freud's writings, only with the most extravagant license and the greatest abuse of logic could one say that one would ever conceive of the id as a co-operator in the work of liberation towards autonomy and responsibility.

Freud notes that two specific periods are critical for the inculcation of values: infancy and adolescence.[84] At these times the person is taught the values and traditions which eventually make them a contributing and mature member of the culture-subject. But, if these critical periods are missed or the effort is thwarted or aborted, persons will be undisciplined and narcissistic. He or she would be of little benefit or positive value to their culture-subject, but would look for every opportunity to gratify primary object-cathexes, since the anti-cathexes formed were either too few or too weak. Moreover, the consequences of self-gratification for the group as a whole, whether positive or negative, will seem to be of little significance by and for individuals whose superego are underdeveloped. Culture and civilization will benefit little or not at all from their existence, for their participation will be greatly reduced by poor displacement patterns incapable of shunting libidinous energy to secondary or tertiary object-cathexes. Thus, dissipation of energy can take place only at the primary level. Any linguistic or ritualistic articulation of values and traditions would be jejune--a mere parroting perhaps for the manipulation of the culture-subject for personal ends. This is individualism, in the light of which communication is perverse and distorted.

The generation born during or after a successful Marcusean revolution of the id would lack the articulated morphological and syntactical matrix from which societal and cultural structures are evolved and through which they are transmitted; they would thereby be permanently debilitated. The damage suffered by the destruction of values and tradition would have an overall deleterious effect upon the culture-subject due to a catastrophic collapse in meaning for lack of the hermeneutic structures of articulation. Being of little benefit to anyone, the victory in such a transformation would be a pyrrhic one; the sought-for liberation would prove to be a chimera. Indeed, there would be a continuous threat of worse oppression and exploitation from other sources due to the loss of self-identity and a derivative loss of self-understanding and self-formation, resulting in a possible historical selection.

Collapsing the values and traditions of the culture-subject would be counterproductive to the overall commonweal due to the unbridled forces loosed. The People's Republic of China was wise to see the destructive potential in the Cultural Revolution which, spearheaded by youth motivated by dogmatism and given impetus by unbridled energy, almost resulted in cultural suicide. In the post World War II period, North American and European society tended towards a free expression of selfish, narcissistic, collective id impulses based upon a positivistic-objectivist perspective, which expressed themselves at virtually all levels of society. Fortunately, the radically centrist quality of the people and their adherence to their own values and traditions as a culture-subject reasserted sociality in a subsequent more conservative shift. Self-reflection leading to self-understanding allowed it to move toward reestablishing the linguistic and ritualistic fabric of its self-identity in a continuing and self-determined formative process.

Nevertheless, this conservative shift must also be critiqued in order to mitigate its negative impact upon social justice issues. This is the vortex where the contradictions meet, i.e., on the one hand, progress toward greater autonomy and responsibility through a self-determined, self-reflective critique, and, on the other hand, correction of the negative elements within the values and traditions of the culture-subject. Here, it is crucial to maintain the positive aspects of these values and traditions in order to preserve one's own identity and avoid selection through their collapse. Maintenance of these positive aspects does not appear to be protected by Habermas, while in Marcuse it seems to be neglected, though in a different manner.

Although Marcuse could not have envisioned it, in the long run the effect of his revolution would be the same as the systems he desired to transform; that is, deindividuation as a result of a positivist-objectivist reductionism. This deindividuation of the members who constitute the culture-subject would result through the collapse of values and traditions, for what could the culture-subject or its members say about themselves? Without an articulated, linguistic, intra-psychic structure the culture-subject would have no more identity than the person but would be truncated and lost. Being alienated from values and traditions by a disruptive and negative process which begins at the point of negation rather than from the original organic unity constituted by its values and traditions, the culture-subject would have no identity.

Bereft of cultural wisdom, it would undergo historical selection through being totally oppressed, exploited and absorbed into another more powerful culture-subject, or through stronger factions within the very culture-subject. The process of deindividuation resulting from the loss of values and traditions is in point of fact a loss of identity and, therefore, a collapse in self-understanding that effects a paralysis in the formative process as self-determined. Others would then define and direct the culture-subject, much as in capitalist systems propaganda seeks to generate through advertising a need for essentially unnecessary products, or in communist systems a dogmatism imposed upon the culture-subject often results in wasteful and unfulfilling production. Both define and direct the culture-subject in ways that are manipulative and exploitive; both are reductionistic and oppressive.

CONCLUSION: DOGMA VS DOGMATISM

In truth, values and tradition should act as a mechanism which generates, not dogmatism, but dogma, that is, the basic principles passed on in the process of history which define the self-identity of the culture-subject as autonomous and responsible. Dogma could be likened to a systemic cultural antibody inasmuch as it manifests itself as a defense structure. It persistently opposes any foreign linguistic intrusion into the culture-subject that would overwhelm its specific cultural self-identity and, thereby, wreak havoc with the culture-subject's self-understanding and its process of self-formation. More precisely and positively, dogma is the linguistic and ritualistic articulation of self-identity which it asserts with insistence in order to maintain the autonomy of its self-understanding and self-determined formation.

Dogma always stands in contradistinction to oppressive and exploitative dogmatism, which is the authoritarian articulation of a power structure in order to maintain or impose a status quo which is neither just nor 'true.' Dogmatism is a distorted and perverse linguistic structure which diminishes the culture-subject's ability to articulate its self-understanding and self-formation, and thereby reduces its autonomy and responsibility. Authoritarian dogmatism, based on oppressive and exploitative interests which articulate the culture-subject's identity in a broken and distorted manner, is resisted and rejected precisely through self-understanding based upon truth. Linguistically structured in dogma, this renders the culture-subject autonomous and responsible. This truth is achieved through the transcendental process of self-reflective critique.

Because it is simple to identify authoritarianism and dogmatism imposed from without, flaws in the very values and tradition which constitute one's own linguistic and ritualist self-understanding are the more dangerous. There is particular need for identification and correction through self-reflection as a liberative process towards increasing autonomy and responsibility. The morphological and syntactical matrix of the linguistic structure of value and tradition must be examined for the purposes of diagnosing and remedying any inherent oppressive and exploitative elements of authoritarianism. This could be the coercive force of a power elite or a dogmatism expressed as rigidified abstractions and rationalized as values and tradition.

In the process of liberation, the culture-subject critiques itself to eliminate such oppression and exploitation within, while dogma assists by articulating linguistically the self-identity of the culture-subject. This provides continuity to self-understanding and self-formation as these move through processes of analytical self-reflection towards self-correction. As the process of critique continues, authority expresses itself as that force of truth which emerges through consensus and moves the culture-subject from oppressive authoritarianism and exploitative dogmatism towards ongoing liberation for continued growth in autonomy and responsibility.

This continuing abductive process of historical-hermeneutical scientific inquiry examines the oppressive and exploitative elements within the values and tradition of a culture-subject. It makes manifest the way in which elements of rigidified abstraction promote and promulgate distortions and perversions within the utopian illusion, trap creative energy and thereby maintain the status quo for a power-elite. Through such a transcendental process of critique the culture-subject is enabled to self-correct so that values and tradition can come forward and give birth to new life for a self-determining, autonomous and responsible people. Such a resurrection is liberation.

Oblate College
Washington, D.C.

NOTES

1. This chapter is centered upon Habermas's analysis and development of a critique based on a criticism and development of the ideas of Karl Marx, Charles Sanders Peirce and Sigmund Freud. Nonetheless, it attempts to move beyond Habermas. This is true particularly in its stress upon the reality of the person in society (see note 2); the need of stable values and tradition for a viable self-identity; the vital necessity of both dogma and authority as positive forces of liberation and resistance to oppression, and their distinction from the negative forces of--what will be termed in this paper--dogmatism and authoritarianism, both defined as means of oppression. As Jurgen Habermas does not think along these lines, this work attempts to push beyond his parameters, while drawing logical conclusions from his premises.

2. Precisely because the question of the human person is epiphenomenal to the human species in Marxism, Habermas does not give adequate weight to the role of personal conscience or conscientious objection in ethical considerations. For him, it is not the human person who is free to act, but the human species. Therefore, the establishment of a normative ethics and the freedom to act reside within the group as a consensual reality.

No one can will or be self-conscious for another. Yet, the human person is a creature of sociality and, as also asserted by John Paul II, realizes him/herself only within the context of community with other persons--a communion of self-determined, self-reflective subjects. Within the truth of this intersubjective relationship, each person progresses in a common identity with the others in a cultural or social group. This, in turn, can be said to exhibit self-reflection, self-determination, and communication only inasmuch as it is a mutual effort of free, self-conscious individual subjects within whom freedom and consciousness essentially reside.

In developing this chapter the problem arose of avoiding epiphenomenalizing the human person to the group, while yet depicting the person as social by nature and, therefore, as related to, and participating in, a cultural group within which he/she develops and freely contributes. This corresponds to the problem of isolating each person at the expense of the group, as if their intersubjective relationships were of little importance or weight. What was needed was a term which would bring the two realities to mind almost simultaneously so that the subject was not lost in the group and the importance of the group relationship was not ignored. Such a term would help in avoiding both 'individualism' or 'totalism,' while expressing the cultural group of free, self-conscious subjects. As no term was found, one was coined: "culture-subject." Its purpose in this chapter on Habermas is precisely to avoid, on the one hand, ignoring the individual subject within which the primary human reality resides and is realized in personal acts and, on the other hand, isolating that very person from those intersubjective relationships (*communio personarum*) which are essential to the full realization of personhood.

3. Edward G. Hall, *The Silent Language* (New York: Doubleday, 1959), pp. 69-71.

4. Manley Thompson, *The Pragmatic Philosophy of C.S. Peirce* (Chicago: Univ. of Chicago Press, 1959), pp. 160-163.

5. Jurgen Habermas, *Knowledge and Human Interests* (subsequently *KHI*), trans. J. Shapiro (Boston: Beacon Press, 1968), p. 196.

6. *Ibid.*, pp. 274-285.

7. *Ibid.*, ch. 12.

8. *Ibid.*, pp. 59-60.

9. *Ibid.*, pp. 164-165.

10. *Ibid.*, 110-111.

11. Jurgen Habermas, *Communication and the Evolution of Society* (henceforth *CES*), trans. J. Shapiro (Boston: Beacon Press, 1971), p. 163.

12. Sigmund Freud, *Civilization and Its Discontents* (henceforth *CD*), trans. J. Riviere (London: Hogarth, 1930), p. 66.

13. Anna Freud, *The Ego and the Mechanism of Defence* (New York: International University Press, 1946).

14. *KHI*, pp. 52-54.

15. *Ibid.*, p. 279.

16. Herbert Marcuse, *Negations: Essays in Critical Theory*, trans. J. Shapiro (Boston: Beacon Press, 1968), pp. 251-252; *KHI.*, pp. 280-284.

17. *KHI.*, pp. 43-44.

18. *Ibid.*, p. 310.

19. *CES.*, pp. 171-175.

20. *KHI.*, pp. 308-316.

21. *Ibid.*, pp. 34-35, 43-44.

22. *Ibid.*, pp. 62-86.
23. I. Kant, *The Fundamental Principles of the Metaphysics of Ethics*, trans. O. Manthey-Zorn (New York: Appleton-Century-Crofts, 1938), pp. 78-83.
24. *KHI.*, pp. 197-198.
25. *Ibid.*, ch. 9.
26. James K. Feibleman, *An Introduction to Peirce's Philosophy* (London: Allen and Unwin, 1959), pp. 324-325.
27. *KHI.*, pp. 113-118.
28. *Ibid.*, pp. 91, 121-135.
29. Max Black, "Induction," *Encyclopedia of Philosophy*, IV, 176-177.
30. *Ibid.*, pp. 116.
31. *Ibid.*, pp. 137-139.
32. *Ibid.*, pp. 127-131.
33. *Ibid.*, pp. 137-138.
34. J. Feibleman, p. 238.
35. *KHI.*, pp. 195-198, 316-317.
36. S. Freud, *Moses and Monotheism*, trans. K. Jones (London: Hogarth, 1932.
37. A.A. Brill, *The Basic Writings of Sigmund Freud* (New York: Random House, 1938), p. 12.
38. Freud, *Moses and Monotheism*, pp. 182-184.
39. *KHI.*, ch. 10.
40. *Ibid.*, pp. 276-277.
41. *CES.*, pp. 116-118.
42. *KHI.*, pp. 137-139.
43. S. Freud, *Beyond the Pleasure Principle*, trans. J. Strachey (London: Hogarth, 1961), pp. 2-4.
44. Brill, pp. 518-520.
45. Freud, *Beyond the Pleasure Principle*, pp. 3-4.
46. *BWSF*, 535-536, 12-13; *KHI.*, pp. 243-244.
47. *CD.*, pp. 64-65.
48. S. Freud, *Moses and Monotheism*, trans. K. Jones (London: Hogarth Press, 1932), pp. 183-185.
49. Eric Fromm, *The Crisis of Psycho-Analysis* (Greenwich, Conn.: Fawcett, 1970), pp. 58-59; *BWSF*, p. 299.
50. *KHI.*, pp. 263-267, and 314-315.
51. S. Freud, *The Ego and the Id*, trans. J. Riviere (New York: Norton, 1960), pp. 15 and 46; *BRP.*, pp. 18-26.
52. *CD.*, pp. 34, 40-42.
53. *KHI.*, pp. 279-283.
54. *CD.*, pp. 23-24, 33-34; S. Freud, *The Future of an Illusion*, trans. J. Strachey (New York: Norton, 1961), p. 7.
55. Freud, *The Ego and the Id*, pp. 37 and 49.
56. *KIH.*, pp. 283-288.

57. Freud, *The Future of an Illusion*, pp. 46-51.
58. Freud, *Beyond the Pleasure Principle*, pp. 14-15, 17.
59. John Milton, *Paradise Lost* in *English Minor Poems* . . . (The Great Books; London: Brittanica, 1952), pp. 152-153.
60. Freud, *The Ego and the Id*, p. 41.
61. *KHI*, pp. 223-228; S. Freud, *Five Lectures on Psychoanalysis*, trans. J. Strachey (New York: Norton, 1977), pp. 37-38.
62. Freud, *The Ego*, pp. 45-70.
63. Freud, *Five Lectures*, pp. 24-25, 37; *KHI*, pp. 237-242.
64. *KHI.*, pp. 274-279.
65. *Ibid.*, 219-220; 238-242.
66. *Ibid.*, pp. 224-242; ch. XI, 254ff, espec., 261-271.
67. *Ibid.*, p. 269.
68. *Ibid.*, pp. 246-254.
69. *Ibid.*, pp. 266-269.
70. *Ibid.*, ch. XII, pp. 274-290.
71. J. Androde e Silva and G. Lochak, *Quanta*, trans. P. Moore (New York: McGraw Hill, 1969), pp. 150-151.
72. *Studies in the Philosophy of Charles Sanders Peirce*, E.C. Moore and R.S. Robin, eds. (Amherst: Univ. of Mass., 1964), pp. 232-235.
73. Freud, *The Ego and the Id*, pp. 24-27.
74. *KHI.*, pp. 290-300.
75. Fromm, *The Crisis*, pp. 42-43.
76. *Ibid.*, pp. 51-52, 112.
77. Fromm, *The Crisis*, pp. 12-25.
78. *KHI.*, pp. 133-135, 308-311. Again, it should be noted that the previous section, while drawing upon Habermas for the general analogy of social critique to psycho-analysis, attempts to maintain a much more positive attitude to tradition and values.
79. *Ibid.*, pp. 314-317.
80. Fromm, *The Crisis*, pp. 25-31.
81. Herbert Marcuse, *An Essay on Liberation* (Boston: Beacon Press, 1969), pp. 10-11.
82. Marcuse, *Negations*, p. 251.
83. Fromm, *The Crisis*, pp. 29-30.
84. Freud, *The Ego and the Id*, p. 38.

PART II

VALUE HORIZONS

AND

LIBERATION IN SOCIETY

CHAPTER V

ON TECHNOLOGY AND VALUES

LUIS A. CAMACHO

INTRODUCTION

For centuries there has been an ongoing discussion concerning the nature of values: are they objective, subjective, or both, and in which way? Are they the subject of intellectual knowledge or of emotive perception? Fortunately this is not my concern here: what I want to say about the impact of technology on values should be valid, even assuming different theories regarding their nature. I take for granted only that the expression, "value-change," has a referent in reality in the sense that the modification of values corresponds to features which can be analyzed in an objective way. By "objective" I mean open to independent verification by different people in diverse settings and times. Although the idea that values exist independently of human beings could be true--at least it is not logically contradictory--I am not supposing that to be the case. As far as this paper is concerned, the possibility of establishing some correlation between technology and values is understood as an empirical matter involving human behavior, including of course verbal utterances. It is very important for me to assume that the proper place to look for values or, if you wish, for the manifestation of values as known by the agent is human behavior.

Yet, this is not a purely empirical investigation of the way a pre-technological society modifies its values as contemporary technology becomes more prevalent. The focus of this paper is not only factual, but ethical. In other words, I will be making moral judgments on value-change, which is the same as saying that value-judgments will be made on value-changes. In particular there is one very important question: which type of technological decisions must we make if we take into account the implications of technology for values? Value-change is, in a sense, a sociological and psychological issue. But some philosophical considerations are of paramount importance, and the general approach followed here is one of second-order questions: what do we mean by "value-change"? How do we find that something or other is valued? What is the way to find out if a particular value-change has taken place? What do we mean by "technology"? And, above all, what are the criteria for making moral judgments about changes in values?

The reader may object that many of these second-order questions are by no means philosophical, but rather sociological.

Though I must grant that some of these questions, taken separately, may be dealt with by particular sciences, nevertheless the clarification of the whole picture (i.e., the answer to these questions taken together as a whole) requires the intervention of philosophical perspectives and insights.

VALUE CONFLICTS

Values are related to behavior and, consequently, to culture and institutions. Verbal behavior openly expresses preferences, be they learned or otherwise, which correspond to value judgments and which should be the basis for action. It is obvious that conflicts between verbal and non-verbal behavior, as well as between separate verbal and non-verbal acts, are very frequent. This is one of the first difficulties: in order to give an adequate account of value-changes one must take into consideration all kinds of behavior. At least three types of conflict come into focus: between words and deeds, between words and words, and between deeds and deeds.

In addition, human beings do not act as lonely fully-conscious agents since their behavior cannot be explained simply by individual conscious motivations. As psychologists are well aware, very often an explanation of our acts has to refer to social and unconscious factors, perhaps more than to personal decisions. In fact, the agent very frequently is unable to explain his/her own behavior. The tension between publicly proclaimed values and acts privately performed in opposition to those values is present in most societies, perhaps in all. Since society operates through such institutions as the family, the school, the church, the state, etc., value-conflict is frequently some kind of opposition between institutions and individuals. For institutions embody values, while individuals act according to them. Agreement between institutional values and individual behavior is not guaranteed by the fact that institutions publicly proclaim their values and try to enforce them by all means at their disposal: discrepancies are always possible.

There is a fourth type of conflict: the values embodied by an institution may not correspond entirely with the values of other contemporary institutions which affect the life of the same individual. For example, the values of the home may not be those of the marketplace; the values of politicians and those of scientists may not coincide.

Sometimes the conflict is only latent, as between the values of the family and those of advertising agencies as reflected in commercial propaganda. But at other times there may be a head-on clash, as is the case when the school, supposedly devoted to preparing the child for a productive career as a professional, tries to instill in him/her a set of values which do not correspond to--in fact sometimes squarely oppose--the values of corporate business or of the government, in which the individual will later on find him or herself as a worker.

Value-conflict, on the other hand, is a necessary condition for moral improvement. Perfect agreement between institutional values and personal behavior would exclude not only hypocrisy but, at the same time, any possibility of change and improvement. In any society ruled by unjust laws value-conflict is highly desirable. Mankind has progressed morally in a slow and haphazard way; very often progress has taken place after a clear-cut conflict between mores and laws, on one hand, and a better moral insight on the other.

In his excellent book *Technology and Society*,[1] David M. Freeman distinguishes two types of conflict from the viewpoint of the individuals and groups involved: *overlapping* and *crosscutting conflicts*:

(a) Overlapping conflicts are characterized by separation and difference on all important sets of values, so that adversaries on one issue become violent enemies on all. Individuals opposed on one issue do not have any attachment to common values and, consequently, do not have any common ground for compromise. Typical of this kind of conflict is condoning violence as a means to avoid the possibility of the adversary imposing his/her values. Moreover, the adversary is seen as less than human.

(b) The crosscutting type of conflict, on the contrary, presupposes coincidence on many value fronts. Since adversaries share many attachments there is room for dialogue and compromise. Freeman thinks that this kind of conflict is highly desirable.

A general principle may thus be established: in the assessment of technological innovations it is very important to take into account the type of conflict they may bring about. Freeman's position in general may be stated thus: avoid overlapping conflicts and, if they exist, do not introduce any technological innovation which would exacerbate them.

TECHNOLOGY

As recently as the 1976 Philosophy of Science Association Symposium[2] there had been doubts as to the justification of assuming technology as a proper subject for philosophical investigation. Even today, most philosophers in the standard analytical and post-analytical tradition would reject any particular topic as a subject for philosophy, be it culture, technology or whatever, since they see the task of philosophy being to explore the conditions for knowledge and not the characteristics of any particular object known. Without entering into such discussion, we may profit from an historical fact: philosophers within several different schools have dealt with technology as a proper subject, and have developed what may be called a "Philosophy of Technology." At least three philosophical systems (called "nonstandard" by some North American philosophers) have developed particular positions on this topic: Existentialism (mainly Heidegger), Thomism (e.g., van Melsen)[3] and Marxism (especially Engels). In addition and more recently, well known and highly respected philosophers of science like Mario Bunge have written on this theme.

According to their viewpoint four approaches may be distinguished in the philosophical literature on technology.

(a) *Engineering*: here the emphasis is on the machine and other technological products. When Dessauer, for example, asserts that for every technological problem there is one and only one optimal solution which is found and not created,[4] or when Butler in *Erewhon*[5] seems to champion the idea of doing away with all machines, attention is focused on the most visible and immediate aspects of technology.

(b) *Sociological*: here technology is seen as a collective activity, as something that presupposes the organization of human labor in factories, usually geared to urban and mass consumption. The emphasis is on human organization with its laws and historical institutions: the factory, the city and the state.

(c) *Anthropological*: although closely related to the sociological viewpoint, this approach enables us to pose another set of problems: are human beings primarily tool-making or symbol-making animals? What is the relation between technology and culture?

(d) *Epistemological*: the least developed of all approaches, philosophically this should be the most important. Some of its typical problems are the following: what is the relation between science and technology? Is there some kind of "technological" knowledge? Is there such a thing as a technological theory?

What is technology? So many definitions have been given that it is hard to keep track of them. In some languages (e.g. Spanish) it is customary to make a distinction between *techniques* as the use of tools in general and the series of procedures whereby practical aims are achieved, and *technology* as a modern state of affairs brought about by the Scientific Revolution of the XVII Century and the Industrial Revolution in the XVIII Century.

I will try to organize some of the definitions according to the four approaches mentioned above.

(a) From an engineering perspective:
- Transformation of matter by application of energy under the guidance of information.[6]
- A set of means by which man puts the forces and laws of nature to use, with a view to improving his lot or modifying it.[7]
(b) From a sociological viewpoint:
- The result of combining knowledge and know-how with the organization of labor, usually in an artificial environment, with centralization of decisions.
(c) From an anthropological perspective:
- Everything that gives corporeal form to human will.
- Mechanism or means for achieving one's ends.[8]
(d) From an epistemological perspective:
- Providing the arts with intellectual rules.[9]
- A system which includes the following elements: applied science, technological theory, technological model, technological action, technological object, use of technological object and satisfaction of the desired function, with two possible entrances: pure science and "soft" technology.[10]

Some of these definitions are too broad; some of them, literally applied, would include any symbolic activity. For our purposes the best is the second under heading (d), although it must be explained since it includes the very word for whose definition we are searching. If by the noun "science" we mean modern and contemporary theoretical knowledge of nature and man, and by the adjective "technological" we mean the type of situation which takes place when all activities, both intellectual and practical, are oriented toward the solution of a problem of a practical nature, then our definition will be more precise and more useful.

It should be clear that many standard remarks on technology (that it is demeaning or, on the contrary, that it is life-enhancing, for example) become meaningless if technology is equated with the totality of human activities. Strangely, many writers on this topic want both to keep a very broad definition and to make supposedly meaningful observations.

TECHNOLOGY AND VALUES

From some of the preceding definitions we can draw some conclusions:
(a) Knowledge as such is good, at least in general; but not every application of knowledge is good as such.
(b) Contemporary technology would be impossible without modern science.

(c) Technology increases the number of possibilities at our disposal to an extent unheard of in centuries past. Accordingly, the consequences of our actions have increased to the point where one cannot even imagine all their possibilities and end results and such unpredictable consequences often take place in social matters. On the other hand, decisions must now be made with far more rapidity than ever before. This is one of the most important sources of the problems of our time: more speed in decisions with less knowledge of results and consequences.

Another important question arises: what is the relation between technology and man's daily life, not only today but throughout history? Two main lines of thought are to be found.

(a) Engels and, in general, the Marxist tradition: the invention of tools is all-important in human evolution; without material tools there is no human work and without work there is no evolution to successively more human degrees of existence. Mankind's most important activity is the production of means for survival; this includes tools and instruments as extensions of one's organs so that one can master natural forces. This is what sets a human apart from other animals after a long evolutionary process ruled by Lamarck's principle that necessity creates the organ.[11]

(b) Mumford, and to some extent Ortega y Gasset and the existentialists: tools may be exclusively human, but the social organization of work is common to humans and many species of animals. There is no historical evidence for an incessant and ever-expanding creation of instruments from the very beginning of humankind; on the contrary, many well-documented civilizations have flourished with very little technological bases. Symbolic activity (language, rites, dance, etc.) is far more important in organizing human life--to such an extent, indeed, that this type of organization is a necessary condition for the invention of machines later on. In other words, machine-like organization of work in social settings precedes the invention of machines. Mechanical labor was performed by huge numbers of people, organized like ant hills, many centuries before the Industrial Revolution.[12]

As far as our topic is concerned, it seems safe to propose the following hypotheses:

(a) If Engels is right, then value-change should be a function of technological processes and, ultimately, of economic changes. The difference between the values of one society and those of another should be traceable in the last analysis to a difference in the mode of production, which essentially includes its technological underpinning.

(b) If Mumford is right, on the contrary, value-change

should be a far more complicated proposition, since it would depend on many factors.

Let us take the first position and formulate it in a very strict form, what we may call the "strict economic principle": *When the economic cost of maintaining a value becomes too high, society necessarily drops it.* Opposition to the "strict economic principle" may adopt very different degrees, according to the emphasis placed on other factors. The extreme position would be the denial of any clear-cut correlation, even a weak one, between value-change and any other aspect of society.

Most persons would agree, in fact, with a "weak economic principle" which may be formulated thus: *When the economic cost of maintaining a value becomes too high, society tends to drop it.* It is understood that this tendency works in conjunction with many other factors, which accounts for the fact that in some cases the change takes place and in others it does not; in some the change is fast-paced, in others slow.

Two remarks are in order here:

(a) Neither the "strict" nor the "weak economic principle" suffice to explain the *adoption* of new values; both refer only to the elimination of old ones.

(b) It should be clear that the difference between the two is not a mere matter of degree; in the former economic determinism rules out freedom, whereas in the latter there is ample room for freedom. The "weak economic principle" calls forth another, which we may call the "principle of personal valuation," to be formulated as follows: *When society tends to drop a value, individual agents may react by considering change to be good or bad and by trying to influence society accordingly.*

Which principle shall we accept, the "strict" or the "weak"? If we accept the former, many of the preceding and following considerations would become empty. One thing seems clear: the "strict economic principle" seems to lack sufficient confirmation. After all, starving people in India do not eat sacred cows.

There is no doubt that technological innovations modify social conditions and arrangements. The introduction of the typewriter, for example, changed secretarial work to such an extent that today's office is very different from that of the 19th century before 1850.[13] A similar change is taking place today with the introduction of small computers. The introduction of the typewriter was not a mere change of equipment; women entered the labor market after 1850 in large numbers precisely because of that technological innovation. Analogously, we may expect that the introduction of microcomputers will bring about social changes as well.

How does this process take place? The mechanism whereby

a technological innovation alters roles in society has been pointed out in detail by Freeman.[14] He distinguishes four stages or levels:

(a) Specific actions: there is an alteration in the behavior within the role, without any adjustment in the overall structure of roles and organizations. The worker is required to use new techniques, but everything else remains the same--for the time being.

(b) Decision rules: requirements and specifications for roles change. New knowledge and abilities are needed to fulfill the expectations associated with a role within society. Without them the worker cannot find a job and the self-employed businessman cannot compete in the marketplace.

(c) Decision structure: at this level relationships between role-sets change; authority is reallocated. Concrete people gain or lose authority because the relations within the social structure have changed in a significant way. Tension and conflicts may follow; people find that new responsibilities have been thrown upon them, while others feel that they have been demoted.

(d) Goals and rationale: this is the most profound level of change; here the very purpose of the structure is questioned. Society reorganizes itself according to new goals and priorities; many jobs simply disappear while others, unheard-of before, come into being. Obviously, many people cannot stand this level of change; fortunately, this is the last stage in a series that usually takes some time.

Contemporary society is technological through and through, both in capitalist and socialist countries. In the former, technology operates as a commodity protected by patents and franchises which constitute legal forms of property. The whole production system, on a global scale, is based on the use and expansion of technology. Underdeveloped nations are technologically dependent upon developed ones; technology flows as a commodity from a small group of countries (around 20) to a large number of countries (more than 100). Many developing countries try to bridge this gap by promoting scientific research with public funds on the assumption that technology will follow from, or is the same as, applied science, and that socio-economic development would automatically result from the introduction of technological innovations.

Technology and development, consequently, are highly valued. So far we have mentioned the impact of technology on values. But technology and development may influence values only after values have influenced *them*. If no priority is assigned to development, and to technology as a means for it, society would remain rather stable. This would be small comfort to a nation plagued with misery, disease, illiteracy, etc. Thus the conflict and antagonism between technology (as a dynamic factor) and culture (as the stabilizing force in society) cannot be solved *a priori* in favor of culture. Although it may be persuasively argued that culture is a necessary condition to avoid alienation, by no means can it be considered a sufficient one.

In many developing countries today maximum priority is given to socio-economic development as the most important social goal and to technology as the instrument to achieve it. This includes planning as the way to reallocate resources with the purpose of reaching a stage where a highly sophisticated economic system would guarantee satisfaction of basic needs for the masses. For some people, consequently, socio-economic development, technology and planning become the ultimate values: anything that increases the GNP is good, anything that decreases it is bad. Of course, this simple equation between economic development as measured by the GNP and goodness may not appear in such stark terms in the consciousness of politicians and their constituencies; in fact--and, we may add, fortunately--complexity of valuations remain and influence decisions at all levels. There may be an additional reason: the economic development of a country is not necessarily reflected in its GNP.[15]

Is technology good or bad? The question has sense only if we mean by "technology" a particular aspect of human life, within space and time boundaries. (If, on the contrary, we mean by it all types of uses of tools and instruments, any symbolic activity or any deliberate action, then the question becomes meaningless or, at best, trivial. Without technology so broadly defined there would not be human life as we know it and, consequently, there would not be any question about its goodness or badness). But we suppose that the question is meaningful and that an adequate answer is very important for the orientation of human life.

A general consideration seems relevant here: if we value diversity of behavior, tolerance of opposing opinions and openness to innovation, then we should value also those elements that make possible the type of society where those characteristics are to be found. In contemporary society technology seems to be one of the historical elements that have helped to create that kind of social situation. However, the relation seems tenuous: an open society could exist without contemporary technology and the latter can be used--in fact, it is used very often--to impose uniformity of behavior and to suppress dissent. Thus the dilemma: while technology makes possible many dreams, it also is instrumental in transforming those dreams into nightmares.

CONTRADICTIONS AND PARADOXES

The disagreement as to the goodness or badness of technology may stem from the incontrovertible fact that technological society is full of contradictions. The way these contradictions are solved in particular places and times determines the general direction in which a society moves in terms of a more or less rational and just situation. Let us mention some of these contradictions.

(a) Between science and technology: whereas science is a public possession, whose main value is truth and whose aim is the increase of knowledge, technology functions as a commodity, privately owned through a system of patents and franchises whose main value is efficiency and whose aim is profit. The ethical codes of the scientific researcher and of the technologist in a factory are, therefore, frequently in conflict, although there is a strong resemblance between the work of the former and of the latter.

(b) Between two concepts of human nature, both present in contemporary society: on the one hand, man as an individual consumer driven by an infinite desire to possess and, on the other hand, human beings as free agents who are able to develop uniquely human attributes. Utilitarianism and personalism, therefore, operate at the same time within the same society--but in opposite directions. Personalism implies the maximization of human possibilities, which can take place only in a democratic structure where people participate in the process of making decisions concerning matters that affect them. The individualistic consumer of utilities, however, motivated by an infinite urge to possess and consume, keeps alive the economy by buying goods and services even when there is no clear need for them. Whereas increased consumption seems to be a necessary condition for an increased GNP, a more democratic society in the sense already defined is not a necessary condition for an ever-increasing GNP and, in fact, may be deemed an obstacle by those who would prefer fewer personal liberties and larger expenditures *per capita.*

(c) Between two types of rationality: that of the private decision-maker, who tries to appropriate for himself maximum benefits while imposing on others as many costs as possible; and the rationality of society as a whole, according to which costs and benefits should be shared by all, with minimum destruction of the environment.

(d) Between technology and culture: whereas the former tends to homogenize all human beings on the principle that maximum diffusion also means maximum profits, the latter essentially seeks to differentiate individual human beings by providing the means for identification with a distinctive group.

In addition to these contradictions, some paradoxes arise in modern industrial societies.

(a) Technological development seems justified insofar as it responds to human needs; yet it has engulfed mankind in a quagmire of unwelcome complications.

(b) Any technological change should be valued according to the real advantages it brings about, but in fact advertising very often is able to promote changes merely on the basis of novelty. Since understanding takes time, the increase in the novelty rate means a decrease in the ability to grasp how things work. It also means a reduction of the possibility of developing a stable relationship between different groups of human beings on the basis of the use and knowledge of common technological products and processes.

(c) Urban life was developed as an answer to human needs; yet it often becomes an inhuman place.

ATTITUDES TOWARD TECHNOLOGY

Partly as a consequence of these contradictions and paradoxes, contemporary attitudes toward technology are not uniform. To go back to the original question of whether technology is good or bad, answers range from those who pronounce it neutral to those who passionately advocate its overthrow.

"Technology is neutral" is, at best, a very misleading expression. If by it we mean that there is a collection of possibilities available to individual persons which in themselves are neither good nor bad, then the sentence is simply false on most counts, since there is no such thing as a freely available technology just waiting to be used by individuals. Patents and franchises, as well as the rules of the market, effectively excludes that. If a country wants to profit from technological wealth it must pay dearly either in terms of industrial rights, trademarks and so on, or in terms of strong boycotts, legal suits and even economic blockades if it does not play by the rules of the game.

If, on the other hand, we take into account that technology is used because individual men or collective institutions make decisions on these matters, then there is no such thing as a neutral choice, since at least its consequences will be either beneficial or destructive.

In sum: technology could be labeled "neutral" only when considered very abstractly, but then we would not be talking about anything existent in the real world.

"Technology is good, but . . ." seems to be the most common attitude, and probably the most logical: without technology we cannot live, and yet in many ways rather we live with it. We need medicines, communications and so on; we do not need pollution, overcrowding, stress and other consequences of some technological innovations. It is clear that we cannot just say that technology is an unqualified good and then complain about conditions in industrial societies.

What should be done, then, about unwanted consequences? Here positions differ. Victor Perkiss has systematized them as follows:[16]

(a) Romantic conservatism: there must be some kind of control of technology, together with a conscious decision to accept only those aspects which do not disturb the status quo. But since this status is defined in economic terms, and usually includes many aspects which constitute the vested interests of those who propose the above mentioned control and selection, a new conflict arises: who will decide the type of control to be imposed, the criteria to be used, and the selection of technologies whereby some are accepted and some are rejected?

(b) Moderate conservatism: this position deplores the results of technological change but, at the same time, can do nothing because of a commitment to an open market society: to impose controls would amount to interfering with the laws of the market economy, with the "invisible hand" that guides individual consumers toward a greater good for humankind as a whole.

(c) Liberalism: since technological change is seen as a natural outgrowth of intellectual freedom it is widely accepted. Anti-social side effects are then mitigated by *ad hoc* measures.

(d) Socialism: we find an ambivalence here because of the contradiction between expectations and reality. Technological change was supposed to bring about the socialization of production, which in turn would lead to socialization of ownership. But, somehow along the way, oppressive bureaucracy has evolved as a side effect, giving rise to new elites linked to new technologies, whose political power is guaranteed by a one-party system.

(e) Romantic revolutionaries reject the compromises made by different states, including the socialist ones. At the same time, this group lacks political power and its tenets remain purely rhetorical proclamations relevant to some kind of simpler, pre-technological communities. Small scale experiments have sometimes succeeded for short times. Only those groups with strong ties, usually of a religious kind, have succeeded in freezing technological stages by deliberately choosing to remain in one and to exclude innovation.

Interestingly enough, there has been no dearth of authors who oppose technology in the most violent terms. Some of them attack the whole fabric of modern industrial society; others concentrate their attacks on particular aspects. Even if *prima facie* their criticisms seem exaggerated, some of their warnings have come true. This is why we cannot dismiss them lightly, for some of the descriptions made by them as factual situations may be taken as hypothetical scenarios which could become realities given certain conditions.

(a) The worst-case scenario would be a mixture of the following elements:

- the irrational thrust of the most primitive passions;
- the calculated greed and power lust of modern industrial man, with all the resources of planification at his disposal;
- the extraordinary, some might say "godlike," powers granted by contemporary technology.

We would then face the ultimate monster, geared to the satisfaction of greed and lust, moved by blind passions and endowed with all the powers of technology. It would be a nightmare, different from previous ones in being precisely a technological nightmare; a collection of marvels at the service of monsters for the oppression of peoples. Nazism comes to mind; Orwell's *1984* and Huxley's *Brave New World* are but different versions of this same horrible possibility.

(b) Some authors have flatly condemned technology on different grounds:

(1) Samuel Butler:[17] machines will evolve according to the laws of Darwinian evolution and eventually will enslave mankind.

(2) Friedrich Georg Junger:[18] technology is based on dead time, functionalism and a mechanical mind. It creates bureaucracy and reduces everything to mechanisms, thereby killing true life which is characterized by spontaneity and diversity.

(3) Leo Tolstoy:[19] although talking about science, technology is included as part of an effort he considers misguided. Only religion can decide what is important, including, of course, practical matters.

It would be foolish to dismiss these worries as altogether unfounded. Technological societies may become mechanistic; human beings may become slaves to machines; decisions concerning technological matters should transcend purely technological considerations.

(c) We have mentioned a modern, horrifying monster born out of the conjunction of three elements. There is another which is far less horrible but more pervasive: technological change as the ultimate value. We began by posing the problem of the impact of technology on values. Now we come to the most interesting aspect of that problem: the fact that change itself has become the ultimate value. From value-change we have come to change as value. The consequences of this travesty should be clear by now: if change itself is the determining value there is no possibility of understanding and of culture. Understanding takes time and aims at achieving permanent truths; culture needs time to develop the unifying ties that bind together different persons in common purposes and institutions. Change as a value in itself, without reference to what is changed, must be rejected if we want to live a fully human life.

CONCLUSION

The struggle for a more just society, not only within one's own country but internationally as well, should be the guiding principle in making decisions that transcend the merely individual spheres of life. Decisions on technological matters constitute a part of the whole of decisions concerning means to achieve specified goals. From this it follows:

(a) Any technological innovation aimed at the personal profit of a minority at the expense of exploiting the many, based therefore on a policy of internalizing benefits while externalizing costs, would inevitably lead to overlapping conflicts.

(b) Technological innovations should tend to decrease those contradictions and paradoxes mentioned above. If, on the contrary, the introduction of technological innovations sharpens those contradictions and paradoxes, the end result very likely will be a disaster in the mathematical disaster-theory sense, namely, a sudden change that brings about the radical transformation of previous conditions.

University of Costa Rica
San Jose, Costa Rica

NOTES

1. David M. Freeman *Technology and Society* (Chicago: Rand McNally College Publishing Co., 1974), pp. 85-88.

2. Frederick Suppe and Peter D. Asquith, eds. *Philosophy of Science Association, 1976* (East Lansing, MI: PSA, 1977), II 139-201.

3. Andrew G. van Melsen *Science and Technology* (Duquesne Studies, Philosophical Series, 13; Pittsburgh, Pa.: Duquesne University Press, 1961).

4. Friedrich Dessauer, *Philosophie der Technik* (Bonn: Cohnen, 1926/7).

5. Samuel Butler, *Erewhon*, or *Over the Range* (London,

1872; New York: Lancer, 1968).

6. Francisco F. Papa Blanco, *Tecnolgíy Desarrollo* (Costa Rica, Editorial Tecnologica de Costa Rica, 1979), p. 32.

7. Nathan Rotenstreich "Technology and Politics," in Carl Mitcham and Robert Mackey, eds., *Philosophy and Technology, Readings in the Philosophical Problems of Technology* (New York: The Free Press, 1972), p. 151.

8. Sir Robert Watson-Watt, "Technology in the Modern World" in Carl F. Stover, ed., *The Technological Order, Proceedings of the Encyclopedia Britannica Conference* (Detroit: Wayne State University Press, 1963), p. 3.

9. Scott Buchanan "Technology as a System of Exploitation," *ibidem*, p. 157.

10. Hugo Padilla "Los objetos tecnológicos; su base gnoseológica," in *La filosofía y la ciencia en nuestros días* (Mexico: Editorial Grijalbo, 1976), pp. 157-170.

11. Friedrich Engels, *The Role of Labor in the Transformation of the Ape into Man*; *El papel del trabajo en la transformación del mono en hombre*, in K. Marx-F. Engels, *Obras Escogidas* (Moscú: Editorial Progreso, n.d.), pp. 371-382.

12. Lewis Mumford "Technics and the Nature of Man," in Carl Mitcham and Robert Mackey, *Philosophy and Technology, Readings in the Philosophical Problems of Technology*, pp. 77-85.

13. Vincent E. Giuliano "The Mechanization of Office Work," *Scientific American* (Sep., 1982), pp. 125-134.

14. David M. Freeman, *op. cit.*, p. 58.

15. Francisco F. Papa Blanco, *op. cit.*, p. 19.

16. Victor C. Ferkiss, *Technological Man: The Myth and the Reality* (New York: George Braziller, 1969), pp. 57-70.

17. *Erewhon*, especially the three chapters under the heading "The Book of the Machines."

18. Friedrich Georg Jünger, *The Failure of Technology* (Chicago: Regnery, 1949).

19. Leo Tolstoy "The Superstitions of Science," *The Arena*, 20 (1898), in John G. Burke, ed., *The New Technology and Human Values* (Belmont, Calif.: Wadsworth Publishing Co., 1966), pp. 24-30.

CHAPTER VI

AESTHETICS IN THE CONTEXT OF HISTORICITY, MORAL EDUCATION AND CHARACTER DEVELOPMENT

RAUL LOPEZ UPEGUI

This chapter concerns the significance of aesthetic values in the constitution of our historicity, and their relation to other values. Such a study must be grounded in the roots of our essential human condition. If any dimension is capable of enabling us to understand the openness of human existence it is that of creativity, for it is by this that we are historical. People appreciate themselves as being historical when they recognize themselves in the flow of happenings.

It was through poetry that the comprehension of being began in the occident: Homer founded what we call a "nationality," the Greek poets shaped the early forms of thought concerning truth, and Virgil by his verses gave roots to a "barberous people." Today it is the poets, writers, musicians and painters who, through their creative work, uncover the temporality and roots which enable us to appreciate that we belong to a time and space. They set us before our very selves and help us to assimilate the effects of recognizing our true nature, to work out our proper agenda, to erect a world and to construct a dwelling place in history.[1]

THE LOCATION OF AESTHETIC VALUE IN THE CONTEXT OF CULTURE

Taking into account the semantic diversity implied by the concept of culture, let us approach it in a way that will most enlighten our subject. By culture we understand "the realization of values for man." It was Heidegger in his "The Epoch of the Image of the World"[2] who singled out this meaning in order to indicate it as one of the five great phenomena of the modern world. In turn, there followed an interpretation of art as what one sees with the distinctive interiority of human sensibility. Thus, in the modern age there arose that distinctive philosophic discourse called aesthetics, though the term has its origin in the Greek concept *aisthesis* or sensibility. (Alexander Baumgarten attempted to elaborate a logic of sensibility parallel to the logic of understanding.)

It seems clear that values belong to, and envelop, human existence. (Thus, we share the point of view of Jean Ladrière who holds that, however the discussion regarding the proper existence of ethical values be resolved, they are objective qualities.[3] We are immersed in values and concrete evaluations at each step of what we call human experience, namely, contact with being in all its manifestations and the renovation of oneself in this contact.

In essence this is a vital experience which consecrates as "value" all those conditions which concern one's own "conservation and growth." A value is therefore an objective correlate of the appreciation found in life experience. We can understand this vital experience under three perspectives: a) linguistic, b) perceptive and c) practical. To the first pertains logos, speech, expression and naming; to the second belong all the various forms of sensibility; and to the third belong praxis, production, work and in general all the forms of action.

It is culture which *orders and codifies,* (in the linguistic sense), all this vast experience with attention to its "products" or results. On this basis, it allows for different experiences and different realities, and finally for the diversity of cultural codifications and valuations. The concrete realization of such different values as justice, truth, religiosity, beauty, honesty, etc., gives birth to a multiplicity of cultural configurations. Thus, the value of justice generates in history a configuration we call the juridical or legal order, while that of truth generates the sciences, philosophy, etc. In this order of ideas the realization of aesthetic values, such as beauty, harmony, proportion, and their contraries, generates a configuration which we call art.

It does not take much effort to note that art and the values it has incorporated through time have had a prominent place in the life and expressions of peoples, whatever be the value hierarchy which shapes their overall experiences.

On the other hand, the person is a totality which includes, as a requirement of one's biological and historical existence, the tendency to express and "respond" to the requirements of one's environment. This is witnessed from the most remote times--and "today with greater force" by the distinct forms and manifestations of this ontological reality. (Note, for example, Lasceaux, Altamira, Machu Picchu, etc.)

Within these expressions I would locate what has been identified as a cultural configuration--or better, such artistic realizations are the configuration itself and express a profoundly human experience. Whether based upon a material, symbolic, religious, magical or political need of whatever type, this always includes an effort to transform the whole of life, society and history. In the very first instance its specific purpose is to realize "within some matter a concrete configuration in a singular and indissoluable manner according to an individual essence, even if this be the simple gestures of a dance. This distinctive mode of appearance gives the object its unity and provides the basis of its visible structure. In other words, the aesthetic object as a realization of value transforms the matter, "informs" it and brings it to that distinctive uniqueness in which value is shaped in the concrete as what is referred to as a work of art. This implies some type of "violence" or "struggle," for Heidegger notes that there is included always a permanent play or "polemic," namely, the dialectic of the hiding and unveiling of being. But above all, a work of art "exists" and is such in the concrete history of men and their cultures.

We are heirs of peoples who have been profoundly engaged in this creative and transforming activity of art. It has always had its place and its muses; on many occasions in history it has served to unite events of different orders. The works of Homer and the tragedies of the Greeks catalogue the ethos of their people, uniting their religion, politics, wisdom, ontological conception of the cosmos and of nature, justice, and the formation of the citizens as *paideia.* All this was brought together in an artistic manner in terms of beauty: Pericles would say "We love beauty, and are not for that less human." In its many forms this is the heritage of the West. Although the times have changed and our "enthusiasm" may be different, the values of art and aesthetic values are not newcomers. In addition there has been the eloquent witness of our pre-Columbian cultures: we are descendents of goldsmiths, artisans, weavers, etc. On every side we note that aesthetic values were highly developed, shaped in concrete works of art, both material and spiritual, and related to other cultural realities.

With the development of philosophy in Greece there arose ways of interpreting these "productions" of the culture from different perspectives. Thus we have theorizing regarding, among others, politics or forms of communitary organization, types of knowledge or forms of understanding, and art or the creative reproductions of matter. Philosophy opened a distinctive space for thinking about art and its works, just as it opened space for meditation on being, truth, justice, good, physics, the physical, etc. More radically one might say that being creates its own space of meditation through human existence.

Plato was typical of the development of these multiple horizons. His effort to exclude the poet for creating fantasies, illusion and dreams showed only the essential importance and radical strength of artistic experience as an experience of "power." He guarded against this as a menace to his project of searching for truth. Thus he tried to exclude art as subversive of the static order which he sought to impart to the conception of the state. This shows how deep is the relation of art and creativity to life, change and openness to new dimensions.

As Plato[4] could not integrate the transforming activity of artisans and artists with his goals and system, in the end he declared them irrelevant. As idols and images were without ontological foundation he considered them condemned to perpetual trickery and corruption, to temporality and ruin; he saw them as movement without transcendence and hence as destined to choke on themselves. In this the philosopher erred, for even he could not avoid employing Greek artistic forms inasmuch as his dialogues were undoubtedly poetic.

In more recent times one notes the vital renovating and liberating thrust, especially of art and music, and the threat these constitute to unjust and oppressive regimes. All Latin America has witnessed this artistic flowering reflected, among so many, by Victor Jara and those who live his memory.

THE DEVELOPMENT OF ART AND WESTERN RATIONALITY

New forms of interpretation of the world and of reality were developed by the modern sciences of the seventeenth and eighteenth century and their reflection in the "philosophy of subjectivity." These elaborated a distinctive form of occidental rationality, characterized by domination, conquest, measurement, order, calculability and the objectivity of nature. The fundamental thrust of all this was "effective work in the world," that is, the search for productivity at all levels. One could no longer interpret this new rationality according to prior categories of knowledge as pure contemplation or theory (in the Greek sense of *theorein* or contemplation), and of nature as something sacred with which we identify or at least try not to violate.

On the contrary, the new rationality, called technology, science, calculating reason, etc., was to uproot and dissipate the mysteries of this world and of nature which we hold "as a given" or object. In the place of Heraclitus' "nature loves to hide itself"[5] was substituted Bacon's "I attack nature to force out its mysteries."[6] To undertake this task a notion of "subject" was elaborated with a "natural light of reason"--about which Descartes marveled--which had the ability to constitute its objects; it had the power to represent, found, and "think out" the physical environment.

It has been the task of modern philosophy to clarify this double movement on the basis of its comprehension of "substance," for which Descartes attempted to lay a new "foundation." On the one hand, he subjectivity constituted objectivity, whose existence increasingly became the pure subjective interiority of the thinking thing: to think was to seek, to remember, to feel. On the other hand, the extended thing became an objective projection of this subjectivity developed, on the basis of imagination, into an increasingly objective world.

Hence, man's historical project gradually began to shape nature through a "mechanical" or technological age whose ultimate objective was to produce "values of use."

Art and the Need for the Absolute

What then are the implications of these developments--thus far but briefly sketched--for interpreting and implementing art and aesthetic values. A first indication is found in G.F. Hegel's "Inaugural Lecture" for his course on aesthetics: "Art is something past for us."[7] This discouraging thought must be understood in context. Hegel had already arrived at the idea of the Absolute as consciously converting itself into the work of history. He understood the new and inexorable test of modern times to be transformation, achievement, work, efficacity and productivity, in sum, the values which are well known to us today. Within this horizon art loses its significance or purpose in the pattern of people's lives. It is not capable of satisfying the new needs of history, and for that reason no longer responds to the "need for an absolute" which it fulfilled in earlier times. To be more explicit, in other epochs it was sufficient for man to produce art; this was a major activity which endowed him with meaning. Painting and sculpture served the gods, who spoke through poetry. If these imaginary beings transcended time, they did not value services rendered through temporal means. Much less did politics value oratory, rhetoric, music, and drama; politics was not at the service of action,[8] indeed action had not gained "an awareness of itself" as a universal exigency. Indeed, according to one Hegelian interpretation it was only with Descartes that consciousness achieved a firm grounding in complete self-awareness.

With the development of the new rationality and consciousness, it is understandable that other priorities would arise; there would be other goals to realize and other dilemmas. As a result of this spirit, anxieties and priorities required that art be converted into pure aesthetic phenomena. In the words of Hegel, these would be "relegated within ourselves" as a new sensibility. They would be considered to be our representation and hence a matter of aesthetic taste or of interior preference, and were reduced to that alone. Artistic activity, which had already been reduced, would then cancel itself out as inefficacious and useless before the imperative of immediate and unrestricted action.

On the basis of this interiority, art attempted to regain its sovereignty. It is a "value which does not value itself" in the words of the poet René Char, for it asserts itself in terms of its own interior sovereignty as accepting no law and repudiating all power. The artistic ego affirms that it is its own measure or rule, the unique justification for what it has and what it attempts; this was romantic culture reduced to the purest individualism.

As a result of this self-affirmation art now frees itself and demands recognition and realization in the broader realm of human work. It moves beyond subjective passion which did not seek to participate in the world because that was ruled by goals, measures and order, in other words, by science, State, and technology. Art is breaking into this world; it is reaffirming its essential place and proper value as that by which man has affirmed his presence in history through painting, music, architecture and the plastic arts; and it is reaffirming its distinction from objects produced for human consumption. This is the explosion of contemporary art, especially of literature.

To sum up thus far: if one is concerned about efficacious action in history, if this is the project which absorbs men and their destiny, if in an Hegelian manner the Spirit or absolute is the conscious transformation and work of the world, then art or artistic activity does not satisfy this historical need. But must art be declared therefore to be inefficacious and transcendent, are those values which pretend to erect a world in terms of use, function and consumation sufficient? Is the historical moment so sufficient that it can exclude and condemn the values which pertain to human sensibility?

Artistic Activity versus Transformative Activity:
  The Apparent Contradiction

Effectively, some assume that this reigning antithesis or contradiction between activity transforming the world and artistic activity is real and must be resolved by the elinimation of the second member. Let us examine the question in greater detail, for the antithesis itself can be interpreted in various ways.

1. Efficacious and transformative action can be understood as a "revolutionary" work, as political action which pushes for a change from less just to more just structures. This necessarily will be a political work carried out by the masses and by popular organizations. Such moments of profound mobilization do not permit the moments of pure contemplation and leisure supposedly required for that "certain comprehension and interpretation" essential to artistic activity. Nonetheless, if one understands this from a dynamic "liberating" perspective, the vanguard

of the movement of transformation requires mobilization of all resources: words, sounds, images, space, etc., to promote and sustain the ends sought through efficacious and transformative action. One cannot have an antithesis without a profound unity of action from different fields and from distinct perspectives converging in the same intentionality. Such coordination and direction has undoubtedly taken place in history, and one could cite many concrete cases in which art has unveiled the truths which the forces of subjugation and domination struggle to hide.

2. One can interpret transformative and efficacious action as effectively suppressing aesthetic values in favor of the goals of technical rationality and the modern cares it imposes. That is to say, it is claimed that what is necessary at the present time is material development, and that what is pressing is the preoccupation with technical progress. Thus the priority is to achieve ever higher levels of productivity, with the greatest return for the minimum investment. The values which guide this orientation are profit, productivity, efficacity, money and domination. Hence, in developing a hierarchy of values, the aesthetic values of sensibility and creativity appear as antithetic to, and are excluded by, the others. This constitutes a contradiction which can be resolved only through the radical elimination or reduction of the aesthetic values which block the affirmation of the others as values. In more common terms: art does not produce money; sensibility is obsolete; one who does not exploit the situation is a fool; one who does not produce should be locked up; artists and poets are a parasitic and idle class. Extrapolating this to other dimensions: one who thinks is dangerous, one who criticizes is a non-conformist.

It is pretended that this is really a contradiction between values themselves, whereas what is truly at play are interests which lie outside the terms of the discussion but intervene efficaciously in their evaluation. For a certain form of power is inherent in rationality and masks itself under other values which it orients exclusively towards function and manipulation, directing them according to its interest in the domination and alienation of mankind. This does not promote authentic realization or development, indeed ultimately it slows and diminishes one's capacity to work, for on this basis creative capacity and imagination are considered impediments to the realization of one's goals.

For such a human being, menaced by the alienating power of the modern world, art holds a unique possibility for recuperating the sense of life, one's self-affirmation and identity. It assures the fullness and unity lost under the influence of the above forces. These include science itself, which undoubtedly held out the promise of great advantages for man, but whose immutable, impersonal, abstract, insensible power--when it does not destroy life--tends to impoverish it and to paralyze the development of properly social human capabilities. In this context one can appreciate the full power of the famous words of Nietzsche's *Will of Power*: "We have art in order not to perish before the truth."[9] Any contradiction seen between technical rationality and the aesthetic is merely apparent, for throughout history artistic activity has totally transformed matter, recreated forms, liberated humans from alienating abstractions, and generated in imagination a memory and sense of life.

Not in vain then have aesthetic values been taken up, realized and conserved in the history of people. Works of art, with their continuity through time, preserve truth and meaning. They constitute a subsistent reality replete with insights received from distinct epochs, and are diversely drawn upon according to the various cultures and exigencies of history. Works of art are subjected to the sensibilities of "each present moment" and to the interpretive categories of the historical subjects who contemplate them, appreciate or depreciate them. In any case--however they be treated--they are signs in a language which can be spoken at each moment and to each person. It is the person who displays and puts in motion their power to give birth to a world in which values can come into play once they are but unveiled.

Thus, in the work of art what seemed pure internal coherence or immanence becomes communication to others. What may have seemed not to have meaning, truth or value, is nonetheless that whence all appears as full of meaning. It is a language which distinguishes truth and falsity and by which we are instructed so that we can understand reality better and   cultivate ourselves.

What then is contained in such works of art, what values have they assimilated? What special reality do they possess which gives them such invaluable richness that they cannot be reproduced or repeated, as is the case, for example, with a Pieta of Michelangelo or a Ninth Symphony of Beethoven. To what special condition should one attribute their power to escape and transcend their own point in history so that time seems to fall away and they become permanent and atemporal? What constitutes their proper essence as different from objects of daily use and from instruments by which we transform the world by work?

It seems sufficiently clear that works of art are different and have distinctive characteristics; they are not "mere things," but are distinguished from other forms of human work and from activity in general. Let us analyze this difference. A useful object which is fabricated or manufactured on a production line does not relate back to the one who has made it, much less does it refer to itself. It disappears in its use; it never tells what it is but only that which it is meant to serve. It has no absolute visibility which presents strength and generates confidence, as Heidegger has well said. In order that such an object "appear" it is necessary that there be a breech or rupture in the circuit of use, some anomaly by which it rises up out of the world of pure objects, and appears as what it is. It is then converted into appearance, into what it was before it became something useful, so that it is available to be converted into a work of art.

In the "usual" or useful object the material itself is not an object of interest; the more the material is apt for its use the more it is appropriated and approximates nothingness. At the limit, every object thus becomes immaterial and disappears without an echo in the rapid circuit of interchange; it vanishes into action which is itself pure becoming.

The work of art on the contrary is what it is made of; its nature and material is visible, stands out, seeks recognition and glories in its reality. This is characteristic of the exultation of the verbal rhythm in a poem, of the sound in the music, of the speech in a novel, of the colored light in a picture, and of space in architecture. The work of art makes to appear the very reality which disappears in a mere object: the temple glorifies the marble, the painting is not made without the canvas and other material ingredients: without the painting the canvas or material factor would remain hidden. A poem is not made of ideas and words as common sense believes; a poem is that which from words brings into appearance the elemental hidden profundity they express. For this reason the work of art cannot be satisfied with the mere reality of the "thing" it places before one. Thus, if a sculpture makes use of stone as does a worker, the sculptor utilizes it in such manner that it is not negated, but instead is affirmed and brought out of its obscurity. This enables it to be a revelation of truth and an affirmation of itself as these elements are liberated and then revealed in their essence.

THE CONSTITUTIVE VALUES OF THE AESTHETIC DOMAIN AND THEIR REAFFIRMATION

The Aesthetic Experience

Let us begin from the simple premise that works of art express radically human value: the aesthetic exists only because it is created and it is admired only from the point of view of the artist or of the one who contemplates. Above we had noted that there is an essential difference between objects of common use and works of art. It is important now to clarify the base for this distinction by identifying that by which things have their distinctiveness, and by which works of art are not simply reducible to other types of works.

One reason can easily be identified: works of art "constitute" a proper sphere of values which men make and by which they are inspired. They promote these values at the same time that they are liberated by them. That is to say, in a work of art one has imagination, while at the same time the work involves images.

The reality which appears in the work of art unchains and stimulates effects which are quite distinct from those occasioned by simple things of this world. (This is not to depreciate the vast field of ordinary things, which has its own way of being and its own dimension of thought. It is simply that in the present context we are directing our attention elsewhere.) We can ask why there are such effects, that is, why in this sector of the world--or of matter and forms--something else is in play which requires of men a special focus or a particular state of awareness. One discovers a mutual difference: art opens an area of feeling and an horizon of new representations which, in turn, evoke a response from the imaginative, emotive and ecstatic dimensions of man.

This response, which is not had by everyone with the same intensity, has the character of aesthetic experience, that is, it is contemplation in which perceptive sense experience has priority--but is not alone. Aesthetic experience begins in this, and is never detached from it. The distinctive nature and dimensions of this experience are the following.

1. There is a predominance of the human capacity of wonder, though this is often insufficiently appreciated. Aristotle has rightly given this a basic role in the development of philosophical meditation.[10] Because in the presence of beauty or of some other aesthetic value wonder erupts suddenly without any warning and without being hoped for it has two distinctive characteristics. On the one hand, it is a break in the ordinary daily pattern of the world in which we are usually submerged, for it is a step from practical to contemplative experience. On the other hand, it is an "appeal" because it is located in a region that is short on emotion and thus has a beneficial and welcomed impact. Wonder opens and gives access to this experience.

2. Once habituated to wonder we enter the second phase, analytic perception in which we contemplate sensible and imaginative data. For example, we encounter poetry as a powerful

universe of words whose composition and powers are affirmed through sound, figure and rhythmic mobility in a unified and autonomous space; or in a sculpture we encounter the polish of certain surfaces, the contours of certain plains, the fullness of certain associated images, etc.

Everything is realized in a new and unified object of perception whose quality demands our attention. This qualitative order presents us with a demand for a complement, a certain coherence with new perceptions; we proceed to form the aesthetic object of our contemplation. In a way we dissolve what we see in order to reintegrate it into an image which lifts us up.

3. The third phase is contemplation. Enjoyment plunges us into pure contemplation and we no longer think either of the matter with which the work was constructed, for it is not a real and common object, nor of anything exterior to the work. Instead the aesthetic object constitutes a world in itself, an object which exists solely in its appearance or representation in the imagination. The one who contemplates becomes pure admirer and in this obtains his fullness.

We can understand thus why some authors hold that what is contemplated is not Reality but a co-reality, and that this co-reality is essentially appearance. Nicholas Hartmann, for example, holds that a thing is an aesthetic object only when "it subsists solely in relation to the subject which contemplates it aesthetically: it exists not absolutely in itself, but only by aesthetic contemplation; the essence of beauty consists, not in something which appears, but in its very appearing."[11]

In sum, from first wonder to the active and analytic grasp of sensible and imaginative qualities, and from these to synthetic vision, to the formation of the aesthetic object and to contemplation, we experience ourselves both as submerged in violent emotion and at the same time as calmed by what some call aesthetic enjoyment or even inebriation.[12] This inebriation, which totally submerges the person in the contemplation of the aesthetic object, appears first of all as "being lost to oneself." It indicates a profound union with the object, though it is a matter not of possession, but of radical admiration. In a letter from Dremtke to his brother, Theo, Van Gogh commented that "from morning to evening I was so absorbed in that melancholic music . . . I had forgotten myself in this symphony.[13]

Much less does this inebriation appear as a desire of the body or for anything; it is absolutely gratuitous and disinterested. It is a loving experience, indeed, its beauty and value cannot be perceived without love. Thus, one can call this drunkenness a fascination. Seeing supposes a certain distancing, a decision that separates and has the power to avoid the confusion of contact while nonetheless converting this separation between the observer and the work into encounter. Despite the distance, what one sees appears to draw us into an astonishing contact, so that the manner of seeing is a type of testing. To see is a contact at a distance, when what is seen imposes itself upon our wonderment as if this were held, touched and put in contact with appearance. It is not a clear and active contact as occurs in the action of physically touching, for in this experience wonder is pulled down, absorbed into an immobile movement, into a depth without profundity. Certainly through contact at a distance what is given is an image, and our fascination is the passion of that image.[14]

In fascination we no longer perceive any real object or figure because what is seen pertains, not to the real world, but to the indetermined realm of the fascinating. In fascinated contemplation works touch us with an unmediated directness: they receive power from us and while remaining absolutely at a distance, enable us. This experience submerges us in the world of forms, of plasticity and of dreams, while not signifying at any moment the loss or alienation which some claim. On the contrary, an exultation of the sense of life is manifested through our "pathos," which in that instant grasps the fullness of being.

Thus, aesthetic feeling is vividly personal; it is inconceivable except as the fruit of the profoundly living collective values of a shared culture. Works of art are an expression and synthesis of the sensibility of the society and culture in a concrete epoch, in terms of the person of the artist, his symbols, etc. Their true originality is derived entirely from being rooted in the soil worked through by many persons, in regard to which, says H. Taine, "the work of art is determined by the general state of the spirit and of the customs which surround it."[15]

One could call upon many examples of this statement in history to illustrate this spirit of collective participation and common feeling. Tolstoy commented regarding Gothic art in the Middle Ages:

> The artists of the Middle Ages who shared the same basis of feeling and the same religion as the people and translated their (the people's) feelings and emotions into architecture, sculpture, painting, music, poetry and drama, were true artists. Their activity, based upon the most elevated vision of that epoch and expressed in terms shared by the whole people, was authentic art, the art of an entire people.[16]

As a collective creation, realized through the cooperation

of all the forces of the community and sustained by a single spirit of solidarity, the Gothic cathedral was not only the symbol of the creative power of the people, but its very image. Today in our towns the literature and music of the troubadours, singers and jugglers are a vital example of this vision; their truly popular expression, rich in local traditions, reflects a whole experience and life of feelings, illusions and hopes.

Aesthetic Values

We have seen how the aesthetic experience constitutes a cycle: it is produced through a process in which there has been a play of values, which it in turn produces, discovers and stimulates. Launched into the realm of the imagination we find that we are free from the weight of the given, static, fixed and immobile reality which surrounds us: the world around us, things in daily use, the daily routine, what is absolutely familiar, evident, unquestioned and permanently accepted. Which of us has not experienced instants of marvelous power which liberate us from our needs, deceptions and limitations, from the forces which hold us captive. This capacity to free us is to no small extent the effect of what today is called the seventh art. One example for youth today is rock music in which the body is one with the rhythm, sound and in general the whole surrounding ambient. Who on hearing a symphony does not feel to some degree what we are attempting imperfectly to describe? In turn, the aesthetic frees us from impulses and resolves tensions which cannot be liberated by other means. (The ancients expressed this profound truth in their myths as can be seen in Orpheus.) The aesthetic directs us beyond time which exercises an oppressive tyranny over our fantasies, subjecting them to the requirements of production, work and profit. By suppressing the rule of time, aesthetic vision enables us to regain contact with our more original interior life.

This experience, in turn, opens our whole capacity of fantasy and dreams, the magic vein which lifts our spirit. Today, as in no other epoch, we experience this need which is intensified by the mechanized, controlled, programmed and directed world in which we live. This is the message of Latin American literature and the magic realism of Garcia Marquez, who reflects our original make-up and purest identity. It is the message which America gives to the world through its multiple artistic expression. However, it is not ours alone; what we say has a worldwide resonance that can be heard, for instance, in the musician, Stokowski: "For some of us this intimate life of dreams, imagination and vision, is the authentic life; this is what we live intimately. Though the external appears precise, consistent and concrete, in reality it is remote, the least real life."[17]

This is in no way an escape from the historic responsibilities we must all confront. It lies rather in the depths of our being, in the play of possibility and reality for whomever would take definitive account of existence; it is the dialectical play of dream and crude reality. Without fantasy one has no further possibilities, because it is fantasy that produces the distance from what has already been achieved and can no longer be made because it is already determined and realized. Imagination is the source of all inspiration and our access to that which is inexhaustible and permanent. A people without the values of the imagination and of spontaneity is condemned to perish.

If there is anything which reveals this aesthetic experience it is the creative power of human existence, namely, in art we discover this exceptional capacity in its most radical and essential form. This is expressed in the creative invention of a microcosm which acquires its proper life thanks not only to manual ability, external action or mere technical control, but to an immanent direction of all the spiritual forces which move to transform matter in order to express feelings, anxieties, sadnesses and social situations. The artistic creator attempts to make this entire ample range of possibilities appear and shine through his works.

For some this creative process will be a slow, difficult, painful, discouraging and rending gestation, interrupted by the forces of the surrounding world which impede its self expression. The literature of all parts of the world contains examples of this. Artistic creation is the invention of forms marked by an integrity which nothing can dissolve and by perfection which nothing can compromise. Although the world which it creates is very different from that of our everyday experience it is more real. Heidegger observes that in "the work the being-created is expressly introduced by creation into what is created, so that 'being-created' expressly results."[18]

Thus, it is artistic forms which have full and total meaning, at least they appear so to us: in this things achieve their full human meaning and value. Let us look at an example: The chair which I see in my room is related to things on all sides. When I photograph it immediately it assumes the character of something curtailed and fragmentary. Were the chair to be seen by a painter, such as Van Gogh, however, his gaze would begin from the chair itself and develop a process in which the chair would become a center around which all else in space are gathered so that these parts acquire an existential mode. As a result what would appear in the painting would form a whole. Thus, the meaning of the life is had by one who grasps it aesthetically: nothing is denied; all is given in its fullness. Eugene Delacroix wrote in his *Diary*:

> The artist, with elements which are without value as they stand, composes, invents a whole, creates. In a word, he impresses the imagination of men with the spectacle of their creations. In a peculiar manner he resumes and makes clear for the average man the sensations which things awaken in us, but which we do not see or only vaguely sense in nature.[19]

This creative impulse often is expressed in terms of "interior necessity": more often than the artist seeks the work, it is the work which seeks its own realization in him or her. This necessity is united to a sense of fullness and freedom, of luminous liberation. Paradoxically, in the artist necessity is united with a freedom of spirit which he is able to transfer to his work and to those who really feel it. There are many testimonies to this existential state of the creative act. We are the masters of our creation"[20] says Matisse; Rilke in his letters to a young poet wrote: "a work of art is good when it has been born of necessity."[21] Thus the creative necessity imposes itself as a value in its own right and pervades all aesthetic production.

Although this chapter has insisted upon the aspect of sentiment or feeling in every aesthetic experience, the development of our thematic brings us finally to exalting this as an aesthetic value in its own right. This emerges and reveals itself in artistic experience for, as an aesthetic object, the work of art always presents this dimension of sensible reality.

M. Dufrenne probably has insisted the most luminously upon the importance of the sensible, as well as upon the immanence the unreal in the sensible: which he calls "the apotheosis and apogy of the sensible."[22] The aesthetic object is an intransitive symbol: rather than refer to another thing it contains a relation of "self in self." Its truth is manifested uniquely by its presence: it is an "in itself for us" and its being consists in this "appearing."

Thus far we have completed a picture of values which manifest themselves in what we might call "aesthetic experience." We do not propose that there is a single form of the experience we have described in this chapter. In fact, each historical epoch has its own which enriches the preceding ones. If anything is characteristic today, it is precisely the absence of rigid aesthetic canons, or perhaps the very absence of canons. Our proposition is intended only to show that this experience exists, that it is personal although it cannot be had without the collectivity, and that it reveals profound values which we must draw out, revise, sustain or promote, above all in those historical moments in which life must affirm itself once more. Art and all that it expresses and represents is a profound affirmation of life against death, which is present in the multiple forms of irrational struggles for power, in all manners of tyranny, in the control and manipulation of men and their minds and coercion over all forms of expression, especially those which manifest feelings.

AESTHETICS AND FORMATION: THE RELATION TO ETHICS

Human life implies a pluralism of values which must be recognized before attempting to unify them. It has been possible to see that through aesthetic values and their forms a fundamental part of human existence is brought into play. Obviously man is more than sensibility; nonetheless, this holds immense possibilities as the source of realizations which, through their quality in turn can be a point of meeting with other human values. In other words, we have seen how art involves truth, justice, love, freedom; it is a dimension which can serve one in embracing and synthesizing one's great powers of expression. Whether we seek it or not, consciously or unconsciously, art always has a message; it always moves the spirit or "turns ones head around"; it informs, conforms, educates and promotes.

One can ask to what hidden reason, if there be one, the perceived increase of violence and of its effects can be traced. Undoubtedly the problem is very complex and involves a great multiplicity of values and antivalues. On the basis of the focus of this work the following response might be suggested. There is a torrent of emotivity, a species of "excess" in this historical moment, which man seems to be directing towards destruction rather than creativity. Today a destructive spirit seems to be in motion, exploiting those hidden forces. For example, what can be hoped of a child who cannot observe his/her world without finding him/herself surrounded by conflict, hypocrisy, dishonesty, moral cynicism and falsity. What affirmation of life and of his/-her existence can be proposed if approximately 80% of the scientists work on projects which directly or indirectly lead to the increase of death. For this reason we hold that until we recover the beauty of life, until we appreciate and promote the beauty of nature, we will not love either life or nature. Hence, an educative process which would take up values in all their importance and significance cannot overlook aesthetic value. If we teach love of life, rather than its devaluation as is the present reality, we will eradicate violence or at least one of its causes and avoid submersion in the nihilism of the contemporary world.

This seems a utopia, but why has this conception not received new elaboration rather than seeming to be a challenge to man? This is the challenge for humanity today: either to destroy itself by developing an increasingly predatory animality or to build up the values of justice, love and aesthetic creation, recuperating or building thereby man's authentic stature.

It is not in vain that in certain countries they have understood the need for an "education in sensibility" related to the characteristic elements and aesthetic productions which the collectivity can develop on many levels. We must be concerned lest our schools cut off the infinite capacity of fantasy and creativity which every child possesses. Fortunately, this begins to be corrected by teachers.

Through sharing creative activity with others, children can develop excellent levels of socialization, respect, help and identity, and discover their own capacities. In emphasizing this difference in attitudes and inclinations through clarifying values we should arrive not at incompatibility, but at a greater complementarity. By taking account of the human as a whole, the development of evaluative capacities can be more balanced. It is obvious that one person will tend to realize one value more than others as he/she develops powers, preferences, inclinations and tendencies. This is only natural, but we must not for that reason fall into a value blindness depreciating anything that is not to one's taste. The idea of a hierarchization of values which is so familiar to us can easily degenerate into incomprehension, disequilibrium and intolerance, for when power concentrates upon one determined value, this receives all the emphasis and attention, at the cost of all the others: this is precisely unilateral valuation.

It is not strange that many young people today clearly prefer activities or professions which can enrich them in the immediate future, and thereby promote their social mobility. Though these also are values, as no one would deny, one who begins to hold a questionable ethical view employs all other values simply as means or instruments to obtain these ends. In such a manner, it makes no difference if they must sell their conscience; it is the outcome which counts. This historical reality which we live seems due largely to the valuative unilaterality which technical rationality has imposed upon us. It would be wrong, however, to attempt to identify one source for all our evils in which one could deposit all the responsibility for the present situation, much less one which would devalue the importance of the achievements to which technical rationality has contributed.

More to the point are the contradictions that have developed within these values and which lead progressively to irremediable collapse. As one among many such causes, I would signal the division and depreciation of constitutive human values. It is time to understand that without these values no historicity is possible. We must try to form sensibility in our youth by urging them to rediscover a world other than that which we have constructed. This world of their dreams, of their restlessness, appears impossible today, but in it they might find more justice, love and beauty. It is possible that they will have a second change on this earth.[23]

Universidad Pontificia Bolivariana
Medellin, Colombia

NOTES

1. See the Heideggerian writings on poetry and the work of art, especially the work, "El Origen de la obra de arte" in *Sendas Perdidas* (Buenos Aires: Losada A.A., 1969), pp. 13-67.

2. *Ibid.*, p. 68.

3. Jean Ladrière, *Les enseux de la rationalité* (Paris: Aubier Montaigne, Unesco, 1977), Ch. VII, "L'impact sur l'esthetique," p. 161.

4. *The Republic* is relevant to this aspect and recalls the poetry of Homer.

5. Frag. 123.

6. In *Instauratio Magna*. ". . . la naturaleza no puede conquistarse más que obedeciéndola," cited by Felipe Cid, *Historia de la Ciencia* (Barcelona: E. Planeta, 1977), II, p. 174.

7. Cited by Martin Heidegger in "El origen de la obra de arte," *op. cit.*, p. 66.

8. Machievelli introduced into Western thought a profound distinction and differentiation between what for the Greeks had been a unity: politics, religion and morals. As a result the modern world differentiates the three so that politics is seen as having its own ends and being very distinct from morals and religion. See the work of Umberto Cerroni, *Introducción a la ciencia política*.

9. *Voluntad de poder* (Madrid: Aguilar, 1962), n. 882.

10. Aristotle, *Metafísica* (Madrid: Aguilar, 1969), I 982 b.

11. *Aesthetic* p. 77, cited by J. Plazaola in *Introducción a la estéica* (Madrid: B.A.C., 1973).

12. Juan Plazaola, *op. cit.* See especially the texts cited, p. 311.

13. Vicent Van Gogh, *Cartas a Theo* (Barcelona: Seix Barral, 1972), p. 114.

14. Cfr. Maurice Blanchot, *El espacio literario* (Buenos Aires: Paidos, 1969).

15. Hipolito Taine, cited by J. Plazaola, *op. cit.*, p. 543.

16. Leon Tolstoy, *Qu'est ce que l'art?*, trad. T. de Wyzewa. (Paris: Perrin, 1898), p. 234.

17. Leopoldo Stokowski, cited by J. Plazaola, *op. cit.*, p. 332.

18. Martin Heidegger "El origen de la obra de arte," in *op. cit.*, p. 53. Note that in the Heideggerian interpretation art is not conceived as the creation of forms. Its nature has more the height or stature of truth. Creative production is "a receiving and drawing out of the interior of the relation, for the unveiling of being; creating should be conceived as drawing out from the source."

19. Eugene Delacroix, *The Journal,* trans. by W. Pach (New York: The Viking Press, 1972), p. 421.

20. Henry Matisse, cited by W. Hesse, *Documentos para la comprension de la pintura moderna* (Buenos Aires: 1959), p. 258.

21. Rainer Maria Rilke, *Cartas a un joven poeta* (Madrid: Alianza, 1980), p. 26.

22. Mikel Dufrenne, *Phenomenologie de L'experience esthetique* (Paris: P.U.F., 1953), p. 41.

23. Gabriel Garcia M, *Cien años de soledad* (Argentina: Sudamericana, 1969), p. 351.

24. John Farrelly, "The Human Good and Moral Choice," in G. McLean, F. Ellrod, et al., eds., *Act and Agent: Philosophical Foundations for Moral Education and Character Development* (Washington: The Council for Research in Values and Philosophy and The University Press of America, 1986), pp. 223-269.

CHAPTER VII

THE PERSON
EXPERIENCE OF TRANSCENDENCE
THROUGH IMMANENCE

RUBEN DIAZ

The title of this chapter expresses a philosophical position in relation to the problem of historicity and values. The focus of the chapter will be in large part phenomenological, although often this requires that one enter the fields of sociology, anthropology and theology. I shall seek to contribute my own reflections from a religious point of view in the broader sense of that term.

The focal point of this chapter is man as the subject of his/her history. It will survey this history, proceeding from the immanent to the transcendent, in a manner both personalized and personalizing. I shall draw upon such classical works as *The Phenomenology of Religion* by Gerard van der Leeuw, *The Holy* by Rudolph Otto, and *The Sacred and the Profane* by Mircea Eliade. To these will be added the very important contributions of such modern and contemporary authors as Brede Kirstensen, Jacques Maritain, Ludwig Feuerbach, Frederich Schleiermacher, Paul Tillich and Bronislaw Malinovski.

The first part of the chapter will treat the more universal facets of the theme, describing the human phenomenon in its multiple and complementary dimensions. Man as "being-in-relation" projects himself, progressively opening to nature, to his peers, and even to the Transcendent. Throughout the work the Transcendent will be referred to indifferently as: Power, The Holy, The Sacred and The Transcendent. However, without hiding my point of view as a believer which is an aspect of my own historicity, the chapter is written in an attitude of openness in the painful search for truth.

The second part will undertake a description of some experiences whose ultimate meaning is absolutely different from other values. This will bring forward diverse ways of understanding the meaning of existence which lead in turn to very different ways of defining ethics.

The last part will concentrate upon the family, understood as the specific place where man realizes his historicity. In and through this dimension the human being comes gradually and fully to realize his/her radical relatedness.

In sum, our philosophical reflection will follow the concrete route of the human effort at self-realization. Since a question about the human person requires a response for the person in the concrete, if we follow the pattern of human rationality we should discover the historical forms taken by this basic human dimension.

MAN: A CONSCIOUS PRESENCE IN THE WORLD, WITH THE OTHERS AND OPEN TO THE TRANSCENDENT

Man, A Conscious Presence

This section will reflect the psychological focus of Richard Knowles' chapters in *The Psychological Foundations of Moral Education and Character Development*, and his usage of the terms body, ego and self.[1] This reflects, in turn, the work of Erik Erickson in his *Childhood and Society*. "A human being, thus, is at all times an organism, an ego, and a member of a society and is involved in all three processes of organization: . . . somatic, psychological and social."[2] These three processes need to be developed also in relation to their original and more Freudian conception.

The original process, to which we allude in this part, will be understood in the sense of Sebastian Samay as affectivity "to signify the fundamental orientation, propensity, adherence or tendency by which individuals attend to their ambience."[3] However, we will attend more to the human experience of openness in the concrete circumstances which surround us.

From Aristotle's definition of man as a "political being" to the Sartrean vision of the person as a "useless passion," there has been a continuing search for the sense or meaning of human beings. Innumerable philosophical and humanistic currents of thought have tried by many means to discover the philosophical stone, the key to the destiny of man. This "stone" has often transformed itself into a Pandora's box or Alladin's lamp, the wings of Icarus, a sword of Damocles, or the Cross of the Nazarine; into number, speech or idea; or even into the "Whole."

Men of every epic who have questioned themselves profoundly have asked "Is it possible that all has lost its meaning?" Paul Tillich recounts this search for the ultimate meaning of things through religion.

> Religion comes to fulfill a moral function; it knocks at the door, and is well received, not rejected. But the moment religion makes claims of its own, it is either silenced or thrown out as superfluous or dangerous for morals.[4]

The religious sense is welcomed by an ethics which is always trying to form good citizens, good spouses, good workers, good governors, good military men, good everything--understanding by "good" all that is in agreement or functional for the system. When this does not succeed, there occurs what Tillich describes as follows: "Religion must look around for another function of man's spiritual life, and it is attracted by the cognitive function. Again religion is admitted, but as subordinate to pure knowledge and only for a brief time."[5]

As soon as reason through scientific knowledge feels itself sufficiently capable it demotes the religion to a pre-scientific stage. By that very fact religion becomes obsolete for all who wish to be part of the scientific and technological process. "Once more religion is without a home within man's spiritual life. It looks around for another spiritual function to join. And it finds one, namely, the aesthetic function."[6]

However, when religion is reduced to a mere contemplative state it seeks a new refuge by centering itself upon feeling. As a result, rather than being a critical and rational reality, it is subjected to the whims of emotion. Man thus converts himself into a "useless passion," without meaning or direction. In this state we fall to the depths of subjectivism, as stated by Feuerbach. "If feeling is the essential organ of religion, the nature of God is nothing else than an expression of the nature of feeling; . . . it is already clear from this that where feeling is held to be the organ of the infinite, the subjective essence of religion, the actual data of religion lose their objective value."[7]

At this point, having made historicity our only mode of transcendence, we are trapped in the immanence of time and space. This is the platform which, in conjunction with the dialectical conception of Hegel, would serve as the foundation for Marx's dialectical materialism for which religion would be "the cry of the appeased creature, the opium of the people."

How can we escape from this intricate labyrinth in which the positive sciences have entrapped us in order to obtain meaning and direction for human existence? On the one hand, we must try to rescue the value of human experience in its incessant search for new horizons, avoiding all absolutization of partial aspects, however important they may seem. On the other hand, we must return to the subject of this experience as historical, limited, situated in time and place without losing sight of his limitations. We cannot close our eyes to the frontiers of human knowledge and experience if man is a concrete subject; as situated he must keep his external frontiers. The critical point is to know the form in which man assumes these frontiers.

Turning to the very center of this experience we note that man, being distinguished through his historicity from the other beings about him, perceives himself in different ways without thereby losing his identity or absorbing identities other than his own. Man perceives himself as a body with spatio-temporal dimensions which is the meeting place with surrounding extended and temporal beings. This level of experience is shared with other living beings who are able to perceive their individuality in nature. Here man, along with the animals, senses that it is his individuality that is affected by an external body in a pleasurable or painful manner. What is more, the surrounding bodies influence his feelings of proximity or distance. Man, along with the animals, enjoys or suffers the presence or absence of others of his species. This is the level of primary feelings.

> My body marks out the situations in which hope is entertained and nurtured. I am a sentient creature insofar as I am embodied. Further, the body is the locus of my action. Through my body I appropriate the world as a field of activity. My body is whenever there is a task to be performed or project to be carried through.[8]

In addition, among those things which move themselves, man distinguishes himself through his reflective ability to perceive his individuality. His "ego" senses that it senses, thinks that it thinks, and knows that it knows. One's ontological differentiation from other living beings begins here. Thanks to this level of perception man has a greater capacity for satisfaction or frustration. Though both a man and a beast can be satisfied, only the man can be frustrated because his expectations have not been realized and he knows this to be so. It is here that the good of the valuable--or better, the good of value--begins to stand out, for man begins to make his own valuations and to know when his satisfaction can be increased.

The perception of one's self does not stop here, but continues in the direction of individualization as one perceives him/her self as an individual among other realities and other humans. This experience includes and gives meaning to previous experiences so that one perceives oneself as entirely unique and irrepeatable, even though submerged or challenged by a determined situation. It is then that one perceives what Ortega y Gasset calls "I and my circumstances" to be the proper being of man; Knowles calls this the "self." Appreciation of this does not require an academic preparation or a superior level of abstraction; it is a primordial act, indivisible from self-consciousness itself. Existential philosophers have directed a great part of their reflection to this aspect of human life.

We have described in this part the different phases of an individual's perception, while attempting to avoid an individualistic rationalism. The social dimension of man implies that the ego and self be contemporaneous with the perception of others. In relation to reality, it is thus more appropriate to speak of ourselves (*nosotros*), rather than of a solitary "self." On this point we share the more communitary focus of Max Scheler and Gabriel Marcel who, in general, refer more to the experience of ourselves.

> This is what makes it possible to perceive 'us' (*nosotros*) when one describes or evaluates a personal project. The I is contained in the 'us', although in the ecological perspective the sphere of 'us' is supposed and not made explicit in its referential significance when the monodic 'ego' has been constituted.[9]

As regards values one perceives not only what befits himself, but also what is fitting for others; thus one perceives that much of what seems suitable enters into conflict with what seems suitable to other human beings and, even more, to beings on lower levels of consciousness. This introduces responsibility: one knows that one's conduct must respond to his/her desires without contradicting or negating the desires of others. Simple adaptation to the environment is at the first level of awareness, but it is necessary to go beyond that in a continual effort to readjust the balance between one's individuality and the whole: from this stems the work of ethics.

Man: A Conscious Presence in the World

Moving ahead in our reflection we arrive at the first experience of man: awareness of distance and of proximity in relation to our surrounding universe. We limit ourselves here to the human experience of the physical and biological world which lacks self-reflection. Man senses himself to be part of this spatio-temporal reality of which he is aware through his own bodiliness. From the first moments of life the human being reacts as an individual to nature; from the fetal state he reacts, though in a limited manner, to the exterior space which is the womb of the mother. Along with one's fetal development comes an increasing interdependence, or better, differentiation.

Many studies and experiences in the field of biology provide significant data on this, but who more than the pregnant mother can witness this as she senses the many diverse signs of life on the part of her child. The umbilical cord is both an active and a passive means of communication with the mother and the external world. With birth, direct interaction with the environment begins: the first cry is the first symbolic and meaningful articulation of this dialogue with one's environment. From then on a human being senses him or herself as both surrounded by, and at the same time distant from, things in a process of increasing communication. For this the role of the family is most important, especially the role of the mother during the first months of existence.

Following the analysis of Richard Knowles, which in turn paraphrases the work of Erickson, it seems appropriate to note that the basic relation of the person with his/her environment is in terms of proximity-distance creating in the subject a sensation of security or of threat. "The bodily experience of this stage is one of vulnerability and helplessness, an almost complete dependence on one's caretakers, and the gradual establishment of feeding and caring patterns."[10]

What Erickson has articulated for this stage of life can be extended to the whole of his bodily existence. One always seeks a refuge (proximity) in the world, while at the same time sensing its strangeness (distance). This paradoxical experience accompanies one through one's whole life in different forms and circumstances.

One's "being-in-the-world" (*Gegenheit*) as a vital experience of the human being is perceived also on the second or "ego" level of the person. Here one senses oneself as distinct and at the same time dependent upon the surrounding reality. This is the stage of taking positions; "yes" and "no" are the paradigms of a sense of freedom by which one is searching to differentiate oneself from the environment. The physical world which surrounds one is not definitive because the human being has passed the threshold which differentiates him or her from nature. This is the stage of the will, of wanting or not wanting; it is also the level of reflective reason which "knows" and "knows that it knows." The physical world is perceived as a workshop or showcase. One knows that he/she has influence on the environment and, in turn, is influenced by it. One's "yes" or "no" will be either transforming action, constructing or destroying nature, or passive contemplation, admiring and praising nature. Obviously, there are means between these two extremes, but the "yes" or "no" are generally in function of one's "ego," and hence affirm oneself. Thus, the person takes an active role here; one is no longer limited to passively "feeling" or "perceiving" what is distant or proximate, but enters actively into relation with one's world. This is the dominion of one's will for power and by power which can submit the other to the ego.

As regards values, in contrast to the bodily level where the valuable was what pleased, here the valuable is what is useful. One attempts to instrumentalize nature and relate to objects by means of instruments. One studies, investigates and analyzes reality in order to know it by means of science so as to be able to treat it instrumentally and technically. Here what is good and what is not is decided according to the functional criteria of instrumentalization: nature is good inasmuch as it serves the purposes of the human "ego."

> After the evolution theories, nature cannot be conceived any more as a machine ruled by its internal laws and principles, nor as an object totally external to man but as a process of continuous development. Organismic wholeness is thus the indispensable presupposition of evolution. We consider nature as a dynamic organismic system comprising a continuous range of wholes at levels of progressively increasing complexity and integration.[11]

This text brings us to the third level of the relation of man with nature, that of the conscious and responsible self, inasmuch as the person is aware of being both part of, and apart from, nature. Here the human being is fully conscious of the proximity and distance. Through the sense of proximity, as "the conscious vortex of evolution" in the words of Teilhard de Chardin, one perceives belonging to nature with which one feels a solidarity. The human being experiences him/herself as part of that "protension" of reality which tends toward love in its fullness.

Many mystics and philosophers have elaborated their experience in terms of living this proximity with nature. However, one also has a feeling of distance and contemplates nature as an indecipherable world which confronts him. One experiences the reality of the "boundary" (Paul Tillich) which separates and differentiates him/her from nature, which questions and implores, which attracts and repels, and which unites and separates. This is the full weight of "the other"; nonetheless it is perceived as part of oneself, relating more to the ambit of one's spatial and or quantitative character. One's bodiliness is thus the point of union with the measurable and the point of interconnection with the world of objects. One begins thereby to perceive the implications of historicity and of one's own temporality, sensing oneself as involved in an interactive dialogue with the physical environment.

As this is the level of responsibility, one develops what can be called a "response" to nature by which one is challenged. One's will to dominate is transformed into a search for significance, direction and meaning.

In hoping I open myself to the many perspectives of

life situations; in willing I take a stand in the phase of this ambiguity; in imagining, I begin to move in certain directions. I imagine myself doing something and this image invites action which is smooth, integrated and purposeful.[12]

Hope, will and creative imagination are man's progressive responses in his dialogue with nature. At this level value includes a sense of the future inasmuch as man is aware, not only of the partial realizations in the present, but also of the possible fullness of the future. His action must have meaning and direction; value will consist in the progressive realization of one's interaction of nature.

Man: A Conscious Presence in the World with Others

The experience of distance and proximity is sharpened through one's relation to one's peers. One gives continuous and dramatic witness to this from the time of infancy when one feeds anxiously at the breast of one's mother until in old age the sick person presses with desperation the hands of loved ones. (In contrast, and from his existential perception of distance, John Paul Sartre would say that "others" are "hell," for their stare reduces me to an object of scrutiny. This experience of alienation has been a dominant theme of existential philosophy).

One experiences "others" at different levels of proximity and distance as one's bodiliness differentiates and limits one in the world with others. Spatio-temporal characteristics are a permanent sign of this limitation. At the same time, however, thanks to this bodiliness one has access to others. Without my body I would be nowhere; bodiliness constantly summons me to the world of other physical beings. The danger is that I might remain at this level of "being-with-others" at which others are a "solitary multitude" and I an "anonymous" being among and before them.

Bodiliness is lived most strongly in a sexual relation. If there is no "ego" or "responsible and conscious self" here the other is greatly estranged or distant, even in the act of greatest physical proximity. In legal codes such a relation would be considered a violation or a mere commercial transaction.

When the "ego" is involved in our relations with others we pass from simple pleasure or sorrow to the level of rationality and the field of logic; our actions are oriented functionally according to our role. This is the case of professional physical contact in which there is a fulfillment of roles according to certain norms. The patient accepts the doctor being cold, efficient and manipulative during an operation.

As an "ego" I have a certain distance from others.

My ego functions primarily in terms of reflective thinking and willing. I reflect rationally on a situation, think about it, and then make a decision. I attack reality in terms of a problem-solving situation and I am in control of what I am doing.[13]

Being thus "in the situation" I see others also as "situated."

At this level my conduct is basically that of accommodating or rejecting. I produce things because I want to have them without any personal commitment. My relations with the others are managed within the limits of politeness, courtesy, convenience or laws. With conduct that reflects all these I will be an honorable member of the society; if not I will be a misfit, a dangerous delinquent, and penalized as such.

It is when the "conscious self" enters one's relations with "others," that we are really in the world of interpersonal relations with its classical dimensions of presence and distance, of immanence and transcendence. At this level one becomes conscious of belonging to the human community and assumes attitudes of responsibility, autonomy and obedience, of solicitude and love.

I as self have a respectful reverence for another person. I have the propensity to give to, and to be one with, him. I have no need to manipulate or dominate him, nor do I need to reduce him to satisfy my own needs. I am not reduced by his sensuality, nor do I analyze him. I feel a spontaneous and centrifugal inclination to accept, affirm and understand this person.

In love, the most fundamental and highest form of self-interaction, I reveal and offer the most intimate dimension of my being-my self, . . . I take off my everyday masks to be-myself-for-the-other.[14]

At this level one has an authentic experience of the distance/proximity of others and the "protension" is almost totally completed. I say "almost" because what is significant does not stop here; one looks for meaning "beyond" this encounter.

The Person: A Conscious Presence in the World of Others and Open to the Transcendent

Such disparate expressions as potension, vital impulse, opening, living spirit, collective unconscious, spirit of the nations, dialectical materialism, ultimate meaning, society without classes, nirvana, transcendence, samsara, history, eschaton, pleroma and God all bring us to man's great existential question:

"What is all of this for"? The final sense of the history of humanity presents itself to us partially in its vivid historicity as the continual search for plenitude.

The human person's experience of transcendence is realized on the same basis as one's immanence, namely, in one's circumstances and at the very center of one's historicity. One experiences one's bodiliness through those who are external. Similarly, sensing an "openness" beyond bodiliness does not choke off one's existential being, but enables one to transcend their corporality. Through one's ego one is open, not only to others who are similar, but much more to that which transcends.

The same thing happens with one's experience of the "conscious self." This experience of transcendence implies being both something and nothing at the same time, being in the extended world but not simply a part of it, being with others but not totally submerged in them. One senses one's existence constantly as menaced by nothingness and at the same time as attracted or protended toward a greater plenitude of one's "existent nonexistence." This "thinking reed" (Blaise Pascal) tries to affirm him/herself despite the fact that one's supports drift before the winds and torments of nothingness.

Religious writers have written graphically and artistically of this experience of the boundary of being and nothingness, between "being" and "Being." The book of Wisdom places in the mouth of the impious his permanent captivation with the bodily dimension of reality and his resultant loss of "relationality" and "transcendence."

> Brief and troublous is our lifetime: neither is there any remedy for man's dying, nor is anyone known to have come back from the nether world.
> For haphazard were we born, and hereafter we shall be as though we had not been; because the breath in our nostrils is a smoke and reason is a spark at the beating of our hearts, and when this is quenched, our body will be ashes and our spirit will be poured abroad like unresisting air. Even our name will be forgotten in time and no one will recall our deeds. So our life will pass away like the traces of a cloud and will be dispensed like a mist . . . for our lifetime is the passing of a shadow.[15]

Without a sense of transcendence, the relation of the person to the whole would lead to a merely bodily ethic--one of pleasure--as in the text cited. Its logical conclusion is: "Come, therefore, let us enjoy the good things that are real and use the freshness of creation avidly."[16] Stoics, Epicureans, materialists and positivists all pursue philosophic reflection with the same attitude.

Taking up once again the pattern of phenomenological reasoning let us turn to Rudolph Otto, Gerard van der Leeuw and Mircea Eliade who have devoted special attention to the human experience of transcendence. The religious experience of openness to transcendence and to the Transcendent is described particularly well by religious authors on the basis of their own experience.

> When I behold your heavens, the work of your fingers, the moon and the stars which you set in place, what is man that you should be mindful of him, or the son of man that you should care for him? You have made him little less than the angels, and crowned him with glory and honor. You have given him rule over the works of your hands, putting all things under his feet.[17]

In a parallel vision of totality and the quest for meaning, Taoism, for example, sees this unity in the person's belonging or proximity to the Whole.

> Obtaining the One, Heaven was made clear.
> Obtaining the One, Earth was made stable.
> Obtaining the One, the Gods were made spiritual.
> Obtaining the One, the valley was made full.
> Obtaining the One, all things lived and grew.[18]

In some manner human beings grasp a relation which transcends the limits of themselves, of nature and of others. Having gone beyond the level of bodiliness, without suppressing it, they move to the level of the Ego and of the Conscious Self where they perceive a "presence" which no longer leaves space for "absence." Non-rational beings are not capable of this experience; only persons, as standard-bearers of this open search for the fullness of reality, can experience the presence of the Other, which is "totally different" from any experience cited above. The perception of this Other is highly complex and ambiguous; one feels both strongly attracted and in turn repulsed for it is perceived at the same time as both "fascinating" and "tremendous." These two primary facets of the perceived object are categorized by Rudolph Otto as "The Numenal," a concept which, in any case, seeks to express sharing in something radically different from the rest of reality.

The proximity of the Other is felt as a sense of "fascination" which impels one to a total ecstasy in what we sense as "the ground of our own existence" (John Robinson) or as "the ultimate concern of my own being" (Paul Tillich). This was the experience narrated by one of the evangelists regarding the transfiguration when the disciple Simon exclaimed: "Rabbi, it is wonderful for us to be here; if you wish, I will make three tents here, one for you, one for Moses and one for Elijah" (Mc. 9,5).

Simon Peter was hardly thinking of himself or of his companions, but was fully absorbed in the vision which he contemplated. In this field of religious experience it is difficult to distinguish the participation of the "ego" and of the "conscious self" inasmuch as all these sentiments experienced by the human person in contact with the "Totally Other" are by nature totally enveloping. Religious experience is an experience of wholeness in which one perceives nature and him/herself as surrounded by a "nouminal" reality which gives meaning to all that has been said above. This does not signify that the totally distinct or "Other" is only the sum and conjunction of the parts. Some religions which have experienced self-transcendence in the sense of Absolute Transcendence seem to run the risk of canceling the individuality of the Other in my own subjectivity or of submerging my subjectivity in the great Whole.

> Religious experience, further, is that experience whose significance refers to the whole, it can therefore never be understood from the standpoint merely of the moment, but only and always from that of eternity. Its meaning is an ultimate meaning and is conceived with the 'last things,' its nature is eschatological, and transcends itself; while for man it implies an ultimate, a boundary.
>   Like all experience, nonetheless, religious experience is related to the object, and this indeed in a pre-eminent sense. . . . In religious experience, however, this orientation is a presence, subsequently an encounter, and finally a union. And in this presence not he who experiences is primary, but He who is present; for He is the holy, the transcendently Powerful.[19]

The awe which man feels before "the sacred" (Mircea Eliade) is a clear indication that what is experienced is distinguished and distanced from the experience itself as well as from the one who experiences. "The Holy" (Rudolph Otto) is not therefore a projection of my own subjectivity, as Ludwig Feuerbach would have us think: "In the object which he contemplates, man becomes acquainted with himself; consciousness of the objective is the self-consciousness of man."[20]

Much less is it a projection of one's frustration in relation to possible and future possibilities, as Marx held in his *Communist Manifesto*, cataloging all religion as "the groan of an oppressed creature, the opium of the people." Nor is it a "collective obsession" derived from an "original traumatizing frustration" as Sigmund Freud would suggest. Finally, "The Holy" is not, as Edward Taylor projected, the self-projection of an "animist" experience by man as "soul" or the "idealization" of existing social structures as Emile Durkheim suggested in his work, *Elemental Forms of Religious Life.*

The Holy is perceived as "totally distinct" from the subjectivity of man, from nature and from other human beings. The ambiguity arises when this "Transcendence" is perceived through immanence. This leads many to see themselves as "The Other," to perceive nature as sacred, or finally to sacralize some social system as absolute. This rationalization of the religious experience through the "ego" transforms religion into a "mechanical domination," a matter of "Power" by means of fetishism and magic. Often this is in conjunction with a "sacred mandate" which sacralizes the political power or in ritual practices for purification or for the propitiation of evil powers. We will return to this point with greater detail in the third section of this chapter.

When a person in one's totality as a "conscious self," places oneself before the "Other" as the fullness of being and meaning, one comes to a better understanding one's situation of total dependence and creatureliness, on the one hand, and the completion of all value, on the other. Spontaneously there arises the supplication: "You alone are Holy; You alone are Lord; You are alone the most high." Adoration is one's spontaneous response, which transforms itself into prayer rather than mere evocation or ceremony.

> The 'Holy' will then be recognized as that which commands our respect, as that whose real value is to be acknowledged inwardly. It is not that the awe of holiness is itself simple 'fear' in the face of what is absolutely overpowering, before which there is no alternative to blind, awe-struck obedience. 'Thou alone art holy' is rather a paean of praise, which, so far from being merely a faltering confession of the divine supremacy, recognizes and extols a value, precious beyond all conceiving.[21]

Thus, we have come to the point of attributing the highest possible value to reality through the immanent experience of the

"Transcendent" as absolute value which gives full meaning to all the other values of reality. Through historicity one sees value manifested in its totality. It is the "openness" of reality or its "protention" that makes this epiphany possible. Thus, Mircea Eliade dedicates a large part of his reflection to the human experience of "sacred time" and "sacred place" which is expressed synthetically in the celebration of the religious "fiesta" and even more in the "sacred banquet," all of which are symbols which express at least partially man's living the sacred. The symbols of sacred time and sacred place draw us to a comprehension of "The Holy" in history, while at the same time its radical distinction from profane time and place puts us on guard before any immanentist reductionism of the religious phenomenon. Thus, what is manifest simply as present should not be taken as an "epiphany." The sacred is perceived historically, but without being identified with history. (The category of sacralization will be utilized to signify any absolutization of the relative.) Authentic religious experience surpasses the categorizations of the "ego" and is located in the context of the personal and social communication of man with "the Transcendent."

In the categories of Knowles, not hope or will, but love will be the basis of the true encounter of man with The Other, and through that with nature. (This is the theological principle of "sacramentality" or "mediation" clearly explained by Edward Schilebeeckx in his work *Christ, Sacrament of Encounter with God.*) Mircea Eliade concludes:

> The non-religious person rejects transcendence, accepts the relativity of 'reality', and comes to doubt even the meaningfulness of existence. The modern non-religious person assumes a new existential situation: he sees himself as the sole subject and agent of history and rejects all appeal to transcendence. . . . Man makes himself, and he can make himself completely only to the degree that he desacralizes himself and his world. The sacred is the major obstacle to his freedom and he will not become himself until the moment he is radically demystified: he will not be truly free until he has killed the last god.[22]

The God of Israel defines himself to Moses as: "I am who will be being" (Ex 3,4), understanding by this that the Israelite people will experience his presence in the history to follow.

From the Consciousness of "the Other"
to the Existence of "the Other"

In the above sections we have perceived the form in which

the person's consciousness is made present to himself and open to the presence of others.

There is danger of a subjective relativism in the move from thought to existence found in the well known Anselmian argument to prove the existence of Being Itself on the basis of the convergence of possibility with reality. Some of the above quotes might give the impression that we take the existence of the Transcendent as proven. In fact, such biblical citations have been used from an anthropological perspective without either engaging our personal religious option or negating other forms of religious experience.

The dialectic of Hegel refers fundamentally to the relation of the subject with the object, or to a dialogue between consciousness and any existent external to that consciousness. Feuerbach limited this dialogue to subjects and their projections, and thus to a monologue of the person with oneself. On this basis religion would be but a gigantic projection of the being of the human person. Only thus can one understand the process of secularism which believes it has definitely uprooted God from the ambit of existence and reduced Him to an illusion in order that man might achieve his/her proper autonomy. This is the solemn announcement of Thomas Altizer who proclaims: "We must realize that the death of God is an historical event, that God has died in our cosmos, in our history, in our *existenz*."[23] (We will not argue here with the theology of the "death of God" because it assumes to conclude where we started. Besides, Harvey Cox's *Secular City* would end in postulating a secular God very similar to the Transcendent.)

The traditional arguments of causality, order and justice have been used for centuries to prove the existence of God by those who accept them as valid. But we do not seek here to prove the real existence of The Other with the same scientific criteria as positive sciences. The only thing that we have sought to establish has been the reality of our experience of the other and of The Other. We have not tried to demonstrate the objective existence of each of the objects of our perception, although to treat of The Other it seems necessary to affirm once again the essentially "relational" character of our being. However, this directionality to others would not make sense if it did not have an existing and inclusive goal or object. Our epistemological position is that with the human type of reality comes a disjunction: either men and existing ontological reality have a sense, direction, and meaning or, on the contrary, everything is without sense, direction and meaning: all is absurd.

Jean Paul Sartre opts for the second alternative and, coherent with that option, affirms that "man is a useless passion."

Nothing could convince Sartre of the contrary because he had already assumed the existential posture that all is meaningless.

However, this posture does not seem correct for most humans; the absurd does not appear to be the permanent result of our experience, for which--against Sartre's "No Exist"--there should be a way out. Paul Tillich assumes in his work, *The Courage to Be*, this "existential anguish" through which the being is conscious of the possibility of not being. This is "the expression of finitude from within" in its ultimate consequence which pushes one to the very boundary between being and non-being. On the basis of facing this anguish of senselessness and meaningless, and acting despite it, Tillich postulates the existence of an "ultimate sense of our existence." The very consciousness of fault projects "the courage to accept oneself as accepted despite being unacceptable."

Contemporary man, no longer impressed by causal proofs of the existence of the transcendent, searches rather for the meaning of life than for its cause. He looks more for an ultimate meaning than for an explicative principle, more for foundation than for exaltation, more for an experience of mystery than for its comprehension. Thus John Robinson speaks of God as "the ground of our own existence" and St. Augustine defined the divine as "interior to myself." "Creation is not a description of an event which took place sometime before, but the basic description of the relation between God and the world."[24]

Thus we have returned to the beginning of the chapter where we established man's experience of relatedness. Here we have added the ontological foundation of this relationality as the analogical participation of beings in Transcendent Being. If beings are, it is because they are in an analogous manner to "He Who Is." "Relation is a basic ontological category. . . . God as being-in-itself is the ground of every relation, in whose life all relations are present beyond the distinctions between potentiality and actuality."[25]

SACRALIZATION OF VALUE

Value and the Absolute

The first part of this chapter was essentially phenomenological, the second part was principally descriptive and historical regarding what happens when any of the poles of human relation--ego - world - society - the Sacred--is taken as the sole value in terms of which all the others have their meaning. Now we shall describe different "scales of values" which can be given by fixing serially upon one of these as the fundamental value of life.

We have spoken of sacralization in the etymological sense

of "secare" with its sense of separating, breaking off, or differentiation. Thus "the sacred" becomes the different, the transcendent, or the valuable, which by right separates itself from every other value as the most important--as the first and ultimate value which founds all others. This makes one value absolute in contrast to the relativity of all the rest. We refer to value in terms of "valuable" on the basis of its having a significance in itself and on this basis being perceived by us as attractive and worthy of our possessing and holding it. Our attitude and conduct will be determined by the object we have valued, by the specific form in which it has been valued, and by us who perceive something or someone to be of value.

Value as "Myself"

The selection of the individual as the central and absolute value basically will be at the level of body and of ego inasmuch as the conscious and responsible self by definition does not restrict the ultimate sense of reality to the conscious subject. The assumption, with the philosopher Protagoras, of "man as center of all things"--the pivotal point of existence--has generated results that are at once fascinating and deceptive. From mythic man, who rejected all heteronomy in order to concentrate in himself, up to the contemporary military-industrial complex, which rejects the other as a pole for human relations, we have examples of the absolutization of man as individual above all other values. Religions see this situation as "sin"; philosophers make different qualifications, generally positive; while science or technology are employed to provide such an individual with a sense of security in the face of the menacing realities which surround it.

Where corporality is the focus of one's values, innumerable types of thinking and practice exalt the body as the absolute: from the tantric cults and practices to contemporary grotesque sexual orgies, from mystical valuations of the body to its commercialization as merchandise, from beauty contests to the glorification of physical force in boxing. "Therapy" groups practice "letting go" and "turning on"--"whatever might help reawaken the life you are capable of living, in yourself, with others.[26]

It is not surprising that in contrast to these exaggerations of the body there should develop contrary movements which tend to castigate the body as something evil in order to elevate, redeem or liberate one from the bonds of space and time, and so to float in a mystical ecstasis of spirituality. Here one finds some ascetical schools which see the body as the first enemy in the search for "transcendental unity" and employ fasts, flagellations, and pain in the attempt to force the body under the dominion of the spirit. Thomas a Kempis warns us regarding corporeality:

> Truly it is a misery to live upon the earth. The more spiritual a man desires to be the more bitter this present life becomes to him. . . . For to eat and to drink, to sleep and to wake, to labor and to rest, and to be subject to the other necessities of nature is truly a great misery.[27]

From focusing upon oneself as the center of one's universe of values and reducing all the rest of reality to one's unconditional service there arises a series of individualist currents of thought: subjectivist, idealist, emotivist, voluntarist, nihilist, existentialist or relativist.

In his encounter with nature those centered in themselves submit to their whims all resources and all the laws and forces of nature, creating of themselves a demiurgic and omnipotent image. Lacking an ethics of responsibility they subject to their ego all persons beyond themselves. Others are good or evil inasmuch as they serve or do not serve their interests. This leads to the creation of individualistic social structures where the competency and survival of the strongest is the sole law of life. Consumption begins to be for the sake of consumption, art for arts sake, and science for the sake of science: these among others are the slogans with which the search for self-realization without limit is undertaken. "Time is money" and "space is where I live well" are the slogans of such a vision (Alan Touraine). This is the "one dimensional man" of Herbert Marcuse who works out his life in a gigantic structure that ends by flattening him: he is the solitary man in the lonely crowd.

In these terms one admits the existence of the Transcendent only in order to search one's own favor and utility through magical practices and rituals which submit "the power of the gods" to one's personal will and benefit. Any intention on the part of nature, of others or of the holy to retrieve their autonomy would be strongly repressed, simply ignored or, in the best of cases, borne stoically. The proclamation of the death of God is the final recourse of this pretended absolute autonomy. Such are the persons who set themselves up as the supreme value of existence.

St. Augustine depicted with magisterial lines the construction of two worlds centered on distinct values. "Two loves give birth to two cities: the earthly city, developed the love of itself at the cost of the love of God; in the celestial city its God was

developed at the cost of the love of self."[28] These are two absolutely different positions regarding the ultimate values of
existence and they call for entirely different conduct on the
part of persons. "This city called Babylon has also those who
hoped only for an earthly peace, imagining all their happiness in
its terms and working indefatigably for the realization of this
earthly republic."[29] "Those who search the true peace, obedient
to God, and reconciled with men, live by faith which works by
love."[30]

A common characteristic of all the ethics which arise from
a vision of the world ultimately grounded in humans is their
phrenetic race for happiness in any and every form provided it
does not imply the loss of their individual enjoyment and possessions.

Value as Nature

In the search for knowledge the attitude of contemporary
scientists with their positivist and pragmatic roots is not a new
posture, for hedonism and empiricism have always based all
upon a physical and tangible encounter with the world of things.
For the scientist, whatever cannot be tested by the instruments
of positive science cannot be considered real. Dialectical materialism follows another systematic method in searching for
truth. At the root of all these approaches, however, there lies a
radical and exclusive option for matter as the sole developing
reality. In the last analysis they consider nature to be the axis
of the whole of reality.

When one subjects metaphysics to economy and to politics
one follows the praxis of all such theories according to which
progress is the ultimate objective of human activity. Well-being
and development are the goals which modern man pursues by
whatever means, convinced that the greater the benefits extrac-
ted from nature the greater the well-being of the human race.
This pragmatic vision of progress is bound intimately to blind
credence in the power of science and technology.

Paradoxically, the belief in the capacity of the "Homo
Faber" concludes by submitting mankind entirely to the super-
human power of technology. A dramatic example of that affirmation is the disturbing and absurd possibility of the destruction
of the planet through the uncontrolled function of the mechanisms of nuclear strategy. Persons need not even take part in the
fatal act of "pushing the button"; the machine itself could in-
itiate the lightening process of world holocaust. "In the past it
was possible to destroy a village, a town, a region and even a
country. Now it is the whole planet that has come under
threat." With these words Pope John Paul II at Hiroshima sum-

marized the anguished worry of the contemporary world.

In this way we have paradigmatically come to the same situation as that of the primitive peoples who sacrificed innumerable victims to mountains, rivers, animals, woods and nature. Now, however, one sacrifices millions of men and women to Industry, Progress, Security, the Balance of Power, Western Christian Civilization, Society without Classes, Science and-Technology. The temples of the new gods are the impressive highways, supermarkets, sky scrapers and nuclear plants among others built upon the deterioration of nature and the submission of humankind to a permanent insecurity psychosis.

> We are a society without ideas, and a society without ideas is a society without hope and imagination. We have fallen into the trap of violence, militarism and competitiveness, which is the world that people without ideas have to resort to because it is the world where there is no freedom.[31]

Sacralizing and absolutizing nature leads to a loss or diminution of other dimensions of human rationality, of one's own person, of others and of transcendence.

Value as Society

The theme: "Values and Myself" developed above should be extended. There we noted the implications for the individual of making the human absolute. Here we shall consider briefly its socio-political dimension, namely, when society in any of its structures sets itself up as absolute in human existence.

With reason the first Christians were considered the "atheists" of their time because they refused to render cult to the emperor of the Roman world. "Imperium was originally the unlimited power possessed by the divinely approved early kings, who fulfilled a number of roles: lawgiver, priest, military commander, judge. The emperor was a living law on earth."[32]

Although the Romans lived in a political dualism between absolutism and constitutionalism, they remain paradigmatic for Western history in that they placed political power above all. Their political model of the theocratic order repeats itself in the twenty centuries of history which follow. It has as its common characteristics: the absolute and unquestioned power of authority, the divine character of its origin, a capacity for absorbing all other aspects of society, a pyramid structure of power, an invarying pressure to orient the changes of persons, and imperialist and conquistador tendencies.

It was a wise politician of the sixteenth century, Nicholas Machiavelli, who counseled the princes to note that "reasons of state" were above all moral or religious considerations, but that both of these could be used in order to make their rule more efficacious and lasting. The Prince might not be religious, but it was best for him to seem to be so if it helped to strengthen his authority. "One does not govern men by the power of 'Our Fathers'," counsels Machiavelli; the church counsels only resignation and humility. Political value was for him virtue par excellence; it was nothing other than the possession of all the qualities leading to political success. "It is therefore the duty of princes and heads of republics to uphold the foundation of the religion of their countries, for then it is easy to keep their people religious, and consequently well conducted and united."[33]

This mode of utilizing religion in politics conforms to the golden rule of all theocratic governments: "Whose kingdom, his religion." That is, the governor does not take into account the religion of the people, but imposes his own. The wars of religion and the religious separation of England would be only corollaries to the general sacralization of political power, as well as a reaction to the politicization of the Catholic hierarchy.

Many politicians who seek political power, do so in the name of "others," but when they attain power their altruistic horizon often disappears--if indeed it had even really existed-- and a Machiavellian egocentricity of power for power's sake shows through. This critique is equally valid for the socio-economic political systems, both individualist and collective. In the first system political power is generally at the service of the dominant class; in the second system it is in the hands of a bureaucratic minority which claims for itself a transitory power which in reality is interminable, namely, until the proletariat is installed in power.

The law is another idol of a sacralizing and sacralized politics. It is claimed to be "the sovereign will of the people": "voice of the people, voice of God." The great offenses against such a god-state are rebellion, disobedience, robbery and conflict. The good is agreement with the law; evil is all that is against the law: "A hard law, but a law" is the supreme reason for all authoritarian imposition and the will of power becomes the fundamental principle of all human social life.

> Life itself is essentially appropriation, injury, conquest of the strange and weak, suppression, severity, obtusion of peculiar focus, incorporation and, to put it most mildly, exploitation . . . because life is precisely Will to Power. . . . Exploitation does not belong to a depraved, or imperfect and primitive society: it belongs to the nature of the living being as a primary organic function; it is a consequence of the intrinsic

Will to Power, which is precisely Will to Life.[34]

In this way the apparent altruism of the political order is in reality enthroned and idealized power as such. Hence, every means is valid for achieving and maintaining it (Machiavelli): all reality is fundamentally nothing other than the "will to power" (Nietzsche).

The "other" human being, which in principle was taken as the absolute value and final purpose of political action, turns into the "valued." One is valuable to the degree that one is functional and useful within the structure of power. "The value or worth of a man, as of all other things, is his price, that is to say, so much as would be given for the use of his power; therefore it is not absolute, but a thing dependent on the need and judgment of another."[35]

Once again the human has become a simple object, a thing at the service of power. One seeks to subject the other to one's own goal of satisfying one's anxiety for power, thereby converting man into "a wolf for man," according to Hobbes' expression.

The Other as Absolute

This last part of our second section will focus upon the absolutization of any *form* of the Transcendent to the exclusion and elimination of all other values. Later we will return again to this theme, though with a more inclusive and integrating focus.

At times the search for The Other as the Totally Distinct, Power, Holy, Sacred, Foundation of Being, Subsistent, Highest, All Powerful, Creator, etc., wrongly tends to annul all the rest of reality by omitting all immanence, and hence all relative existence. Historically, this tendency is had whenever one sacrifices the human person, nature or society "in the name of God." Every pantheistic vision of reality absorbs all into the One, of which all is the necessary manifestation or "unfolding" in history.

In distinction from the "historical absolutes" previously noted (the ego, the world and society), the Transcendent as absolute is above and beyond all reality and nonetheless is the principle of all that historicity signifies. Gerard Van de Leeuw in his work *Phenomenology of Religion* develops a characterization of the different religions according to the criteria of the object of their beliefs. Thus, he classifies religions into: "Religions of detachment and flight, combat, repose, uneasiness, infinity, nothingness, majesty, will and love."[36]

These religious forms follow the underlying image of the absolute. A brief look at such forms brings us to the conclusion that the major part of these assume a distance or abyss between man and the Absolute. In some this distance is totally annulled by transformation in mystical identity. Once again we draw upon the theories developed by Otto of the "fascinating" or "awesome" and the "tremendous" in the sense explained above.

> Islam is in the first, second and third place a religio-social complex, in which equal emphasis is due to each factor of this combination. . . . It develops a colossal power which is rooted in its faith in God, or, in other words, it takes *God's sovereignty in absolute seriousness.*[37]

Religious forms which stress the total distance of the Absolute conclude to an existential nothingness for man. In contrast to such religions of distance are those which stress total "proximity" as do certain religions of India. "The mainstream of Hindu religious sentiment . . . directs itself towards the infinite and attempts to attain it by asceticism."[38]

The various forms of religious nominalism ultimately include either the absolute in the relative or the relative in the absolute, while the forms of religious dualism separate the two irreconcilably as disparate and even contradictory existences. On the one hand, religious practice that is entirely separated and distanced from socio-political life divides human life, binding it to idols in a sanctuary--which ultimately will turn into a prison. This either renders religion entirely innocuous and obsolete or puts it at the service of mere human caprice. On the other hand, socio-political practice socializes these idols and converts them into demigods which are then manipulated for any purpose: holy wars, sacrificial deaths or the elimination of subjected groups.

FAMILY: THE CENTER OF COMMUNION AND PARTICIPATION

Foundations

The title of this last section appears to diverge from what has preceded. The first section was a sociological analysis of the relational dimension of the human person, leading to a phenomenological analysis of the distinct levels of relationships. Later, we showed the real effects of the absolutization and exclusive polarization of any one factor in human relations. By way of conclusion, we will seek now to recover the identity of the person through life in the family as the most distinctive expression of one's "relatedness" and "sociality."

Recent scientific experiments in the field of embryology and human genetics could lead one to the false conclusion that human life is created in a laboratory. In reality there exists no such "creation," for what takes place there is but genetic manipulation. Should a new synthesis of amino acids or a posterior manipulation of already existing human genes be called a recreation of life? Will the family remain the "natural context" for the reproduction and development of the human species? These and other questions will be answered only in the future.

In any case, the ontological and ethical principles will remain the same, though perhaps with different formulations. One principle which arises from the experience of mankind is its "relational being"; another is the "gradual" or progressive character of its realization through history. In the last section of this chapter, beginning with and through family life, we will discuss the relations with one's self, with the world, with others and with the transcendent.

The Family Dimension of Human Beings

> The individual cannot become human by oneself; self-identity is real only in communication with another self. Alone, I sink into gloomy isolation; only in community with others in the act of mutual discovery do I emerge. (Karl Jaspers, *On My Philosophy*.)[39]

What Jaspers affirms regarding the human being as "a relational being" we assert by the term 'family dimension', namely, that the fullness of one's being as human is achieved through intimate relations with other human beings. These relations are first on a biological level, for one's individual life does not begin abruptly, but is part of a process already begun; one's ontological existence is related to prior existences as effect to cause. Thus, references to mythical "first parents" or "progenitor" point to human beings who are the sources of other lives. In turn, this new existence is potentially linked through the same order of cause and effect to subsequent existences. This gives real strength to the term "human family" which, in turn, is "related" to the rest of the cosmos in intimate existential relations.

Beyond this cosmic human meaning there is the family in its literal sense. In it we distinguish such constitutive and complementary relations as those of "paternity," "spouse," "child to parent" and "child to child." No human being is outside these relations, for all are offsprings with relations to parents and vice versa. Of the four relations cited the relation of child to parent appears the most universal both in biological and in ontological terms. Though the others might not have their biological counterpart, they remain ontologically possible.

When we say that we are all sons or daughters we affirm the radical and universal character of filiation as actualized within the family. This is the result of a previous union of human beings who, for different motives, shared their generative powers: one's ability to generate can be realized only in cooperation with another. In turn, this implies two relationships: no one is a child without parents, nor a parent without a child. Like an umbilical cord, this genetic biological line ties us to space and time and, in turn, makes us historical. Thus the "family" dimension of the person is a constitutive factor in one's essence, for all "rational beings" are born from flesh and blood: even the mythic cosmogonies image the origins of all realities through divine births.

The family dimension of the person is so proximate and therefore obvious that at times it is displaced by a desire for existential solitude. This, however, is not done without catastrophic effects. Kafka, (*The Castle*), Dostoyevsky (*The Brothers Karamazov*), Camus, (*The Plague*), Malraux, (*Human Destiny*), Sartre (*Nausea*), and Auden (*The Age of Anxiety*) all attempt to acknowledge tacitly or expressly a great truth about human beings and a great value of existence, namely, that "it is not good that man should be alone. . . . God made man to his own image, made him in the image of God. Man and woman both he created them." (*Genesis* 1,27-2,18).

Sexuality: A Foundational Human Endeavor

All human beings are sexually differentiated. Like the rest of reality, humans are divided into two basic types: masculine and feminine. Being consubstantial to one's nature, our personal being is characterized in an exclusive and complementary manner by one of these two existential forms--we are man or woman, not both at the same time.

Nevertheless, masculinity does not counterpoise itself to femininity: the two are complementary so that one cannot be realized without its counterpart. Ultimately sexuality is defined not by genitality, but by the very being of the person. For this reason sexual complementarity does not necessarily include genital action. Further, when one aspect is separated from the other there arise in our society such common practices as prostitution, free love and commercial pornography. Placing the masculine and feminine in irreconcilible counterposition gives rise to reductionist views and practices which ultimately sacrifice either the person at the altar of society or one's nature at the altar of egoism. "We need to think of ourselves no longer as exclusively 'masculine' or exclusively 'feminine', but rather as whole beings in whom the opposite qualities are ever-present."[40]

Independently of their role in society human beings perceive themselves as either man or woman, thereby promoting their heterosexual complementarity. Thus, the family is the place where the person initially meets him or herself, the world beyond and "the Other." Because these characteristic forms of interrelation are determined by one's being as masculine or feminine, these relations reflect one's individuality and nature and lead to one's progressive human realization.

The Family: A Systemic Unity of Intimacy and Participation

Finally, the family is the priviledged place for the historical realization of the human being. It is in the family and on its basis that one actuates one's "relational being" on its different planes.

> As lonliness and solitude are respectively destructive and creative ways of being alone, so conformity and community are destructive and creative ways of being with others. In conformity and community there is an orientation toward the other, rather than toward oneself in loneliness and solitude. This orientation toward the other can take one of two forms. It can take the form of a self-oriented submission to the look of the other, or it can posture a situation of creative participation. . . . Community is the positive expression and existential fulfillment of the we-experience.[41]

The family makes concrete the possibility for a real encounter of "I" with "thou." This is projected in a "we" that is generative of "others" within a spatio-temporal context. As the priviledged space of personal intimacy the family makes it possible for a person to encounter themselves and others. Other human groups, different from the family, participate in this in a complementary manner, but only in the family does genitality find its full sexual dimension.

The social and religious sanction of family ties is posterior to the family itself, not constitutive of its nature. For this reason there can be integral families which are not recognized as such by the law which attends only to its own formalities. But the contrary can be true as well: a society can sanction positively a determined form of family life which in reality is not a family or a home. Even if recognized by the law as legitimate, homosexual unions can never constitute a family nucleus. The same can be said of certain forms of sexual promiscuity such as "group marriages" or "open families." Monogomy appears to offer the best possibilities for personal self realization. Without qualification we hold that this judgment, though drawn from cultural experience, has universal value. We respect other forms of family organization without, however, considering them to be absolute norms for human self-realization.

In the family one learns to differentiate oneself from the surrounding world. Space and time, the foundational axes of our historicity, find their full meaning in the family. For this reason it is most important to provide physical space sufficient to facilitate family communication, to respect the intimacy of the family and at the same time to provide for its social life: overcrowded lodging, in contrast, is direly prejudicial. Similarly, families need to share their time in a creative manner; without time for itself a family soon disintegrates.

Just as things are at the service of persons, goods are a means for family happiness. As in the animal world, adults strive to nourish their offspring, and this work brings all closer together. Within the family work, whether paid or not, achieves its authentic meaning, whereas salary without a family context is money without value. When these means are transformed into ends, however, the family suffers. Thus, by placing man at the service of progress industrial society has a traumatic negative impact upon family values. It turns recreation, work, vacations, free time and the means of communication into so many sources of enrichment for the few, despoiling the family of its time and space and falsifying its authentic relationship with nature.

> I should like to feel the full force of the sun again,
> making the skin hot and the whole body glow, and
> reminding me that I am a corporeal being. I should
> like to be tired by the sun, instead of my books and
> thoughts. I should like to have it awaken my animal
> existence. I should like, not just to see the sun and
> sip it a little, but to experience it bodily.[42]

This dramatic cry of a prisoner expresses a feeling of being forceably distanced from reality; it reflects a generalized recognition of the "one dimensional man" (Marcuse) in the present industrial era.

As the family is the place of personal meeting with others, the process of socialization takes place in the home. Relations between parents and offspring, spouses and siblings transcend biological dimensions as they project outward in a series of concentric circles each with its distinctive mode and accent. Just as the family is not imprisoned in a biological circle, it need not submit itself to models created by specific social systems. David Cooper, in his work *The Death of the Family*, proclaims the death of a determined model of family due to the deficiencies of the system:

> The burgeois nuclear family unit has become, in this
> century, the ultimate perfected form of non-meeting,

and therefore the ultimate denial of mourning, death, birth and the experiential realm that precedes birth and conception.[43]

The family is not coming to an end, but it is bound up with others in the development of the human being. Though not the final stage of human realization, it is a permanent mode of the unfolding of human existence. Hence, to call the family the nucleus of human society is not to say that other parts of society are unrelated to this nucleus, but only that our mode of being social beings is by means of the family.

The "relational" or social dimension of the person does not end here; it opens to an immense number of possibilities. One experiences one's transcendence in the presence of an "Other" which is totally distinct from oneself and from the surrounding social and natural reality to which one is intimately related. Ultimately, the family offers the greatest assurance of openness to this Transcendent by cultivating values in an appropriate hierarchy. Thus, "The unity between man and wife becomes a personal community that embraces the whole of life and that is an example of every relationship between the I and the thou."[44]

Just as individual humans express in their own language their needs and relations to reality, each family has its own language according to its situation "in" and "before" reality. In the family, through the example and teaching of the parents, the child learns the nature and meaning of life. The cultivation of religious feeling in a family and its integration with other aspects of family life enables its members to have concrete religious experience. In this manner the I-Thou encounter with the Holy is not a solely personal matter, but a communitary experience.

The child who feels sufficiently secure among those who surround him/her does not need to create idols in order to overcome weakness. If no object or person in the surroundings has attempted to elevate itself to the category of the Absolute, the child will know how to distinguish clearly between others and "The Other." Love as the norm of family life establishes equity, plants the commandments and assures the moral dimension of personal growth. If parents live what they believe and manifest happiness subsequent generations probably will follow in their footsteps.

Only an ethic of openness to others makes possible the positive development of the family and its members. Permanent and progressive openness to the mystery of the other person opens the possibilities of revelation in "the other," "others" and "The Other." Education in the family opens up the potentialities for the full realization of its members.

In turn, only those who have experienced fully the reality of being a son or daughter will be capable of being mature fathers or mothers, responsible brothers or sisters, and of realizing a lasting marriage. The human family is the privileged nucleus of intimacy and of participation in these complementary forces which rule the life of a person: possession and gift, solitude and community, persons and society, I and Thou, unity and multiplicity, and intimacy and participation.

> Only an affirmation which reaches far beyond all empirical and objectively discernible ways of living can gain for us a sense of life's fullness and place the seal of eternity upon the perpetually renewed act of creation, enabling thereby the family to maintain its awesome power to complete or repudiate it.[45]

This dialectic of family life continually unfolds in complementary moments of love as giving and receiving, of communion and participation. A family which is continually sustained and fed by love, interrelation and personal communion cannot but project itself in participative and liberating action within its natural and social context. Open and interpersonal relations in the family generate increasing growth beyond the frontiers of one's personal being through participation and openness. This reaches intimate communication with the Transcendent in, and beyond, history.

Paul Claudel confirms that every 'thou' which one encounters becomes an unrealized and unrealizable promise, that every human 'thou' is fundamentally a delusion. No human encounter can escape ultimate solitude; nor can any human person exhaust the infinite capacity of another person.

> When one loves a person, one loves more than a person; one loves the secret that it hides and reveals, and which surpasses one. Love is connected to all and always, that is, to the infinite, the eternal, the absolute . . . to God.[46]

Immanence as historicity is the concrete place of the meeting of man with the transcendent. It is in the human being basically as a family member that immanence transcends itself in that experience of wholeness which is the full encounter with the Transcendent.

Universidad Catolica del Ecuador
Quito, Ecuador

NOTES

1. (Washington: The University Press of America and The Council for Research in Values and Philosophy, 1986).

2. (New York: Norton, 1964).

3. Sebastian Samay, "Affectivity: The Power Base of Moral Behavior," *Act and Agent*, eds., G. McLean, F. Ellrod, *et al.* Washington: The University Press of America and The Council for Research in Values and Philosophy, 1986), Ch. III.

4. Paul Tillich, *Theology of Culture* (New York: OUP, 1964), p. 10.

5. *Ibid.*, p. 12.

6. *Ibid.*, p. 16.

7. Ludwig Feuerbach, *The Essence of Christianity* (New York: Harper & Row, 1957).

8. Calvin Schrag, *Experience and Being* (Evanston: Northwestern University Press, 1969), p. 134.

9. *Ibid.*, p. 188.

10. Richard Knowles, "The Active Person as Moral Agent" in *Psychological Foundations of Moral Education and Character Development: An Integrated Theory of Moral Development* (Washington: The University Press of America and The Council for Research in Values and Philosophy, 1986), p. 248.

11. Errol E. Harris, "Science and Nature" in *Man and Nature*, G. McLean, ed. (Calcutta: Oxford University Press, 1978, p. 28 ff.

12. Richard Knowles, op. cit., p. 258.

13. William Kraft, *The Search for the Holy* (Philadelphia: The Westminster Press, 1971), p. 28.

14. *Ibid.*, p. 19.

15. Wisdom 2,1-5.

16. *Ibid.*, 2,6.

17. Psalms 8,4-7.

18. Tao Tzu, "Tao Te Ching" quoted by Chang Chung Yuan in "The Nature of Man as Tao," in *Man and Nature*, p. 109.

19. Geraidus van der Leeuw, *Phenomenologie del Religion* in the translation of J. E. Tumer, *Religion in Essence and Manifestation* (New York: Harper and Row, 1963), v. 2, p. 462.

20. Ludwig Feuerbach, *op. cit.*, p. 119.

21. Rudolf Otto, *The Idea of Holy* (Oxford: Oxford University Press, 1971), pp. 51-52.

22. Mircea Eliade, *Le sacré et le profane* (Coll. "Idées," 76; Paris: Gallimaud, 1965), p. 172.

23. Thomas Altizer, *Radical Theology and the Death of God* (Indianapolis: Bobbs-Merril, 1966), p. 11.

24. This and previous quotes are taken from: George Mc-

Lean, "Paul Tillich's Existential Philosophy and Protestantism," *The Thomist*, XXVII (1964), passim.

25. Paul Tillich, *Systematic Theology* (Chicago: The University Press, 1956), I, 271.

26. Frederick Steng, others, *Ways of Being Religious* (Edgewood Cliffs, NJ.: Prentice Hall, 1973), p. 552.

27. Thomas Kempis, *The Imitation of Christ*.

28. St. Augustine, *Civitas Dei*, XIV; 26.

29. *Ibid*. and *In Psalmis*, CXXXVI, 2.

30. *Civitas Dei*, XIX, 23.

31. Mathew Fox, *Family Spirituality* (Santa Fe: Besi, 1981) recorded conference.

32. Michael Curtis, *The Great Political Theories* (New York: Avon Books, 1970), V.I, I 218.

33. Michael Curtis, *op. cit.*, p. 224.

34. Oliver A. Johnston, *Ethics* (San Francisco: Holt-Rinehard and Winston, Inc., 1978), p. 362 (quoting Frederick Nietzsche's *Beyond Good and Evil*).

35. *Ibid*. (quoting a text from Thomas Hobbes, *Leviathan*), p. 175.

36. Geraidus van der Leeuw, *op. cit.*, passim.

37. *Ibid.*, passim.

38. *Ibid.*, passim.

39. Cited by Calvin O. Schrag in *Experience of Being* (Evanston: Northwestern University Press, 1969), p. 185.

40. June Singer, *Androgyny* (New York: Anchor Press, 1976), p. 275.

41. Schrag, *ibid*, p. 203.

42. Dietrich Bonhoeffer, *Letters and Papers From Prison* (New York: Macmillan, 1972).

43. David Cooper, *The Death of the Family* (New York: Pantheon Books, 1970), p. 4.

44. Wolfhart Pannenberg, *What is Man?* (Philadelphia, Fortress Press, 1975), p. 93.

45. Gabriel Marcel, *Homo Viator* (Chicago: Harper and Row, 1962), p. 97.

46. Stalo Gastaldi, *Il hombre, un misterio* (Quito: Ediciones de la Universidad Catolica, 1983), p. 129.

CHAPTER VIII

LIBERATION AND VALUES

MANUEL B. DY, JR.

The historicity of values is manifested in our time in the liberation movement of peoples, notably in Third World countries. Theologians have not lagged behind in reflection upon this movement, finding justification in biblical sources, from the Old Testament to the letters of St. Paul. The Christian churches have even gone as far as leading the movement itself. Philosophers, however, are just beginning to be explicit and emphatic in their reflection on this historical experience. But if the concept of freedom is the key to understanding the historicity of values, then the liberation movement cannot escape the philosopher's scrutiny.

Two pitfalls are to be avoided in a philosophical reflection on liberation. One simply equates liberation with violent revolution, with overthrowing a regime, usually unjust, by force. The historical examples of recent times attest that it is not always the case that a revolution liberates a people; rather, in many cases, it leads to further and worse oppression of a great majority of people. Besides, as Merleau-Ponty says, "before being thought (a revolution) is lived through as an obsessive presence, as possibility, enigma and myth."[1] The other pitfall treats liberation in the abstract, as devoid and withdrawn from the complexity and dynamism of the historical situation, by limiting it to either the economic or the political or even to the religious dimension of the situation. But, liberation, after all, "is a historical, not a mental act," says Marx.[2] If our reflection is to be truly philosophical and moral, it must take into consideration the *totality* of the historical situation and focus upon society as a moral agent, a collective or social person.

Our main task is to capture the movement of freedom as found in people, taken as moral agents, and to make explicit the values involved in this movement. This must be done without specifying in a deterministic sense the path and terminus of this movement, for that would be contradictory to the notion of freedom. Our presupposition here is that society is not simply a conglomeration of individuals such that a dichotomy and then conflict arises between the individual and the common good-- though this constitutes a moral problem itself--but that it is constituted by persons who can act freely and responsibly. The person constitutes society just as he or she is constituted by society (as the Confucianists are known to view man). Every finite person is as much a collective or social person as an individual person. In the words of Max Scheler,

> not only does everyone discover himself against a
> background of, and at the same time as a 'member'
> of, a totality of interconnections of experience which
> have somehow become concentrated, and which are
> *called* in their temporal extension *history*, in their
> simultaneous extension *social unity*; but as a moral
> subject in this whole, everyone is *also* given as a
> '*person acting with others*,' as a 'man with others'
> and as 'co-responsible' for everything morally relevant
> in this totality. We must delegate as collective per-
> sons the various *centers of experiencing (Er-lebens)*
> in this endless totality of living with one another.[3]

This paper then is divided into three parts. First, we will
examine the notion and movement of freedom on the level of
the individual person. Second, we will apply this movement on
the societal level. Third, we will explicitate the values and their
interconnections found on those two levels.

THE NOTION OF FREEDOM

Soren Kierkegaard paved the way for a new understanding
of the reality of freedom as reconcilable with determination[4] by
pointing out that the opposite of freedom is not determinism,
but indifference and lack of commitment. But what is the relation of freedom as commitment to the person?

Existential and phenomenological writings abound with
descriptions and discussions on the person.[5] Gabriel Marcel
contrasts the person with the ego.[6] The ego is characterized by
self-enclosure, by an attitude of *having* in its relationship with
things, ideas, persons and God. The person, on the other hand,
is characterized by *disponibilité*, by an attitude of *being*, a
participation in things, ideas, persons and God. *Having* divides,
whereas *being* unifies. Along the same vein, Max Scheler describes the person as a center and unity of diverse acts; he
contrasts this to functions which happen, but are not actuated.[7]
Freedom is the act by means of which the individual passes
from *having* to *being*. More than *having* freedom, we are called
to *being* or becoming free, as persons integrated and whole.
Freedom as a *fact*, as something we as human beings have,
points to freedom as a *value* that we intend. Freedom is not an
end in itself,[8] but as an intentionality points to values of the
person.

Thus, just as Scheler distinguishes values from goods, we
can differentiate two kinds of freedom: free choices or horizontal freedom, and the fundamental option or vertical freedom.

In the Schelerian sense, "values are *qualities* experienced *in* things, but they are not identical, with them."[9] They are given first of all in feeling; strictly speaking, we do not think of values, we feel them.[10] Goods, on the other hand, are carriers or bearers of values and are subject to change. Values as qualities do not change. The color-quality blue is still blue, even if I decide to paint the blue board with red. Friendship as a value remains a value, even if I cease to be a faithful friend to another or become his enemy. This objectivity of values, especially the higher ones, explains why the failure to realize a higher value results in the degradation of the person, rather than of the value itself. (In Plato, "it is worse to do injustice than to suffer injustice.")

When we speak of free choice, we refer to goods. We choose to actualize certain possibilities because we see a value in them or because they carry a certain worth for us. But in choosing horizontally, we prefer vertically one value over another. For example, if I choose to use the remaining three hundred dollars in my possession to buy a colored television set instead of allocating this for the food of my children, I am preferring the value of the pleasant over the values of the vital and of love. Generally speaking, in relation to the task of becoming moral persons, there can be only two fundamental options open to a person: that of love (in Scheler's philosophy, the movement towards higher values) and that of egoism or hatred (the movement towards lower values).

Both forms of freedom necessitate a dialectic with the historical situation or with nature. Again, the presence of human freedom is not the absence of determinism, but active involvement in a situation and commitment to a project. To quote Merleau-Ponty in his classic critique of Sartrean freedom:

> What then is freedom? To be born is both to be born of the world and to be born into the world. The world is already constituted but never completely constituted; in the first case we are acted upon, in the second we are open to an infinite number of possibilities. But this analysis is still abstract, for we exist in both *at once*. There is, therefore, never determinism and absolute choice, I am never a thing and never bare consciousness. In fact, even our own pieces of initiative, even the situations which we have chosen, bear us on, once they have been entered upon by virtue of a state rather than an act. The generality of the 'role' and the situation comes to the aid of decision, and in this exchange between the situation and the person who takes it up, it is impossible

to determine precisely the 'share contributed by the situation' and the 'share contributed by freedom'.[11]

The dialectic of freedom and the situation leads us to see the positive side of freedom, namely responsibility. In the Eastern tradition, freedom is never talked about so much as is responsibility, rights never so much emphasized as is obligation. But to talk of response-ability, to be response-able, is to take up a certain *project* in *time*, a presence to what *is*. This is at once a consciousness of what *was* or *has been* and what is *possible* or *coming-to be*.

> It is by being unrestrictedly and unreservedly what I am at present that I have a chance of moving forward; it is by living my time that I am able to understand other times, by plunging into the present and the world, by taking on deliberately what I am fortuitously, by willing what I will and doing what I do, that I can go further . . . so freedom flounders in the contradictions of commitment, and fails to realize that, without the roots which it thrusts into the world, it would not be freedom at all.[12]

Project then opens up possibilities in the world by the very commitment which binds it. "As long as I do not project anything, I do not chart possibilities within the actual," Paul Ricoeur would say.[13]

The art of taking up a project is at once a determination both of myself and of the situation. In being committed, I bind myself to a future appearance: "I objectify myself in a way, as I objectify myself in a signature which I will be able to recognize as mine."[14] The world is no longer a brute fact, the paper no longer a blank sheet, but contains my gesture. There is no way for me to affirm myself, no way for me to wake up from anonymity except through my acts.[15] The person exists in and through his diverse acts, although he can never be completely identified with any one of them.

Merleau-Ponty's philosophy of situated freedom has often been characterized as a philosophy of ambiguity, for it is impossible to delineate precisely the contribution of freedom in a project from that of the situation. In the end, "what is required is silence, for only the hero lives out his relation to men and the world."[16] Nevertheless, he sees the task of philosophy as none "other than to teach us once more to see them clearly."[17]

It is Paul Ricoeur who picks up this task of tracing the movement of freedom, the dialectic of freedom and the situation which he terms as "nature." He sees the dialectic of freedom and nature as twofold: first, as a negation of nature and second, as a re-affirmation of nature. In each there exist three movements.[18]

1. As a *negation of nature*, freedom affirms itself first as a threefold conquest of nature by means of tools, language, and institution. To protect oneself with the basic necessities of life, the person interacts with fellowmen and physical nature, establishes institutions, produces tools, creates the arts. Society is thus as much a product of the person as the person is a product of society.[19]

The second movement is the mathematization of the real constructed by man through experimentation, science and technology. With the formulation of the principle of inertia, the person is able to establish interconnections of things and effect a causality that is the anti-thesis of natural causality. The technological world in effect is an "abstract" world created by the person to control and harness the forces of nature.

The two movements lead to the third, the negation of *human* nature itself. The domination of physical nature further carries an attempt to negate the nature of human beings conceived as essences, the sedimentation of the self in temporality, with the result that the *Cogito* is an abyss in the world of things. The classic Sartrean assertion "man is nothing but what he makes himself to be" is testimony of this movement.

2. But freedom, on secondary reflection, is also a *reaffirmation of nature*, and again in three movements: Nature is affirmed first of all in action, when the subject affirms his or her own existence by bringing out the possibilities of the body in a concrete project. One cannot act without nature for nature, as Marx would say, is in a way the subject's body. In the second movement, freedom takes on the character of desire, motivation, spontaneous will. Freedom becomes a "way of life"--not an isolated act, but the power to act with consistency. This entails maintaining a relation with nature which is not exhausted in fleeting moments of passions, but a stable persistence of character, a "habitus," virtue, or character, so to speak.

Finally, nature is affirmed in the third movement of freedom as objectification of freedom in the spheres of economics, politics and culture. The "works" of freedom are the products of human activity, the condensation of my ability to work, to relate, and to express myself. Two histories can be detected in any cultural object: the ascending genesis of libido and the descending genesis of freedom. Indeed, nature or situation is the other of freedom; more fundamentally, nature is the mediation of freedom.

What is noteworthy in the above summary of Ricoeur's description of the movement and dialectic of freedom and nature is its historical and social character. Keeping in mind the two directions of freedom, horizontal and vertical, let us follow this movement of liberation in its societal dimension.

LIBERATION OF PEOPLES

On the societal dimension, the movement of freedom is the liberation of people *from* something and *for/to* something. In other words, the negative and positive aspects of liberation correspond to the negation and re-affirmation of nature. This dialectic of freedom and nature in the social dimension expresses itself historically in the search for cultural or national identity by a people, often unarticulated but manifested in the different tensions of the social fabric. In a sense we can refer to these social tensions as diverse "acts" taken in the general sense of the social person, and the search for cultural or national identity as the development of a people--their "becoming" a social person.

Jurgen Habermas has provided us with a conceptualization of these tensions in society through his categories of the three "human interests."[20] Although these interests are cognitive for Habermas, considered from the perspective of the different kinds of inquiry (empirical-analytic sciences, historical-hermeneutic sciences, and critically oriented sciences), they have their basis in the *natural* history of man, and in the socio-cultural evolution of the human species.[21] The three interests correspond to the means of social organization: work, language, and power; to Ricoeur's threefold conquest by man: tool, language, and institution; and to the "works" or objectification of freedom in economics, culture, and politics. In a note of warning to hermeneutic philosophy, Ricoeur himself reminds us always to keep in mind this trilogy of work-language-power.[22]

1. *Technical interest* refers to the drive in the person for instrumental action to master and control nature. The human being learns to acquire and exercise this *purposive-rational* control of the conditions of existence leading to a "fixation of beliefs" and the establishment of a habit. The aim of empirical-analytic inquiry in this regard is the production of technically exploitable knowledge that discloses reality as technically controllable. This is the sphere of labor relations in society that Marx attempted to analyze and comprehend.[23] The failure of Marx, however, lies in regarding the development of the human species as taking place solely in the dimension of social labor in the relations of production, and eliminating theoretically and practically the second interest.

2. The *practical interest* of the social person refers to his or her symbolic interaction in cultural tradition(s). While techni-

cal interest is born from the necessity of the person to work in order to survive in a material world, practical interest answers an equally important need to relate intersubjectively in ordinary language communication. The scientific inquiry involved into this interest is called *hermeneutics*.[24] It is worth quoting Habermas himself in describing this interest:

> In its very structure hermeneutic understanding is designed to guarantee, within cultural traditions, the possible action-orienting self-understanding of individuals and groups as well as reciprocal understanding between different individuals and groups. It makes possible the form of unconstrained consensus and the type of open intersubjectivity on which communicative action depends. It bans the danger of communication breakdown in both dimensions: the vertical one of one's own individual life history and of the collective tradition to which one belongs, and the horizontal one of mediating between the traditions of different individuals, groups and cultures. When these communication flows break off and the intersubjectivity of mutual understanding is either rigidified or falls apart, a condition of survival is disturbed, one that is as elementary as the complementary condition of the success of instrumental action: namely the possibility of unconstrained agreement and non-violent recognition. Because this is the presupposition of practice, we call the knowledge-constitutive interest of the cultural sciences (*Geisteswissenschaften*) 'practical'.[25]

Note that intersubjectivity is embodied in ordinary language, in what Dilthy calls "life expressions," namely linguistic expressions, actions, and non-verbal experiential expressions like gestures, glances, interactions and the like. All three are integrated and interpret one another in a given culture.[26] This is similar to Merleau-Ponty's key insight into language as being, not a clothing of ideas but embodied thought or thinking, or culture itself.[27] The task of hermeneutics is to interpret language and disclose reality for the sake of mutual understanding and recognition, but always against the background of the cultural world.

Technical control and communicative interest, however, are not enough. The socio-cultural world has a tendency to contain invariant regularities and to express "ideologically frozen relations of dependence."[28] Technology and science can become ideological in the sense of dominating the entire sphere of social relations.[29] This calls for the third interest.

3. The *emancipatory interest* criticizes the ideological tendencies of the first two interests. The task of the critical sciences is to unmask the forces of domination, dogmatism, and repression lying behind the reproduction of labor and the institutionally secured forms of general and public communication. Emancipatory interest seeks to break the barriers to open communication between social groups and persons, raising their self-consciousness "to the point where it has attained the level of critique and freed itself from all ideological delusions."[30] Both technical and practical interests are brought to the fore of self-reflection, and subjected "to the criterion of what a society intends for itself as *the good life*."[31] The technical interest of self-preservation cannot be segregated from the cultural conditions of human life: social persons must first interpret what they consider as life. And these symbolic interpretations must likewise be subjected for evaluation to ideas of the good life. This entails an open communication, for the notion of the ideal is not a fixed essence or pure and unconditioned convention, but depends on symbolic interaction and material exchange with nature.[32] Emancipatory interest thus is of the order of anticipation, of hope and of an eschatology.[33]

It would be a mistake, therefore, to isolate these three interests one from another, or even to envisage a simplistically strict one-to-one correspondence of each of them with work, language, and power. The process of liberation is precisely the tension and interpenetration of all three; freedom cuts across these three spheres of human and social existence.

How then are we to describe the movement of social liberation in these three spheres? Since the movement of liberation contains both negative (liberation from) and positive (liberation for/to) aspects, I propose here to cite the negative, without claiming to be exhaustive,[34] rather than the positive. The last section of this paper, societal values, will serve as the positive dimension of the process of liberation.

1. It is to the young Karl Marx of the *Economic and Philosophical Manuscripts* that we credit recognition of the importance of work for the liberation of person. Work is the humanization of the person and of nature; it is that whereby the person becomes more human and nature is humanized or brought under the control of the person. Insofar as person is *body* one needs to work in order to survive, but as embodied *subjectivity* one expresses and communicates oneself through labor; in this sense, work is also culture revealing the worker. To be deprived of work then is to be deprived not only of the means to survive, but also of a means of self-expression.

In the social dimension, the process of liberation involves, first of all, an economic liberation from the material deprivation of hunger, poverty and disease. More often than not these are tied up with unemployment, the lack of opportunities for work, and an unjust economic system of distribution in whatever form, whether capitalism or socialism. Social disparity can, of course, be extended beyond the national level to international relationships where economic dependence and manipulation become the rules of the game. The truth of the Marxist critique of capitalism is based upon the insight that freedom is not without responsibility, that it is not the same as licentiousness, and that in the concrete the laissez-faire system does not necessarily bring about a more equal distribution of goods and opportunities. On the other hand, while in theory socialism promises a common basic security, in practice it equates equality with having rather than being, and the freedom of the person is supplanted by the "freedom" of the state. Be that as it may, both systems give credence to the intertwining of wealth and power, and to the fact that economic liberation is not all of liberation.

Technology as the "scientifically rationalized control of objectified processes"[35] may indeed satisfy the material needs of society, but it can also give rise to what Marcel calls "technocracy." Means can become ends in themselves; and the social person can be reduced to an efficient mechanical tool, if not a number or stage of production. Relationships cease to be interpersonal and become functional; one is identified and objectified by that for which he or she functions. In highly technologically advanced countries work becomes monotony and depersonalizes man. The individual person is subjected to the enormous apparatus of production and distribution and deprived of free time. This repression of the person can disappear from the consciousness of the populace by a kind of legitimation of domination-- the "constantly increasing production of nature which keeps individuals . . . living in increasing comfort."[36] Thus, the domination of nature by technology can lead to the domination of man by man.

2. Technical control has to be subjected to social emancipation, for technical control of physical and social conditions for preserving life and making it less burdensome does not lead automatically to social emancipation.[37] In this sphere, liberation is cultural liberation: Particularly today, it is from a neo-colonialism that is more subtle than the previous territorially expansive colonialism for neo-colonialism takes the form of technology which "provides the great legitimation of the expanding political power, which absorbs all spheres of culture."[38]

The social person must come to an interpretation or reinterpretation of his/her culture in the face of modernization and the imposition of a dominant culture. One must first liberate oneself from being subjected to, and absorbed in a foreign culture if one is to dialogue with it. This "coming to terms" first with oneself entails what Martin Heidegger calls a "creative repetition." Creative repetition is a sort of digging into one's past or tradition, not for superficial externalization, but for inner symbolic meanings and values in the light of present and future possibilities. Language plays a crucial role in this movement of freedom because language recuperates the meaning of the past, carries it forward to the present in act of communication and throws open the possibilities of the future--all in the unity of a mode of thinking, acting, and interacting. The word can compensate for the enslavement of the work.[39]

But words too can be a source of misunderstanding in the sense that they can take the place of action and experience. "Language is only the locus for the articulation of an experience which supports it, . . . everything, consequently, does not arrive *in* language, but only comes *to* language."[40] True, culture is the objectification of the will of our predecessors, but to interpret it from the finitude of the present in order merely to understand it but not critique it, is to remain in the nostalgia of the past. This can lead to a romanticism and, in the extreme, to an ultranationalism of a violent kind. The values unearthed from a tradition may be claimed by an authority in order to bind a people against another class or in order to legitimize itself in power. The problem of legitimation links itself naturally to a different kind of social disparity from that of the economic gap of the rich and the poor, namely the disparity between authority and citizenry, or between the intellectual elite and the masses.

3. The movement of social liberation this reaches its peak in the dimension of power; indeed freedom has always been associated with inner capacity. (Note the Kantian formula for the derivation of the postulate of freedom: "I ought, therefore I *can*.") In this sphere of emancipation, society must be on guard against despotism, the abuse of power, whether of the technical or the cultural type, or both. What this calls for is a critique of ideologies and, with regard to the re-interpretation of one's culture, an act of distantiation that leads to self-criticism with a view to open communication. Self-consciousness and self-reflection which constitute self-criticism are particularly necessary in order to liberate oneself from excessive manipulation by the media and/or a regime that wishes to perpetuate itself. In many developing countries, the masses are depoliticized so that power can maintain itself and prevent the people from exercising their freedom of self-determination. The despot, of course, wants to give a semblance of rationality by means of technical/economic

progress and holding elections that are only appellative in character, if not downright rigged and dishonest. Where these means fail, militarization is utilized to keep the social groups from asserting themselves.

How is one to liberate oneself from the destructive use of violence? The movement of liberation in this sphere necessarily involves the complex problem of the use of violence for the sake of freedom. The question does not have a simple, ready-made answer. What has to be kept in mind is the many forms that violence can take in the human realm and the overwhelming structure of resistance it sets against freedom. In its explicit manifestation, it is murder and war, the will to inflict harm on the other, imperialism and racism. In more subtle forms, it is manipulative persuasion, flattery, blackmail, fraud, monopoly of information and discussion, and even simply the inaction of apathy. But,

> what unifies the problem of violence is not the fact that its multiple expressions derive from one or another form that is held to be fundamental, but rather that it is language that is its opposite. It is for a being who *speaks*, who in speaking pursues *meaning*, who has already entered the discussion, and who knows something about rationality that violence is or becomes a problem. Thus violence has its meaning in its other: *language*. And the same is true reciprocally. Speech, discussion, and rationality also draw their unity of meaning from the fact that they are an attempt to reduce violence. A violence that speaks is already a violence trying to be right: it is a violence that places itself in the orbit of reason and that already is beginning to negate itself as violence.[41] [Italics mine.]

The solution to violence then is meaningful discourse, which is non-violent. Violence is justified only when all recourse to meaning is exhausted and when the taking up of violence is itself meaningful. The state, after all, in the Hegelian sense is the overcoming of private violence by subordinating it to the rule of law, the common will, or universal reason. "Politics exists because the city exists,"[42] the place of discourse. Meaningful discourse is the opposite of violence because meaningful discourse respects the other's freedom. The non-violent man's openness to dialogue is not a surrender to his freedom, but rather an overcoming of a private violence. Against the violence of the other his non-violence serves as testimony of an inner strength, of an inner freedom.

SOCIETAL VALUES

We must now return to our previous distinction between horizontal and vertical freedom. In the dialectical movement of freedom through the interpenetrating spheres of work, language, and power, vertical freedom makes manifest the values that adhere to the historical situation; these are justice, truth, and love or care. Each of these belongs to all three of the spheres of liberation we discussed in the last section, but in an interpenetrating manner.

1. *Justice* is often said to be the overriding value of the social order. Too often, however, it has been mistakenly identified with the legal order. Debate over economic systems betrays a misconception of justice as identified with equity or with an isolated just demand.[43]

What is legal obviously is not necessarily or always what is just. We revise laws and make constitutional amendments precisely to meet the demand of justice, but legalism can be a great source of injustice. The identification of justice with a chart of punishments of some sort raises the question, how just are our laws and the authority that imposes them? In many developing countries the demand for justice is overwhelming in the face of massive arrests of persons without charges, in the savaging or massacre of persons suspected of subversion, in the hamleting of communities away from their land--all in the name of law and order. Clearly, justice has to do with respect for the rights of persons.

Nor can justice be equated with equity or equal distribution of goods. The mother dividing the cake into equal pieces among her children is a classic example of justice misconceived as equity. What if one of her children due to hunger and malnourishment needs a bigger slice? Could it not be the case that dividing the cake into equal parts betrays her fear or playing safe, rather than a genuine spirit of concern? In the social realm, would the socialist system of equal distribution of basic necessities at the expense of individual initiative be, as it claims, more just than the capitalistic system? Would the welfare system in a society meet the demand of justice? On the international level, is it just for a highly developed nation to give economic aid to a developing country in the interest of getting cheap labor and raw materials, or of dumping junk surplus products on their market? These questions among others point to another essential quality of justice--genuine justice is inspired by non-partisan interests.

Nor can justice be equated with the satisfaction of an isolated just demand. To give in to the demand of workers striking for a higher wage in the long run may lead to a greater injustice such as massive lay-offs, higher prices of commodities or foreclosure of the firm. Justice to be genuine cannot remain abstract, but must take into consideration the total existential situation--the concrete relationship of a person with other persons. The relationship of person and physical nature becomes an issue of justice only in the light of this inter-human relationship.

The value of justice, thus, has three features: respect for the rights of the human other, non-partisanship, and consideration of the total existential situation.

2. *Truth as value* is not simply the equation of judgment with reality, but truth for which one is willing to live and die. What does it mean to live and die for the truth? Marcel offers us an enlightening description.

> To live according to truth means not to live according to one's moods. How so? Moods are variable, even for the individual who lives his whole life according to them. But when we use the word 'truth,' no matter how we define it, it always refers to something that shows consistency and absolute stability. In any case, living according to truth means bringing oneself into agreement--but not only with oneself (as this would perhaps mean only a formal coherence). No, it means bringing ourselves into agreement with a demand which has to express itself in us and cannot be stifled. While experience shows that we can stifle it if we want to, it nonetheless resides in the very nature of this demand that it should be clarified. This does not necessarily mean that the demand must press forward into consciousness in entire universal character. Most probably it will only take shape when a particular situation demands it, or when an action is required, regardless of the personal risk involved.[44]

Marcel gives as an example the taking of an oath or the act of freely coming out into the open to testify to something that one has seen, at the risk of death or torture or of harm to one's family.

Truth is not the same as opinion. In opinion, I do not stake my being; but in truth I *participate* in the act of understanding. This presupposes that truth is always against a certain background or horizon, perhaps aptly conveyed in the metaphor of light. No one has the monopoly of truth, just as no one possesses light. There is always an intersubjective quality of truth that is irreducible to the quantification of Gallup polls and the counting of heads. The search for truth is a communal search, a "fusion of horizons." But it will always remain a *search*, for truth is *aletheia*, according to Heidegger, and therefore includes a mixture of darkness, and perhaps of pain. Still, truth as value liberates: "the truth shall make you free."

3. *Love as value* is *care*, in the Heideggerian sense, under the aspect of solicitude. As *dasein* or man is a being-with (*mit-sein*), caring by no means involves only incidental acts of kindness towards one's neighbor. Caring is being-ahead-of-itself, while being-already-in-the-world and being-alongside-entities-which-we-encounter. To care is to be continually creatively responsible for the other in time. (In the parable of the Good Samaritan, the Samaritan did not stop at picking up the victim; he deposited money at the inn and promised to pay for any extra charges.)

One of the paradoxes of love and caring is its quality of being both singular and universal. One never loves humanity in the abstract; one loves concrete individuals in their particularity, and this means giving them the freedom to become themselves. Yet, in willing the free self-determination of the other, one affirms a basic humanity, a common brotherhood (and sisterhood) of mankind. Authentic concern for the other takes cognizance of the uniqueness of the other (whether individual or social) and of his or her own pace and rhythm of growth, which it respects and supports. Love, as Scheler constantly emphasizes, is a movement towards the higher possibilities of a value.

In the language of power, genuine authority flows from an active concern for the total welfare of the community, otherwise authority becomes despotism and obedience becomes servitude. As the abuse of power hides a failure and refusal to take into account the value of the other human person, it is not difficult to see why violence is problematic for the person who is aware of the value of love. Violence may be justifiable at times as an ethics of conviction, but it has to be balanced by an ethics of responsibility.[45]

The notion of responsibility is the key to the link between love and justice--two seemingly contrasting values--and consequently between justice and truth. The cold hand of justice and the warm heart of love can be expressed in the categories of the socius and the neighbor.[46] The socius is the servant of the institution; the neighbor is the person encountered inter-personally. Justice ought to govern our functional relationships, mediated through structures; love spontaneously colors our direct immediate relationships. But justice is genuine only if it is inspired by a non-partisan interest, if it is a beginning love conceived as responsibility. For there can be as much love "hidden in the humble abstract services performed by post office and social security officials" as between friends and intimate persons; the "*ultimate* meaning of institutions is the service which they render to persons."[47] Inversely, love can easily become false charity if the service rendered does not answer to the real demand of justice, or is made an alibi for a lack of justice. Justice is the minimum of love, and love the maximum of justice. The minimum demanded in justice is the basic dignity of the human person which love enhances. Justice and love then have a common root in responsibility.[48]

The dignity of the human person in turn provides the link of justice to truth.[49] Justice and truth (and love) are grounded on the value of the human person as sacred and inviolable. Truth as a value is a *call* to bear witness to some light, a vocation to shed light on what is revealed. Insofar as man as man is given the word, he shares in the sacredness of this revelation and the response-ability to bear witness to it. To refuse to testify is to do injustice not only to others in the community, but also, and worse, to oneself.

What is the ultimate source of this sacredness of the person or the ultimate foundation of the community of persons? Scheler's hierarchy of values offers us a possible answer in the realm of religion. Because a higher value has the characteristic of founding other values, the highest value is the value of the holy because it founds the other values of the sensory, the vital, and the spiritual. If the value of the holy indeed supports the other values, then the Transcendent is immanent in the human values of justice, truth and love, and historically, in the movement of liberation.[50] "The dualistic spiritualities of evasion ought to die."[51] Absolute Value can no longer be thought of apart from the dynamism of man's freedom in history; the Transcendent stands at the crossroad of the incarnational and the eschatological. This is the Person who can ultimately and deeply unite all our divergent commitments, give meaning to our actions, and value to our individual and social persons.[52] The movement of liberation rests on this call to bear witness to the Transcendent. Justice, truth, and love are inseparable from faith.

A word must be said on the nexus of the values mentioned above; these values find their "home" in the family. The family is not just the means for the biological perpetuation of the human species, but the seat of the creative transmission of values in culture. The network of relationships in the family reflects in miniature the interrelationships of work, language, and power in society at large. There is wisdom to the words of the ancient Confucian text found in *The Great Learning*: "If you want peace in the world, you must first have peace in the state; if you want peace in the state, you must have peace in the family."[53] In the same tradition, Confucius says, "The root of *jen* (or love) is filial piety and brotherly respect."[54] Filial piety is the unity of man and man in time, and brotherly and sisterly respect is the unity of man and man in space. As a micro-society and micro-history, we cannot treat the family merely on an animal level as a shelter for our basic necessities. Neither can we deal with it simply in a formal sense as a rational contractual agreement which can be rescinded whenever conditions become unfavorable.[55] It is in the family as *home* that "I am"-- "I become myself" through "I am with." The societal values of truth, justice, love and faith take root and develop in freedom and responsibility.

We have traced the movement of liberation of the person-- in particular, the social person--and the values incarnate in this movement, but by no means have we exhausted the topic. Perhaps, the important lessons in our sketch are the dialectic of freedom and nature in the different but interrelated dimensions of man, and the historicity of values in this movement of freedom. Concretely, the appeal of freedom is the call to *participate* in something or someone other and greater than ourselves: only then can we claim to be on the way to freedom.

Ateneo de Manila
Manila, The Philippines

NOTES

1. Maurice Merleau-Ponty, *Phenomenology of Perception* (London: Routledge and Kegan Paul, 1967), p. 446.

2. Karl Marx and F. Engels, *The German Ideology* (Moscow: Progress Publishers, 1964), p. 56.

3. Max Scheler, *Formalism in Ethics and Non-Formal Ethics of Value* (Evanston, Ill.: Northwestern University Press, 1973), p. 520.

4. Cf. John D. Caputo, "A Phenomenology of Moral Sensibility: Moral Emotion," in R. Ellrod, G. McLean, et al., eds., *Act and Agent: Philosophical Foundations of Moral Education* (Washington, D.C.: Council for Research on Values and Philosophy and University Press of America, 1986), pp. 199-222.

5. Cf. George F. McLean, "The Person Moral Growth and Character Development," in *Act and Agent*, pp. 361-398.

6. Gabriel Marcel, "The Ego and Its Relation to Others," *Homo Viator* (Chicago: Henry Regnery, 1951), pp. 13-28.

7. Max Scheler, *op. cit.*, pp. 29, 62, 77, 85, 288, 370f., 379-86, 390, 430f., 477f., 482, 507, 537.

8. Cf. Frederick E. Ellrod, "Freedom and Moral Choice," in *Act and Agent*, pp. 117-140.

9. Alfons Deeken, *Process and Permanence in Ethics: Max Scheler's Moral Philosophy* (New York: Paulist Press, 1974), pp. 14f. (Italics mine.)

10. Max Scheler, *op. cit.*, p. 35.

11. Maurice Merleau-Ponty, *op. cit.*, p. 453.

12. *Ibid.*, pp. 455-456.

13. Paul Ricoeur, *Freedom and Nature: The Voluntary and the Involuntary* (Evanston: Northwestern Univ. Press, 1966); also in William L. Kelly and Andrew Tallon, *Readings in Philosophy of Man* (McGraw Hill, 1972), p. 291.

14. *Ibid.*, p. 288.

15. *Ibid.*, p. 287.

16. Maurice Merleau-Ponty, *op. cit.*, p. 456.

17. *Ibid.*

18. Paul Ricoeur, "Nature and Freedom," *Political and Social Essays* (Athens, Ohio: Ohio University Press, 1974), pp. 23-45.

19. Peter Berger and Thomas Luckmann, *The Social Construction of Reality* (New York: Doubleday & Co., 1966).

20. Jurgen Habermas, *Knowledge and Human Interests* (Boston: Beacon Press, 1971).

21. Thomas McCarthy, *The Critical Theory of Jurgen Habermas* (Cambridge: MA: The MIT Press, 1978), p. 59.

22. Paul Ricoeur, "Ethics and Culture," *Political and Social Essays*, p. 262.

23. Thomas McCarthy, *op. cit.*, pp. 60-64.

24. *Ibid.*, p. 68-69.

25. Jurgen Habermas, *op. cit.*, p. 176, quoted by Thomas McCarthy, *op. cit.*, p. 69.

26. Thomas McCarthy, *op. cit.* pp. 71-77.

27. Maurice Merleau-Ponty, *Phenomenology of Perception*, pp. 134-139.

28. Thomas McCarthy, *op. cit.*, p. 75.

29. Jurgen Habermas, "Science and Technology as Ideology," *Towards a Rational Society* (Boston: Beacon Press, 1971), pp. 85ff.

30. Thomas McCarthy, *op. cit.*, p. 88.

31. Jurgen Habermas, *Knowledge and Human Interests*, p. 313.

32. Thomas McCarthy, *op. cit.*, pp. 90-91.

33. Paul Ricoeur, "Ethics and Culture," *Political and Social Essays*, p. 257.

34. Cf. chapter VI above.

35. Jurgen Habermas, *Towards a Rational Society*, p. 57.

36. *Ibid.*, p. 83.

37. *Ibid.*, p. 58.

38. Herbert Marcuse, *One Dimensional Man* (Boston: Beacon

Press, 1964), quoted by Jurgen Habermas, *Towards a Rational Society*, p. 84.

39. Paul Ricoeur, "Work and the Word," *History and Truth* (Evanston: Northwestern Univ. Press, 1965), pp. 197ff.

40. Paul Ricoeur, "Ethics and Culture," *Political and Social Essays*, p. 262.

41. Paul Ricoeur, "Violence and Language," *Political and Social Essays*, p. 89.

42. *Ibid.*, p. 93.

43. Gabriel Marcel, "In Search of Truth and Justice," in *Searchings* (Westminster, Md.: Newman Press, 1967), pp. 3-15.

44. *Ibid.*, p. 16.

45. Paul Ricoeur, "The Task of the Political Educator," *Political and Social Essays*, pp. 287-289.

46. Paul Ricoeur, "The Socius and the Neighbor," *History and Truth*, pp. 89-109.

47. *Ibid.*, p. 109.

48. Robert Johann, "Love and Justice," in Richard T. de George (ed.), *Ethics and Society* (New York: Anchor Books, 1966).

49. Gabriel Marcel, *op. cit.*, pp. 15ff.

50. Cf. chapter V above.

51. Paul Ricoeur, "The Task of the Political Educator," *Political and Social Essays*, p. 292.

52. Robert Johann, *The Pragmatic Meaning of God* (Milwaukee: Marquette University Press, 1966).

53. *The Great Learning*, chapter IV (free translation).

54. *Analects*, 1:2.

55. Gabriel Marcel, "The Mystery of the Family," *Homo Viator*, pp. 68-98.

INDEX

THE COUNCIL FOR RESEARCH IN VALUES AND PHILOSOPHY (RVP)

Purpose

Today there is urgent need to attend to the nature and dignity of the person, to the quality of human life, to the purpose and goal of the physical transformation of our environment, and to the relation of all this to the development of social and political life. This, in turn, requires philosophic clarification of the basis upon which freedom is exercised, that is, of the values which provide stability and guidance to one's decisions.

Such studies must be able to reach deeply into the cultures of one's nation--and often of other parts of the world from which they derive--in order to uncover the roots of the dignity of persons and of the societies built upon their relations one with another. They must be able to identify the conceptual forms in terms of which modern industrial and technological developments are structured and how these impact human self-understanding. Above all, they must be able to bring these elements together in the creative understanding essential for setting our goals and determining our modes of our interaction. In the present complex circumstances this is a condition for growing together with trust and justice, honest dedication and mutual concern.

The Council for Studies in Values and Philosophy is a group of scholars who share the above concerns and are interested in the application thereto of existing capabilities in the field of philosophy and other disciplines. Its work is to identify areas in which study is needed, the intellectual resources which can be brought to bear thereupon, and the financial resources required. In bringing these together its goal is scientific discovery and publication which contributes to the promotion of human life in our times.

In sum, our times present both the need and the opportunity for deeper and ever more progressive understanding of the person and of the foundations of social life. The development of such understanding is the goal of the Council for Research in Values and Philosophy (RVP).

Projects

A set of related research efforts are currently in process, some developed initially by the RVP and others now being carried forward by it either solely or conjointly.

1. *Foundations of Moral Education and Character Development*. A study in values and education which unites philosophers, psychologists and scholars in education in the elaboration of ways of enriching the moral content of education and character development.

2. *Cultural Heritage and Contemporary Life: Philosophical Foundations for Social Life*. Sets of focused and mutually coordinated continuing seminars in university centers, each preparing a volume as part of an integrated philosophic search for self-understanding differentiated by continent. This work in the First, Second and Third Worlds focuses upon evolving a more adequate understanding of the person in society and looks to the cultural heritage of each for the resources to respond to its own specific contemporary issues.

3. *Seminars on Culture and Contemporary Issues*. This series of 10 week seminars is being coordinated by the RVP in Washington.

4. *Joint-Colloquia* with institutes of philosophy of the national Academies of Science, philosophy departments or societies in Eastern Europe and China concerning the person in contemporary society.

5. *The Mediation of Values to Social Life*. The development of a four volume study on the mediation of values to social life is a corporate effort of philosophers throughout the world.

The personnel for these projects consists of established scholars willing to contribute their time and research as part of their professional commitment to life in our society. The Council directly sponsors some projects and seeks support for projects sponsored by other organizations. For the resources to implement this work the Council, as a non-profit organization incorporated in the District of Colombia, looks to various private foundations, public programs, and enterprises.

PROJECT ON CULTURAL VALUES
CHARACTER DEVELOPMENT AND
SOCIAL LIFE IN THE XXIst CENTURY

A. Cultural Heritage & Contemporary Life

Series:
I *Culture & Values*
  I.1 Research on Culture & Values
  I.2 Methodology & the Study of Values
  I.3 Reading Philosophy for XXIst Century
  I.4 Relations Between Cultures
  I.5 Urbanization and Values
  I.6 Person and Society

II *Africa*
  II.1 Person and Community

III *Asia*
  III.1 Man & Nature

IV *Europe & N. America*

V *Latin America*
  V.1 Social Context of Values
  V.2 Culture, Human Rights & Peace

B. Foundational Research on Moral Education and Character Development

Series VI *Foundations of Moral Education*
VI.1 Philosophical Foundations
VI.2 Psychological Foundations
VI.3 Educational Foundations
VI. 4 Social Context of Values: Lat. Am.
VI.5 Chinese Foundations
VI.6 Love & Morality: Lat. Am.

C. Educational Methods and Materials

THE COUNCIL FOR
RESEARCH IN VALUES AND PHILOSOPHY

THE COUNCIL FOR RESEARCH IN VALUES AND PHILOSOPHY

CULTURAL HERITAGE AND CONTEMPORARY LIFE

Series I. Culture and Values

Vol. I.1 *Research on Culture and Values: Intersection of Universities, Churches and Nations*, George F. McLean

Vol. I.2 *The Knowledge of Values: A Methodological Introduction*, A. Lopez Quintas

Vol. I.3 *Reading Philosophy for the XXIst Century*
George F. McLean

Volumes in preparation will treat inter-cultural harmony, urbanization and values, and the humanization of social structures.

Series II. Africa

Series III. Asia

Vol. III.1 *Man and Nature: The Chinese Tradition and the Future*, Tang Yi-jie, Li Zhen

Vol. III.2 *Chinese Foundations for Moral Education and Character Development*, Tran van Doan

Series IV. Europe and North America

Series V. Latin America

Vol. V.1 *The Social Context and Values: Perspectives of the Americas*, O. Pegoraro

Vol. V.2 *Culture, Human Rights and Peace in Central America*
Raul Molina, Timothy Ready

Series VI. Foundations of Moral Education

Vol. VI.1 *Philosophical Foundations for Moral Education and Character Development: Act and Agent*, G. McLean

Vol. VI.2 *Psychological Foundations for Moral Education and Character Development: An Integrated Theory of Moral Development*, R. Knowles

Vol. VI.3 A volume by professors of education

Vol. VI.4 *The Social Context and Values: Perspectives of the Americas*, O. Pegoraro

Vol. VI.5 *Chinese Foundations for Moral Education and Character Development*, V. Shen and Tran van Doan

The series is co-published by: The University Press of America (UPA), 4720 Boston Way, Lanham, MD 20706, Tel. 301/459-3366; The Council for Research in Values and Philosophy, Washington, D.C. 20064, Tel. 202/635-5636.

To order: U.S. and Canada: UPA, as above

U.K. and Europe: Eurospan, Ltd., 3 Henrietta St., London WC2E 8LU.

All other locations: Feffer and Simons, Inc., 1114 Avenue of the America's, New York, NY 10036.